Participating in God

Participating in God

Creation and Trinity

Samuel M. Powell

FORTRESS PRESS

MINNEAPOLIS

Participating in God
Creation and Trinity

Library of Congress Cataloging-in-Publication Data
Powell, Samuel M.
      Participating in God : creation and Trinity / Samuel M. Powell.
         p. cm.
Includes bibliographical references and index.
      ISBN 978-0-8006-3602-9
      1. Creation. 2. Trinity. I. Title.
      BT695.P69 2003
      231.7′65—dc21

                                                            2002156637

The paper used in this publication meets the minimum requirements of American National Standard for Information Sciences—Permanence of Paper for Printed Library Materials, ANSI Z329.48-1984.

Manufactured in the U.S.A.
07   06   05   04   03   1   2   3   4   5   6   7   8   9   10

To Terrie

Contents

Part Two:
Understanding the Universe in a Trinitarian Way

Part Three: A Trinitarian Ethics

Preface

Every book is an attempt to solve a problem, and its success depends not only on the significance of the problem but also its solution. The problem I attempt to solve in this book is how to think about the world in a way that is scientifically responsible and also faithfully Christian.

This book is an exercise in systematic theology. My aim is to come to an understanding of the world of God's creation. By *understanding* I mean thinking about the world in a way that is both compelling and intellectually satisfying, at least for those who share my assumptions. Those assumptions are two: first, that the Christian faith is true and, second, that the picture of the world that the natural sciences give us is reliable. The purpose of the succeeding chapters is to spell out in detail the harmony of these two assumptions and the fruitfulness of thinking about the world with both of them in mind simultaneously.

As is well known, theologians in the first half of the twentieth century, especially Protestant theologians, were preoccupied with christological and soteriological themes. Such preoccupation was partly a result of the periodic swings in theological interest, but it cannot be denied that theologians were at a loss to integrate the scientific picture of the world into theology. There were many reasons for this. In the nineteenth century, natural science had come to be increasingly associated with agnostic and even frankly atheistic philosophies. The encounter between theology and the sciences was not an altogether happy one. Moreover, the pace of scientific developments, particularly in physics in the early decades of the twentieth century, proved difficult for even scientists to assimilate. Nonetheless, the fact remains that in this period the doctrine of creation was put on the theological back burner, to await a more propitious time.

The situation began to change in the last few decades of the twentieth century. Theologians such as Wolfhart Pannenberg and Jürgen Moltmann reacted to their teachers by directly addressing the doctrine of creation. At the same time, other theological movements, such as process theism, made the doctrine of creation and related themes the subject of focused interest. Both Pannenberg and process theists made serious attempts to engage the results of the sciences and incorporate them into their presentations of the Christian faith. Meanwhile, interest was growing in the possibilities for a sustained encounter between theology and the sciences that would work at an advanced level of specialization and detail. This interest has born fruit in the form of journals (notably *Zygon*), research centers (such as the Center for Theology and the Natural Sciences in Berkeley), conferences, newsletters, and other customary modes of academic discourse. There is now a burgeoning discipline concerned with the dialogue between theology and the natural sciences. Of particular value have been the numerous books and articles on focused topics, such as the implications of quantum theory for the concept of divine action and the importance of neuroscience for the concept of the soul.

The need for this sort of focused study will continue. It will always be necessary to keep in step with the advancing results of the sciences. A substantial number of theologians and scientists working together will be required to do so in ways that are beneficial to theology. But there is need also for the occasional synoptic view that takes account of the scientific picture of the world in its current state and considers it from the perspective of the Christian faith and in turn thinks about the Christian faith on the basis of that picture. The particular need today is a theology of the created world that takes account of both the scientific world-picture and also the central convictions of the Christian faith. This need arises from the fact that Christian theology is inherently systematic. Each doctrine is systematically connected to every other doctrine. It is a mistake to treat the doctrine of creation in isolation from other doctrines. Creation must be considered not only in terms of the natural sciences but also in terms of the doctrine of the new creation and the trinitarian God of the new creation. This book is an attempt to satisfy that need.

The plan of this book is as follows. In chapter one I suggest that Christian doctrine consists of three aspects: the rule of faith, the hermeneutical dimension, and the ethical dimension. Each is an essential component of the Christian faith, and each appears in the doctrine of creation. Chapter two is an exposition of the rule of faith with regard to the doctrine of creation. My thesis is that the rule of faith expresses the central convictions of Christianity and consequently must be safeguarded in any presentation of doctrine. At the same time, the rule of faith has a somewhat modest scope and is compatible with a wide range of philosophical and scientific theories. In chapter three I introduce the hermeneutical dimension of doctrine and provide some illustrations of its historical development with respect to the doctrine of creation. My purpose here is to show that the doctrine has always been understood according to the prevailing philosophical and scientific picture of each historical era. Accordingly, it is appropriate for us today to understand the doctrine in light of the current state of scientific knowledge.

Chapter four is a presentation of the idea that creatures participate in the trinitarian life of God. I illustrate the growth of this idea in the Bible and in Christian history and argue that it provides us with one of the dominant ways in which the Christian tradition has understood creatures' relation to God. This idea firmly ties the doctrine of creation to the doctrines of the triune God and of the new creation. In this way the systematic character of theology is preserved.

Chapters five through eight are an attempt to interpret the world in terms of creatures' participation in the Trinity. My argument is that the trinitarian life of God is a life of identity and difference, unity and diversity. Since creatures participate in this life, they too should exhibit identity and difference, unity and diversity. They do so, however, under the condition of finitude. This means that the trinitarian dialectics of identity and difference appears in creatures that are temporal and material. Accordingly, identity and difference appear in creatures as the dialectics of persistence and change in time, of generic identity and individualizing difference, of part-whole relations, and of relationality. In every case, the characteristics of creatures are grounded in the dialectical life of the Trinity but under the condition of finitude. At the same time, the finite character of creatures means that the dialectics of trinitarian life is disrupted to some extent in creatures. In the Trinity identity and difference are harmoniously balanced. In creatures, however, they are not harmonious. As a result, creatures are marked by the limitations of finitude in a variety of forms. In the human domain, there is further distortion because identity and difference appear under the condition of sin. At the end of each chapter, I indicate briefly the way in which God's new creation in the kingdom of God represents God's response to the distortions of sin and to the limitations of finitude.

Chapters nine and ten concern the ethical dimension of the doctrine of creation. In chapter nine I argue that the Christian faith has, in addition to a cognitive aspect, a practical and ethical aspect. Christian doctrine is not only a matter of intellectual conception but also a commitment to live in certain ways. The history of Christian thought shows that this ethical dimension contains two impulses. In the first, the world is regarded as ethically and spiritually problematic and we are called to differentiate ourselves from the world. This is the impulse toward transcending the world ethically. In the second, the world is regarded as the good creation of God and we are called to identify with the world. This is the impulse toward participation in the world. In chapter ten I offer a discussion of ways in which these two impulses appear in our contemporary ethical situation. The world-transcending impulse takes the form of overcoming the world of consumer culture. The world-participating impulse takes the form of loving concern for the natural environment on the basis of our identification with it.

Thanks are due to those who helped with this book: The Council for Christian Colleges and Universities and the John Templeton Foundation for sponsoring the John Templeton Oxford Seminars on Science and Christianity; Point Loma Nazarene University for providing a sabbatical; the Wesleyan Center for Twenty-First Century Studies for financial support; the members and staff of Point Loma Nazarene University's Department of Philosophy and Religion for ideas, critique, and moral support; participants in Point Loma's weekly science-religion discussion group for reading a draft of this book and providing many helpful comments; Eugene Harris for photographic help; and, most important, grateful thanks go to my wife Terrie, for her unfailing help and support.

PART ONE

CREATION AND TRINITY

1

The Historical Development of the Doctrine of Creation

The first step toward a contemporary theology of creation is to examine the doctrine of creation in its historical unfolding. This is because Christian doctrine has an irreducibly traditional character. The Christian faith is an ongoing dialogue with its own past. It continues to exist and to be faithful to itself only by engaging the formative steps in its historical becoming. Although it does not owe obsequious servitude to its past, it is nothing without that past. Without standing in that tradition, it is no longer the *Christian* faith. For these reasons, a grasp of the doctrine's past is needed if we are see what the doctrine's present can and must be.

The point of departure for considering the history of the doctrine of creation is the Bible. But it is necessary to consider the special character of the Bible. Convictions about creation scarcely appear in the Bible as systematic and comprehensive doctrines but are embedded in the Bible's narrative framework,[1] with the result that the Bible has no self-contained doctrine of creation.[2] The Genesis account of creation is the prelude to the history of God with a particular people and with the rest of the created order. The creation-event points forward to the ultimate restoration and re-creation of all things, articulated in Revelation, just as in John's Gospel the appearance of Jesus Christ looks back to and recapitulates the creative beginning of God's acts in Genesis. For this reason, the account of creation narrated in Genesis must not be abstracted from its place and function in the Bible as the prelude. It is not appropriate to think of the first chapters of Genesis as *the* biblical doctrine of creation.

This point can be stated more explicitly by noting that the Bible always draws the closest connection between creation and redemption.

Not only is creation the prelude to redemption but redemption is consistently understood in light of creation. For example, Psalms such as 18:16-17 and 124:1-5 describe redemption as rescue from the waters of destruction, a clear allusion to the chaos from which, according to Genesis, God creates the ordered world and by which the world is constantly threatened. In a different way, Second Isaiah represents the return of Israel from captivity in Babylon in terms reminiscent of creation. In 42:5-9 it is the creator who does the new thing of restoring the fortunes of Israel. In 44:26-27 this same creator is the redeemer, who decrees that Jerusalem will once again be inhabited and who overcomes the chaos of destruction as in the primordial quelling of the threatening waters. In 45:18 the creator declares that the world was created for habitation and not to be chaos. Finally, 51:9-11 announces that the redeemed Israelite community will be enabled to return to Jerusalem, just as in the exodus from Egypt God parted the waters of the sea, thus making a way of deliverance. Not surprisingly, Paul's letters (e.g., 2 Cor 2:15) and Revelation (21:1) take up this theme of the new creation in ways that unmistakably refer us back to Genesis and other creation passages in the Bible.

Another creation motif is the image of God. This prominent idea, first enunciated in Gen 1:26, is adopted in the New Testament to refer to Jesus Christ and the saving effects of Jesus Christ. Paul in particular sees redemption as the restoration of the image of God (e.g., Col 3:10) in which humanity was first created, an image that is identical with Jesus (e.g., 2 Cor 4:4 and Col 1:15). Jesus Christ is also prominent in the New Testament as the agent of God's creation. John 1:3, Heb 1:2, and Col 1:15-16 all identify Jesus as the creator of all things, probably reflecting the teaching of Proverbs 8 about the role of God's wisdom in creation.

The importance of these observations is that biblical teachings about creation should not be abstracted from their setting in and connection with the larger narrative scheme of the Bible. The Bible, in short, does not have a doctrine of creation, if we mean an enclosed idea that can be inspected in isolation from other doctrines. Instead the Bible presents the idea of creation as part of an interconnected web of beliefs, each of which can be understood only in terms of the others.

We are now in a position to state emphatically what the doctrine of creation is not and cannot be. First, it is a mistake to treat the doctrine of creation as though it were simply the description of an event in the past. Although one may, on the basis of scientific theories, associate the creation-event with the so-called big bang, the Christian doctrine of creation is not only and not even primarily about the big bang. To identify creation narrowly with a physical event would mean losing the Bible's sense of the intimate relation between creation and redemption and treating the doctrine as a quasi-scientific account of an event in the past. Although *a* doctrine of creation may be identified with a past event in which the universe came to be, the *Christian* doctrine of creation cannot be.

Second, the doctrine of creation itself is not a *theory* about the universe. It is neither testable nor falsifiable in the customary scientific senses of the terms. Also, it cannot be brought into a logical relation with accepted scientific theories; it does not entail any particular scientific theory and is not entailed by any particular theory. Further, it is impossible to adopt the objective and dispassionate attitude toward the subject matter of the doctrine as is required in the physical sciences. Regardless of how passionately a scientist may embrace a theory and how significant the theory is believed to be, the scientific method and community are committed to a dispassionate and critical attitude toward theories. Such an attitude is necessary if theories are to be properly tested in a scientific way. But a doctrine such as creation is held in a different way because it is an integral and fundamental part of the Christian faith and life. With a few exceptions, scientific theories can be changed and belief in them discontinued without extensively altering the rest of our beliefs. Adopting or rejecting the geological theory of plate tectonics has widespread ramifications in the field of geology and related fields, but probably leaves one's overall worldview unaffected and most likely would not alter one's daily practices. Adopting or rejecting the doctrine of creation, however, is existentially a more serious matter, for doing so would affect the full scope of our worldview and, if our lives are consistent with our beliefs, our practice. Of course, the fact that the doctrine of creation is not a theory and not held by us in a dispassionate manner does not mean that believers must cling to it dogmatically and groundlessly in the face of all evidence. Our understanding of the doctrine of creation should be informed by the physical sciences, and it is certainly possible for clear and convincing evidence and arguments to strengthen or weaken one's convictions. Because the doctrine of creation is such an integral part of the Christian faith, however, it is not belief in creation alone but the entire structure of the Christian faith and life that would be strengthened or weakened. In short, the doctrine of creation makes existential and ethical demands on us that go far beyond the cognitive demands imposed on us by a sound theory.

Finally, the doctrine of creation is not a metaphysical account of reality, at least if metaphysics is concerned with the most generic features of reality.[3] Although the doctrine of creation is interested in the whole of reality, that interest is concerned more with the creator of that reality and with the creator's importance for our lives than with the universal categories and features of reality. Naturally, it is to be expected that any particular exposition of the doctrine of creation will, intentionally or not, make use of some metaphysical assumptions. It may even expressly employ a metaphysical theory. There is nothing illegitimate in this; such attempts must be judged by means of the usual canons of philosophical argumentation. But the doctrine itself does not depend on any particular metaphysical scheme and does not entail any particular metaphysics.

What, then, *is* the doctrine of creation? The place to begin is with an understanding of the Christian faith as such. The Christian faith embraces the dialectical relation of thinking and practice. On the one hand, this means that we can draw a distinction between the cognitive and the practical dimensions of doctrine. On the other hand, it means that this distinction is artificial, for there is no authentic Christian thought without a corresponding practice and no right practice without sound thinking. Thought and practice are two complementary components of the one Christian life and faith.

This analysis admits further refinement. We may distinguish three dimensions of the Christian faith. These are the regulative, the hermeneutical, and the ethical dimensions.[4]

The regulative dimension of faith takes the form of doctrines such as we find formally in creeds and official statements and also in liturgies and hymns. In their regulative aspect, these doctrines perform two functions that are pertinent to this discussion. First, any given doctrine may support another doctrine, thus exhibiting the systematic character of the Christian faith. For example, the medieval theologian Anselm argued that the doctrine of atonement makes sense only if the christological doctrine of Christ's two natures is true. Second, doctrines perform a defining function that arises from the need of the community to distinguish itself from what it regards as aberrant views by giving expression to its most central convictions. In this way it defines itself in relation to other communities and worldviews. It defines the boundaries that distinguish it from other systems of beliefs and establishes the rules that regulate appropriate Christian thought and action.[5]

The hermeneutical dimension of the Christian faith is the attempt by the community to understand its beliefs and practices. Understanding occurs when beliefs and practices are thought about through some conceptual scheme. In form, attempts at understanding often appear as systematic theologies, after the model of the great medieval *Summas*. In the Middle Ages there was a persistent and ultimately successful attempt to understand the Christian faith in terms of an Aristotelian framework. This gradually modified the earlier tradition of understanding that incorporated, for the most part, a Platonic conceptual framework. In each case, Christian convictions were understood in terms drawn from a conceptual scheme. In this way, the creator came to be thought of as the first cause of the universe as described in Aristotle's philosophy. Several points deserve note. First, this analysis implies that understanding differs from arriving at the truth. Medieval theologians understood the Christian faith in a certain way, but it would be difficult for us to claim that their understanding was true. Today we are likely to understand the Christian faith in terms drawn from modern physical and social sciences. While it is natural for us to be convinced of the truth of our understanding, an assessment sensitive to the history of Christian thought will compel us to refrain from claiming that our views are true in any sort of absolute sense. Second, whereas the regulative dimension of the Christian faith is an act of the entire Christian community (admittedly, by its representatives), the task of understanding is undertaken by individuals— although these individuals pursue understanding within the community of faith and often for the benefit of that community. Nonetheless, the task of understanding can be highly idiosyncratic. It may not correspond to the traditional understanding of a given community if it draws on a conceptual system different from that on which the traditional understanding is based. Nonetheless, to the extent that it is intended to be a Christian understanding, the hermeneutical dimension will seek to remain within the boundaries of the regulative.

The regulative and hermeneutical dimensions point to what the Christian tradition has always understood by the phrase "faith seeking understanding." Origen, a second-century Christian, asserted that, while the apostles stated with great clarity the necessary doctrines of Christianity, they left the rational grounds of their doctrines unexplained so that the wise people of later generations might exercise their thinking.⁶ This position implies a distinction between the teaching of the apostles and the explanation of those teachings to be offered by intellectuals. Christians were obligated to affirm the apostles' teaching, but no such authority was attached to later expositions. Whether consciously or unconsciously, this attempt at comprehension has always involved the use of some prevailing philosophical or scientific conceptuality. The Christian tradition therefore commonly distinguishes between the faith that consists in the central convictions of Christianity and the understanding of that faith.

The ethical dimension of the Christian faith arises from the fact that the Christian faith is not only thought but also practice. Faith is both a cognitive state of mind and a commitment to a certain way of life. That is why the Gospel of John (3:21) can speak of those who "do" or "practice" the truth. Truth, in the Christian conception, is both cognitive and ethical. Not only does Christian doctrine imply an ethics; it is so connected to ethics that, without a commitment to this way of being, one cannot be said to believe. Accordingly, part of my exposition of the doctrine of creation will show its connection to certain ethical practices and a way of being in the world. The ethical depends on the regulative dimension insofar as it is intended to be expressly and faithfully Christian. It also depends on the hermeneutical insofar as it depends on current states of knowledge, as in the use of natural scientific knowledge to think faithfully about the church's ecological responsibilities.

Several observations are in order about this analysis of doctrine. First, the analysis of doctrine offered here is not necessarily exhaustive. Other analyses are possible. Other dimensions of the Christian faith may be discerned, but these three seem to me to be the most pertinent to the doctrine of creation.

Second, the three dimensions that I have enumerated are distinct only within the analysis. None of these is the whole of doctrine. We can speak of them separately only as abstractions from the concrete examples of doctrine in history. No matter how resolutely we attempt to portray, for instance, the doctrine of creation in its regulative dimension, our portrayal is always necessarily associated with some understanding. In the same way, any attempt to understand the Christian doctrine of creation theologically must remain within the bounds of the regulative dimension by thinking with the Christian tradition about its central convictions. Finally, the nature of the Christian faith demands that every doctrine have a corresponding and necessary ethical dimension. Of course, in any given exposition of a doctrine one dimension may be more prominent than another, but it is the theologian's task to set forth the Christian faith in all three of its dimensions.

Third, this analysis addresses the question of doctrinal authority. What is that aspect of the doctrine of creation that, in the words of Vincent of Lerins,[7] has been believed everywhere, at all times, and by all within the community of faith? Which are the persistent elements and which are the transitory?

It is obvious that a doctrine such as creation is not authoritative in its hermeneutical dimension. This dimension is an attempt, by some within the community, to understand. Although it should be faithful to the central convictions of the Christian faith, the hermeneutical dimension is self-consciously a product of the dialogue between the faith and other bodies of knowledge, such as science and philosophy. It is a highly contextualized activity and thus has a necessarily transitory and contingent quality. Because it arises out of this dialogue and because its dialogue partners (especially the sciences) tend to shift their ground over time, the hermeneutical dimension is historically dynamic. The understanding of doctrine changes over time and culture.[8] For these reasons, although it is a necessary task, it does not provide the community with results that are authoritative for matters of faith and practice.

The ethical dimension likewise cannot be considered authoritative. Christian practice, in addition to being faithful to the fundamental convictions of the Christian tradition, also is carried on in particular cultural and intellectual contexts. Because of the need to engage in ethical practice in an informed way, expositions of the ethical dimension necessarily draw on current states of knowledge and theory. Such expositions therefore are also hermeneutical undertakings and involve the activity of understanding. Accordingly, the ethical task of the Christian faith is dynamic and changing as is the hermeneutical, although not to the same degree. Although some aspects of Christian ethics persist over time, its highly contextualized nature precludes it from being fully authoritative in itself. Otherwise, we would have to continually affirm and live by the sometimes limited ethical sensitivities of the past.

It is the regulative dimension of the Christian faith that is persistent and therefore authoritative. The regulative dimension of doctrine is concerned with drawing boundaries between what is and what is not acceptable belief and practice. As such it gives definition to the community and seeks to state the nonnegotiable convictions without which the community cannot maintain itself without loss of identity. We should note, however, that what allows the regulative function to be authoritative is its modesty. Whereas in seeking to understand, the theologian is allowed to wander considerably beyond the express statements of the Christian tradition in speculative directions, the classical and regulative statements of doctrine—the creeds—impress us mainly by how much they do not say. Creeds assert that God created the world, but none goes much beyond that modest affirmation. The Christian tradition has every right to expect its adherents to embrace this affirmation, but in fact they are not being asked to commit themselves to a full-blown metaphysical system or scientific theory. To put the matter another way, the modest affirmation is compatible with many understandings. All Christians will agree that God created the world, but if we ask about the more specific content of their belief we find a great variety of answers. Nonetheless, the regulative dimension is not vacuous; it definitely rules out some beliefs and practices. I suggest, then, that the authoritative element of doctrine lies in the regulative task, which is the persistent element in the Christian faith.

Before proceeding to the historical development of the doctrine of creation, there remain only a few methodological issues to discuss. The first concerns the scope of the topic. Limitations of space means that the doctrine of creation can be considered only in its broadest outlines. Many other important subjects will have to be passed by.

The second methodological issue pertains to the mode of exposition of biblical passages, an issue that presents enormous challenges to the interpreter. Questions of dating, setting, and authorship remain disputed. As a result, the purpose of the passages cannot in every case be precisely ascertained. Limitations of space prevent a thorough review of the issues and possibilities for interpretation. All that can be done is to indicate the scholarly consensus, where there is one, and to restrict the exposition to those aspects of biblical teaching that appear to be reasonably assured.

The third issue has already been alluded to. It arises from the fact that the doctrine of creation is intimately connected to other doctrines, notably the doctrine of redemption. This means that any attempt to expound the doctrine of creation that overlooks these connections will be led seriously astray. At the same time, practical limitations prevent an adequate treatment that would demonstrate the full array of connections between the doctrine of creation and the other components of theology. All that can be done is to give the reader some sense of the way in which the doctrine of creation is embedded in the larger scheme of Christian theology. In this way we can periodically remind ourselves of the dangers of focusing too narrowly on texts that are overtly about creation and neglecting the way in which creation is merely one part of an integrated body of theological doctrine.

2

The Regulative Dimension
of the Doctrine of Creation

Christian theology has been characterized by the phrase "faith seeking understanding." This mandates that we begin by determining what that faith is. Faith points to the regulative dimension of doctrine. Before we can understand the doctrine of creation, we must be clear about what it stands for and what it stands against. For this reason I begin with a discussion of the regulative dimension as it has developed in the Christian tradition.

The Bible

It is natural to begin with the biblical tradition for two reasons. First, even though the Bible does not in itself contain the church's doctrine of creation in a fully developed form, it provides the foundational materials for the church's doctrine. Second, we can observe the regulative dimension of faith at work in the biblical tradition. This latter point is especially true of the Old Testament, where, at significant places, the writers[1] were concerned to define a normative faith and to distinguish that faith polemically from the beliefs about creation that were prevalent in the surrounding cultures.

The first chapter of Genesis will serve as a case study of the regulative dimension in the Bible. Among its other purposes, there is an unmistakably polemical interest in distinguishing biblical faith from that of the surrounding nations.[2] I will focus on four points in the text in which the regulative function seems most prominent. They are, first, the lack of mythological motifs in the description of the separation of heaven and earth (1:6); second, the status of sun, moon, and stars

(1:16); third, the role of humanity and God's provision for humanity (1:26-30); and fourth, the absence of conflict in the creation story.

According to Genesis God decreed a dome in the midst of the primordial waters, thus separating the waters above the dome from those below. We miss the point, however, if we treat these words about the firmament as though they could be a serious candidate for a scientific account of the universe, as is sometimes done. The way to appreciate the ancient purpose of the passage is to compare it to other ancient accounts on which the Bible depends but from which it distinguishes itself. Behind the biblical passage lies an ancient understanding of creation as an act of separation, but the biblical version represents a considerably less dramatic version than the Babylonian version on which it depends. The latter recounts Marduk's slaying of Tiamat and dividing her body into two parts, one of which formed the dome of the sky.[3] The story of Marduk and Tiamat illustrates an ancient mythological way of apprehending reality. By *mythological* I refer to its role, in conjunction with annual rituals and with the ideology of the monarchy, of explaining the cycles of nature and the emergence of order from chaos. In both the Babylonian and biblical stories there is creation by separation, but it is evident that the biblical writers purposely deemphasized (without eliminating altogether) the mythological elements of the story. The dome is no longer the slain body of Tiamat, overcome by combat with the forces of order, but simply a material structure. Of course, its biblical form is no more scientifically acceptable than is its Babylonian form. At the same time, the purpose of the biblical story was not primarily to explain the workings of the universe but to point to God's power while shifting the emphasis away from mythology and polytheism. This purpose illustrates the regulative dimension of faith. The biblical text demarcates the boundary between normative belief and aberrant belief.

A second way in which the regulative dimension can be seen is in the portrayal of the sun, moon, and stars. Verses 14-18 note rather curtly that God ordered lights to appear in the dome to separate day from night, to mark the seasons, and to illuminate the earth. The modern reader will again be struck by this picturesque manner of representation, the heavenly bodies being attached to the cosmic dome like Christmas ornaments on a tree. But the main point will be missed unless the ancient Near Eastern background of this passage is kept in mind. For the ancients, the astral bodies were not what they are for us—material things that either give or reflect light. They were instead thought of as divinities. A residue of this belief appears in Judg 5:20, which recounts that "the stars fought from heaven, from their courses they fought against Sisera," showing that the notion of stars as gods is not unknown in the Bible. A vestige of this idea may lie behind the statement of Gen 1:16 that the sun and the moon were to *rule* the day and the night. When the writers of Genesis asserted that God decreed the existence, location, and function of the heavenly lights, however, there can be no mistaking the intent. Sun, moon, and stars, in spite of their important functions in God's ordering of the universe, are no longer deities. They are mere creatures with assigned roles to play. Here as elsewhere the biblical text distinguishes creator from the created world decisively.[4] Once again, the regulative dimension is evident, as the Israelites were instructed in how to think rightly about heavenly objects and were indirectly forbidden to worship them.

A third appearance of the regulative dimension is the representation of humankind and the care that the creator shows. Any reader of Gen 1:26-30 will discern that humankind is given special status in God's ordered universe. We alone are created in the image of God; we alone are given dominion over the earth; and only we receive a command from God. The regulative character of this passage is brought into relief when we compare it with the alternative versions of creation available in the ancient Near East. In the Babylonian account, humankind is created for one purpose—to serve the gods by laboring on their behalf. We are to bear the burden of work that the gods would have borne. It is difficult to resist the conclusion that the Genesis account is expressly offering a different and opposing view of humankind and its role in the universe. This account mentions nothing about our serving God. Instead, all our activity is directed toward this world.[5] We do not provide for God's needs; God provides for our needs.

Finally, consider the way in which the act of creation is portrayed. Since the rise of modern science, attention has focused on the sequence of events, with some arguing that the sequence is compatible with the results of scientific inquiry and others arguing that the sequence is not. But this focus misses the main point of the biblical story, which is that God is the sole agent of creation—and through speech. The Babylonian account of creation has a far different view of the matter: the physical universe arises from the dismembering of Tiamat, that is, through combat. The story begins with a plurality of divine beings and with conflict. The conflict is finally resolved through bloodshed, giving rise to the universe. Once again, it is difficult to avoid the conclusion that the biblical writers consciously portrayed the process of creation in such a way as to emphasize the unity of God, to eliminate conflict, and to discount any possibility of rivals to God's power.[6]

This selection of creation-motifs from Genesis 1 shows the regulative task at work, distinguishing the normative biblical faith from incompatible beliefs in alternative ancient Near Eastern accounts of creation. Biblical writers, to be sure, did not reject every aspect of the alternative creation stories. They accepted the motif of creation by separation and apparently endorsed the notion that the earth is covered by a dome on which hang the heavenly bodies and which prevents the upper waters from flooding the earth. This demonstrates the importance of distinguishing the regulative function from the modes of thought and understandings in which it is embedded. Unlike creeds, which present the regulative dimension of faith in a distinctive form, in the Bible the regulative aspect of faith is not separated from the biblical narrative. The biblical writers rejected only those aspects of alternative creation stories that were incompatible with the beliefs that they were prescribing. In those cases in which ideas about creation were available that did not conflict with their views, they willingly incorporated those ideas into the biblical text.

The Christian Tradition

Although the Bible does not present the regulative dimension of faith in a systematic or comprehensive form, we can see theological convictions emerging throughout it. This process, in which convictions move from an inarticulate and inchoate state to an express and developed state, continued into the Christian era, where it found expression in creeds and other writings. The regulative dimension is not a fixed body of convictions given definite form in the Bible but instead arose in a tradition stretching from the Old Testament to the later Christian creeds. At least part of the reason for this dynamic character of the regulative dimension is the fact that the intellectual context shifted. Whereas the first chapter of Genesis drew upon and was directed against Near Eastern mythologies, the early church faced a worldview shaped by the ancient philosophical schools of the Hellenistic period, notably the Platonic, Aristotelian, Stoic, and Epicurean schools. In addition, the church had to contend with the new religions of the Hellenistic period, especially (for the doctrine of creation) Gnosticism. The practical effect of this new situation was to change the character of the worldviews from which the Christian faith must be distinguished, compelling further articulation and development of the regulative dimension.

Irenaeus and the Creedal Tradition

The place to begin with the doctrine of creation in the Christian tradition is Irenaeus (d. c. 200). His main work, *Against Heresies*, is one of the earliest attempts to provide a complete refutation of what was at the time Christianity's main competitor, Gnosticism. Irenaeus unsystematically catalogued the errors of Gnosticism and then refuted them. Whether Irenaeus's presentation of Gnosticism is entirely fair to the Gnostics and accurate is not my concern here.[7] I am interested instead in Irenaeus's contribution to the emerging regulative dimension of the doctrine of creation.

Irenaeus's rambling work ranges widely over Christian beliefs. Among them we can separate out seven affirmations related to the doctrine of creation that became part of the emerging rule of faith: (1) There is one God and creator; (2) the creator is not a lesser god; (3) the creator is the Father of Jesus Christ; (4) creation is an act of God's freedom; (5) creation is by the Word and the Spirit; (6) the world was created from nothing; and (7) the body is redeemable and not to be denigrated.

1. There is only one God and that God is the sole creator. Gnosticism had a fairly complicated understanding of the process of creation, involving multiple and sometimes conflicting gods. Over against the Gnostic views, Irenaeus asserted the unity of God and went out of his way to emphasize that everything created owes its origin to the one God. There were several issues. Irenaeus wanted to ensure that any lesser beings such as angels had no hand in creation and were to be classified as creatures. God's act of creation was performed immediately, not mediated by a chain of subsidiary beings. Irenaeus found all the resources necessary for creation contained in the divine Trinity.[8]

2. The creator is supreme and not subordinate to some higher principle or being. Irenaeus here was countering the Gnostic belief that the creator, although *a* god, is not the highest principle or divinity. Gnostics typically asserted that the creator is actually quite far down on the ontological scale. This world was, for them, the work of an inferior divinity. Worse, at least some Gnostics argued that the creator was so far removed from the highest principle as to be ignorant of it.[9] Against this Irenaeus affirmed the supremacy of the creator.

3. The creator is the Father of Jesus Christ. This issue may strike the modern reader initially as arcane, but it cut to the heart of Christianity's understanding of itself and of its relation to the Old Testament. On the Gnostic view, Jesus was a representative of the highest principle sent to correct the mistakes of the creator. In at least one Gnostic-like system, the creator was identified with the god of the Old Testament. This identification established an opposition between the creator and Christ, and between the Old and New Testaments. Irenaeus found these oppositions to be intolerable. In their place he steadfastly affirmed the closest connection between Jesus Christ and the creator. Not only is Jesus the eternal Word of God, by which God fashioned the universe, but he is also the creator's Son.[10] This affirmation preserved the relation between Jesus and the creator and also between the doctrines of creation and salvation.

4. Creation has resulted from God's free choice.[11] This assertion is a consequence of the prior affirmations. If the creator is in fact the highest principle and needed no help in the act of creation, then creation must have resulted from an act of choice. It could not result from necessity, for there is nothing that could compel the creator to act. Creation likewise was not an accident, for the creator possesses intelligence.

5. Creation occurred by means of the Word and Spirit of God. In one picturesque metaphor, Irenaeus likened the Word and Spirit to the two hands by means of which God created the world.[12] Although Irenaeus did not present a fully developed doctrine of the Trinity, it is significant that already in the second century the creator was being thought of in trinitarian terms. The main point for Irenaeus is that, with these two "hands," God stands in no need of external agents or resources in order to create. The Trinity is the sufficient origin of creation.

6. The world was created out of nothing. This idea, apparently first enunciated in 2 Macc 7:28, ran counter to the assumptions of Hellenistic

philosophy. Virtually every ancient philosophy posited an eternal material substance from which this ordered cosmos arose. The Gnostics also, it appears, posited some preexisting (although perhaps not material) substance. Irenaeus, however, expressed in uncompromising terms that all things, even matter itself, were created by the free act and power of the creator.[13] In doing so, he introduced into the emerging Christian doctrine of creation one of its most prominent features and certainly one that distinguished it with utter clarity from its ancient alternatives. Although later Christian writers would draw on Hellenistic philosophies for various insights, the eternity of matter would never be an option. To allow it would be to question the power and supremacy of God.

7. The body is redeemable and not to be denigrated. Christian writers inferred from Gnostic theology that anything material could only have been the imperfect work of the creator, itself a lesser deity. As a result, material substances such as the body must be of little value in Gnostic estimation. Whether this deduction corresponds to actual Gnostic thought and practice is debatable. What is beyond dispute is that ecclesiastical writers such as Irenaeus believed that Gnosticism implies a low view of the body and of the body's prospects for salvation. Over against this view, Irenaeus insisted that the body participates in salvation. The immediate issues were mainly christological and soteriological, not cosmological. What irritated Irenaeus was the suggestion that, the body being of low worth, Christ could not truly have had a human body and could have received nothing from his mother, Mary. This implied, for Irenaeus, that Christ was not really human, that his suffering was no great accomplishment, and that he cannot truly be the redeemer of humanity.[14] It was important for Irenaeus that Christ recapitulate the history of humanity with God and thus restore humanity to God. But this could happen only if Christ were indeed human. Although the focus of Irenaeus's remarks was on Christ and salvation, they are important also for the doctrine of creation. They give classic expression to the conviction that material substance, as a creation of God, is good and can participate in salvation. Redemption is therefore not a flight *from* the created world but instead the salvation *of* the created world in its physicality.

This selection of ideas from Irenaeus's *Against Heresies* gives us some indication of the direction in which the doctrine of creation, particularly in its regulative dimension, was going. Institutional shape was given to the regulative aspect in the creed of Constantinople (381).

Building on the earlier Nicene creed (325), which had itself built on previous summaries of faith, the Constantinopolitan creed sets forth the most basic tenets of the doctrine of creation. It excludes the Gnostic and pagan belief in a plurality of divine principles by affirming belief "in one God." It reinforces Irenaeus's insistence that the one God, the creator, is the Father of Jesus Christ by enjoining belief in "the Father." In this way it ties together the New Testament and the Old and resolutely decides against the Gnostic inclination to oppose creation to salvation. By asserting that God is the "creator of heaven and earth, of all things visible and invisible." it draws the firmest possible distinction between God and the created realm and announces that the created world has a single source, the one God. It thus rules out belief in lesser, divinities who would be surrogate creators in place of the highest God. The creed also endorses Irenaeus's trinitarian doctrine of creation by affirming belief in "one Lord Jesus Christ . . . through whom all things came into being" and in "the Holy Spirit, the Lord and life-giver." Finally, it repeats the main points of Irenaeus's concerns about the goodness and redeemability of the physical universe by mentioning "the Lord Jesus Christ . . . who was incarnate by the Holy Spirit and the Virgin Mary and was made human . . . [And] the resurrection of the dead." Here Jesus Christ is affirmed as truly and fully human and the resurrection of the body is asserted.[15]

The Nicene and Constantinopolitan creeds were the first official documents that addressed the doctrine of creation. They set forth the basic outlines of the doctrine in its regulative dimension. The regulative character of the creedal statements about creation is seen in the fact they make no express use of contemporary philosophical modes of thought for purposes of exposition. Instead they focus on defining the boundaries of appropriate Christian thought and, implicitly, practice.

Although these creeds established the base lines of the doctrine in its regulative dimension, further development was necessary because, as time went on, it became clear that the chief alternative to the Christian faith was going to be not Gnosticism but the amalgamation of Hellenistic philosophy and cosmology that was taking shape in late antiquity. Among early Christian writers who took account of and responded to this philosophy and cosmology were Athanasius (296–373) and Basil the Great (c. 329–379).

Athanasius

The regulative dimension of the doctrine of creation received further development and articulation in the writings of Athanasius in express response to the philosophical systems of late antiquity.

Against the Epicurean philosophy, with its materialistic and deterministic bent, Athanasius argued for the existence of a creator. He urged this point by drawing attention to the universe's order and by arguing that such order requires belief in the universal Logos, which he identified with the Word, the second person of the Trinity.[16] In his view, not only do rational beings participate in the Logos but in fact all creatures participate by receiving life and order. Without their participation in the Word, the entire universe would revert to the nothingness from which it came.[17] By grounding the universe's order in the Logos and identifying the Logos with the Word, Athanasius argued that the universe depends on a creator, who is the Trinity.

Having argued that the universe and everything in it is the result of a single creator, Athanasius addressed the philosophers' conception of evil. His strategy was to put the onus on pagan philosophy. With the common pagan assumption that evil is a substance, the philosophers had to choose between, for Athanasius, undesirable options. Either they must concede that God has made evil (since evil, being a substance, is among things created) or they must argue that God is not the creator of all things, but only of what is good.[18] The philosophers, of course, almost uniformly decided that God is associated only with goodness. But for Athanasius, allegiance to the biblical tradition and its teaching about the creator meant that neither horn of this dilemma is acceptable. The only alternative, he thought, was to go between the horns by denying the premise that evil has substantial reality. It being exceedingly difficult for ancient philosophers to conceive of reality that is not material substance, the burden was on Athanasius to depict evil in a rigorous, comprehensible way. His approach was to define evil as that which is deficient in being. God being the supreme reality, lesser things are real insofar as they reflect in some way God's nature. Evil, on the contrary, does not in any way reflect God's nature. Accordingly, evil lacks substantial reality and God is in no way responsible for it.[19] This inventive solution, which anticipates Augustine's (354–430) later and more elaborated version, places responsibility for evil squarely on humanity. Whether it is philosophically valid is a different question; its place in the emerging regulative dimension of the doctrine of creation, however, is evident, for it asserted clearly that evil is not a part of the good creation of God. Athanasius thus developed Irenaeus's point about the goodness of physical things in a way that philosophically absolved God of responsibility for creating evil.

Athanasius also tackled the question of the stars' divinity, a thesis affirmed in Aristotle's cosmology. Although difficult for moderns to embrace, this view was common in an era when unforced movement of any sort suggested the presence of life and the regular motion of the stars seemed to indicate a highly intelligent sort of life. Beginning with the axiom, commonly accepted in late antiquity, that the divine must be self-sufficient and not dependent on anything,[20] Athanasius argued that the interdependence of all things in nature argues against anything in this world being divine.[21] The stars, being part of an interconnected system in which each part depends on others, cannot be divine.

But to deny divinity to any given part of the universe left unanswered the question of whether the universe as a whole was divine. Although each part of the universe may depend on other parts, the universe as a whole may be self-sufficient and hence divine. This was roughly the position of Stoic philosophy. Athanasius's retort to this pantheistic option is twofold. First, divinity cannot be composed of parts as is the universe.[22] Second, the pantheistic interpretation attributes bodily characteristics to God, characteristics that, in Athanasius's estimation, contradict what he took to be commonsense assumptions about God's invisibility and intangibility.[23]

Pagan philosophers of all sorts provided another challenge for Athanasius by affirming the existence of eternal unformed matter as one of the basic realities of the universe. In this view, the act of creation was in truth an act of transformation as the creative god shaped the unformed, imperfect, and intractable matter into a cosmos. For Athanasius, however, such a view of the creator is unworthy, for it declares the creator to be lacking in power and more a mechanic than a creator.[24] The only option that was worthy of the idea of God was to contradict one of the axioms of pagan philosophy by postulating the creation of matter from nothing.

Basil the Great

Basil (c. 329–379) was quite clear about the distinction between attempting to understand by means of science and philosophy, on the one hand, and the regulative character of the doctrine of creation, on the other. The former is the product of curiosity, while the latter aims at preserving the church's belief and practice. Focusing on the former would mean neglecting what was for him the more important task of edifying the church.[25] This stricture certainly did not prevent him from engaging in philosophical and scientific exposition of the doctrine of creation. He nonetheless maintained a firm distinction between the task of edification and the attempt to understand, preferring the simplicity of faith's affirmations to the rational proofs offered by the philosophers.[26]

Not surprisingly, he cautioned against undue curiosity in cosmological matters. Touching on the current debate about whether the earth is suspended in space or rests on something else, he reminded his audience of God's mocking response to Job's inquiry into the universe. He encouraged them to restrain their curiosity and to rest in the thought that all things are sustained by God's power. In this way, regardless of which philosophical explanation they found attractive, they would remain true to the faith, which contains truth of unsurpassed reliability and profitability.[27] Whereas, he argued, scientists might become enthused over questions about the shape and size of the earth and the causes of eclipses, the Genesis account of creation completely neglects such matters and focuses our attention on the main thing necessary for our souls, the knowledge of the creator.[28]

In Basil's remarks we can observe the regulative aspect of the doctrine of creation taking shape. While there is a proper task of attempting to expound the doctrine with the help of current science and other disciplines, the regulative dimension of doctrine is distinct. It is not concerned with engaging the world of human thought but instead with safeguarding the church's convictions so that we may know and worship God. As we can see from Basil's thoughts, the regulative dimension of doctrine is far more modest, if more secure, than the results of attempting to understand. Whereas understanding necessarily involves the theologian in all the apparatus of human inquiry and in articulating human knowledge in great detail, the regulative function restricts itself to the most basic affirmations, such as that God's power sustains all things. The individual theologian may be persuaded by this or that scientific account of the universe, but the vital matter is to affirm the regulative convictions of the faith.

Having argued for the importance of the regulative dimension of the doctrine, Basil proceeded to employ it in defending the faith against incompatible philosophical doctrines.

The first of these doctrines is materialism, the belief that no principle beyond matter is required to explain the existence and character of the universe. Here Basil had in mind not only the Epicurean philosophy but also the pre-Socratic philosophers of nature who had posited various sorts of material principles as the foundation of the universe. Failing to grasp the governance of the world by its creator and deceived by their atheism, he argued, they could see the universe as ruled only by chance. Over against these systems he set the biblical account of the universe's creation and rule by a single God.[29] Far from the universe being the result of chance, he asserted, the Genesis account shows that God created it for a purpose, namely, for the advantage of souls who could make use of the physical world to come to the knowledge of God.[30]

Another philosophical doctrine that Basil combated was the eternity of the world. It was particularly tempting in ancient times to assert the eternity of the world on the basis of the regular and circular motion of the heavenly bodies. Circular motion seemingly had no beginning and no end. Unlike the line, the circle has no point that is obviously the starting position. Basil, however, argued on scriptural grounds that, even though circular motion is repetitive, the heavenly courses are part of the created world that had a beginning and will have an end. Moreover, making the universe coeternal with God is a prelude to worshiping the universe as divine.[31] Along the same lines, he rejected the theory of eternal unformed matter, for to ascribe timelessness to matter is to place it in the same category that God is in. Furthermore, to do so is to diminish the power of God, for if matter is eternal then God is no longer the creator but only a craftsman who fashions something ordered out of preexisting material. The universe, therefore, would have two sources, unformed matter and God who contributed the form.[32] Basil had assimilated the argument, arising from the trinitarian debates of his century, that eternity is a mark of deity. Earlier in the century the issue had been the eternity and hence the full divinity of the Word. In the "Hexaemeron," Basil's concern was to deny the eternity of matter on the grounds that doing so was equivalent to considering it divine. Naturally this argument would not have carried much weight with ancient pagan philosophers, who did not regard timelessness as the prerogative of God alone. But his argument does give clear expression to the regulative nature of the doctrine of creation. Given the theological conviction that God alone is eternal, arguments had to be fashioned to convince people that matter could not be eternal but must itself be a result of creation.

Athanasius and Basil illustrate the early church's articulation of the regulative dimension of the doctrine of creation. Building on the work of Irenaeus and the creeds, they brought those resources to bear on the philosophical issues of the day in order to distinguish Christian convictions decisively from pagan beliefs. In so doing, they effectively brought the development of the doctrine's regulative aspect to completion. Although the task of understanding the doctrine by interpreting it in terms of the sciences went on and will go on indefinitely, the end of the patristic period of Christian history saw the regulative function attain virtually its final form. All that remained was for future creeds to state more fully the points already adumbrated in the early centuries.

Some conclusions can be drawn from this review. First, in discussing the normative Christian doctrine of creation, we must restrict ourselves to those beliefs that are matters of ecumenical agreement. Practically speaking, this means assigning a normative status to the doctrinal formulation of the early church. Second, there is a difference between a doctrine in its regulative dimension and the beliefs of the body of Christians at any given time. The rule of faith is not simply a snapshot of beliefs but that body of persistent and normative convictions that are necessary for the well-being of Christian thought and practice. Third, there has been genuine development in the regulative dimension of the doctrine of creation. It is not comprehensively stated in the Bible or in early creeds and writers such as Athanasius. Because it arose in situations of conflict and engagement with alternative systems of belief, it has a historically dynamic character. At the same time, a study of the creedal tradition shows that most development had been completed by the beginning of the Middle Ages.

Summary

Keeping in mind that the regulative dimension is historically dynamic, we can nonetheless identify at least its main components and offer some elucidating comments.

First, the creator is the God attested in the Bible, namely, the Father, the Son (or Word), and the Holy Spirit. This entails, at a minimum, that the creator is the Father of Jesus Christ, that creation occurs through the Word, and that the Holy Spirit is also involved in creation. Admittedly, the role of the Spirit is vague; the creedal tradition has not devoted much attention to this subject. Nonetheless, there is no question that the tradition wishes to affirm that creation is a work of the entire Trinity, even if the details remain far from fully worked out. Above all, no wedge is to be driven between the creator and Jesus Christ, as though they represented different or even opposing principles. For the same reason, creation and redemption must be considered only in relation to each other.

Second, the triune creator is alone the basis of creation. The created world is grounded in a single source, in spite of evil and in spite of the diversity that we observe in the universe. The creator had no need of and made no use of intermediate beings or principles. This means that there is no eternal matter that, independently of God, establishes limits to God's creative activity.

Third, the triune creator is distinct from the created world. Accordingly, neither the universe as a whole nor any part of it is divine. Moreover, the triune creator does not need the created world to supply some deficiency in the divine being, for this would subordinate the creator to a higher principle. Therefore, creation must be represented as resulting from a divine decision. It cannot be represented as an involuntary emanation from the divine being. The creator's distinction from the created world establishes the possibility of the creature turning away from God in sin.

Fourth, the triune creator is related to the world in a way that is compatible with this distinction. The world results from the creator's decision and therefore reflects the goodness of the creator. Everything created is by nature good because it participates in God; therefore evil is not a thing that has been created. Further, creation is not limited to an initial act of bringing into being. Creation includes God's providential care for the world, a care that finally issues forth in redemption. In this way the triune creator becomes the Trinity of salvation.

The importance of the regulative dimension lies in the need to keep the doctrine of creation faithful to its own tradition. Christian theology will always be tempted to portray itself in terms of the prevailing ideas of a culture. Engagement with these ideas is necessary, for the task of understanding is essential to the vitality of the Christian faith. It is also inevitable, because we always find ourselves embedded in a definite intellectual setting that shapes our thinking whether we are aware of it or not. Without fidelity to the tradition whence it arose, however, the doctrine of creation will be transformed into something quite different. Instead of being the *Christian* doctrine of creation, it will be an amalgamation of individual attempts to engage current knowledge in order to fashion an understanding of the world that is perhaps scientifically astute but theologically vague. The regulative dimension keeps the doctrine of creation wedded to the Christian tradition and its convictions.

At the same time, there is the danger of misunderstanding the function of the regulative dimension. This typically happens when beliefs are added to the doctrine of creation that have no ecumenically regulative significance. The insertion of belief in a six-day creation into some Reformation era creeds is an example of this.[33] It was a mistake to make belief in a six-day creation part of the rule of faith. This mistake was a result of another but common mistake—assuming that every seemingly clear statement of Scripture has regulative value and is fully authoritative. This mistake was understandable at a time when every word of the Bible was regarded as divinely inspired. But this view is scarcely tenable today unless we ignore or discount the results of biblical scholarship. The regulative aspect of doctrine is not equivalent to the sum-total or any selection of scriptural statements. Instead, we should regard the Bible as the normative source of a millennia-long dialogue, in which there has been a considerable amount of sifting and weighing. As the church continues this task, the regulative and authoritative dimension of doctrine has slowly emerged as consensus forms on difficult issues. But it is a mistake to canonize scriptural statements as rules of faith without seeing them in their place in the history of doctrinal tradition. As the example of six-day creation shows, sometimes beliefs are proposed as a rule of faith that should not be regarded as such.

The theological task today with regard to the regulative dimension is especially its preservation. Without it, there is no Christian tradition. Without it, a normative dialogue partner is lacking for the ongoing task of understanding doctrine. A related task is to help the church think about the ways in which the doctrine is expounded today. Are they too broad? Should the church state its belief about creation more fully? For example, the Protestant creeds expressly inculcate belief in the providence of God, a providence that extends even to the smallest details of the universe. In light of current scientific views of the universe, belief in God's particular providence has become difficult to sustain. The theological task today is to think through the doctrine of creation and to raise the question of how to state beliefs such as providence in ways that are truly regulative and authoritative and that do not say too much or too little.

3

The Hermeneutical Dimension
of the Doctrine of Creation

The traditional Christian posture toward doctrine is summed up in the phrase "faith seeking understanding." *Faith* designates the regulative dimension of doctrine. *Understanding* denotes the interpretive or hermeneutical dimension. These two, together with the ethical dimension, constitute the substance of Christian doctrine. In this chapter I argue that, within the Christian faith, understanding is always embedded in the prevailing cultural and intellectual ideas of a given era. While seeking to adhere to the received faith, we necessarily think about and understand creation *through* ideas that are common—perhaps so common that they are transparent to us. Examples of this abound. Consider, for instance, the ways people have understood the earth's location in the universe. Prior to the time of Nicolas Copernicus (1473–1543), the doctrine of creation was routinely and universally thought to imply that the earth is the center of the universe. Christians thought about the world by means of geocentric conceptions lingering from the classical and medieval worlds. After some theological maneuvering in response to Galileo, the view became widespread that the earth is not the center. Adherents of the Christian faith sooner or later managed to assimilate this new view into their understanding of creation. Although the regulative aspect of doctrine had not changed (no one felt the need to rewrite any creeds), the ideas and images with which the doctrine was thought about had changed dramatically.

The following pages represent a highly selective look at the development of the hermeneutical dimension of the doctrine of creation. From the thousands of writers who have contributed, a few representatives will be chosen in order to show that theological faith about creation has been persistently joined to modes of thinking drawn from the cultures in which that faith occurred. First I examine the Old Testament and the way it incorporates various ideas of the ancient Near East. I then look at developments under the influence of Hellenistic philosophy and finally inquire into some of the ways the doctrine has been understood under the impact of modern natural sciences.

The Old Testament

As in the case of the regulative dimension, we can detect the hermeneutical dimension already in the Old Testament, in which certain motifs of ancient Near Eastern mythology and other ancient beliefs are used repeatedly.[1]

One salient motif drawn from ancient myth is creation from the primordial watery chaos, often symbolically portrayed as the divine victory over the sea monster. The Genesis account retains a vestige of the ancient view when it presents creation as an act of dividing the primordial waters. The universe is formless until God introduces order and structure by separating the water by means of the firmament. Proverbs 8:27-29 represents the matter somewhat differently, but it retains the importance of God's subduing the primordial water: "When he established the heavens, I [wisdom] was there, when he drew a circle on the face of the deep, when he made firm the skies above, when he established the fountains of the deep, when he assigned for the sea its limit, so that the waters might not transgress his command, when he marked out the foundations of the earth. . . ." Here, as in Genesis, God is portrayed as establishing limits for the unruly sea, lest the universe revert to a watery chaos. In several Old Testament passages, this act was picturesquely described as God's overcoming the sea monster Leviathan. For example, Ps 74:12-17 states that "God my King is from of old, working salvation in the earth. You divided the sea by your might; you broke the heads of the dragons in the waters. You crushed the heads of Leviathan; you gave him as food for the creatures of the wilderness." In this episode God's dividing the Reed Sea (in Exodus) is paralleled to the primordial act of slaying Leviathan and thus subduing the forces of chaos. The primordial victory over chaos is represented as a paradigm for all of God's creative and saving acts. The God who originally wrought salvation by defeating the forces of chaos will continue to act on Israel's behalf. The point is that the text represents all threats to Israel as the eruption of the ancient chaos. God's original victory over chaos is understood not as an event that occurred only in the primordial past but as a recurring pattern of divine activity for the salvation of Israel. The deliverance in Exodus participates in this pattern. In the same way Isa 27:1 represents God's future and decisive act of salvation as the destruction of Leviathan, and Rev 13:1 portrays the great eschatological opponent of God as a Leviathan-like beast arising from the sea. The ancient mythical symbol of the watery chaos, then, recurs in modified form in biblical tradition in connection with God's creative and saving deeds.

The Old Testament also employs a building metaphor to describe God's construction of the universe. In this metaphor the earth is represented as resting on pillars sunk into the depths of the water. In Proverbs 8 God is an architect, who "drew a circle on the face of the deep" and "marked out the foundations of the earth." This picture of the earth resting on foundations is quite prominent in the Old Testament. In Ps 75:3 the shaking of the earth's foundations becomes a symbol for the vicissitudes of life, salvation being portrayed as God's steadying the foundations. Psalm 104:5-8 sees the foundations as evidence of God's everlasting faithfulness:

> You set the earth on its foundations, so that it shall never be shaken. You cover it with the deep as with a garment; the waters stood above the mountains. . . . They rose up to the mountains, ran down to the valleys to the place that you appointed for them. You set a boundary that they may not pass, so that they might not again cover the earth.

Here God's control over the waters of chaos is complete. Although surrounding the earth on every side, they cannot shake the foundations. Instead they meekly go to the places where God has directed them. They subserviently keep their place. The building metaphor is continued in Job 38:4-6, which likens God to a builder: "Where were you when I laid the foundation of the earth? . . . Who determined its measurements—surely you know! Or who stretched the line upon it? On what were its bases sunk or who laid its cornerstone?" Although the book of Job asserts that the human subject is in no position to answer these questions, there is no doubt that the Old Testament regards the earth as in some sense a constructed reality, secure in its place because it has been designed and made by God. Even the heavens are regarded as something produced by God's handiwork, as Ps 104:2-3 suggests: "You stretch out the heavens like a tent, you set the beams of your chambers on the waters."

Another set of ancient beliefs used extensively in the Old Testament relates to the idea of life. The Old Testament regards life as the infusion of God's spirit or breath into inanimate dust. This is portrayed succinctly in Gen 2:7: "The LORD God formed man from the dust of the ground, and breathed into his nostrils the breath of life; and the man became a living being." Naturally, what God gives God can also take back, as Job 34:14-15 indicates: "If he should take back his spirit to himself, and gather to himself his breath, all flesh would perish together, and all mortals return to dust." Death, then, is the event in which the breath that God had lent to humankind returns to its source (Ps 104:29-30).

The Era of Hellenistic Philosophy

From the time of late antiquity until the rise of modern science, the context in which the doctrine of creation was understood was framed by the philosophical systems and rudimentary sciences of late antiquity. This mix of systems included the Pythagorean, Platonic, Aristotelian, Stoic, Epicurean, and Skeptical schools, in addition to scientific work in astronomy.

By the twelfth century the works of Aristotle were being translated into Latin and made available to scholars. Christian theologians were beginning to appreciate the power of Aristotle's philosophy, some showing a willingness to combine Platonism and Aristotelianism, other even preferring Aristotle's philosophy over Plato's. Adjustments had to be made at certain points where Aristotle's teaching flatly contradicted Christian doctrine, but the rigor and precision of Aristotle's method and his clear superiority to Plato in the physical sciences meant that serious intellectuals in the Middle Ages could not ignore him.[2]

Thomas Aquinas's (c. 1225–1274) attempt to understand creation by using Aristotelian concepts is an outstanding example of using Hellenistic philosophy to systematize Christian doctrine.

Aristotle's philosophy presented distinctive problems to Thomas. Although it affirmed a first cause of the universe, it assumed the eternity of matter; it asserted that creation was not a direct act of the first cause but was instead mediated by a series of other causes; it taught that this cosmos is the only cosmos, i.e., that there are no worlds outside this one, a teaching that appeared to conflict with the almighty power of God, who could have created other worlds; and it lacked any suggestion that the first cause exercises providence in the world. In short, the assimilation of Aristotle's philosophy to Christian doctrine was a daunting task. But it was a necessary task, for the Aristotelian system, augmented with the results of ancient astronomy, represented at that time the greatest available body of knowledge. In the thirteenth century, to understand meant to think within the framework of Aristotelian philosophy, just as to understand today means to think within the methods and results of the sciences.

Aristotle's philosophy affirmed the eternity of matter, so that the act of creation consisted in joining form to matter and not in creating matter from nothing. Thomas, wishing to employ Aristotle's philosophy but bound by the rule of faith, had to contrive an Aristotelian rationale against Aristotle's belief in the eternity of matter. He did so by arguing that ancient philosophers had understood creation from only a limited perspective. They were searching only for the causes of particular features, such as whiteness, or for causes of particular individuals. These sorts of causation can be readily understood as the uniting of a form (such a whiteness) with matter. But none of them, he argued, sought for the cause of being as such. To ask for the cause of being as such is to ask for the cause, not only of the form, but also of the matter of an entity. The question of being, then, leads us to affirm the creation, not the eternity, of matter.[3] The point to note here is that Thomas took a component of the traditional doctrine of creation (the denial of the eternity of matter) and gave a rationale for it that draws on Aristotelian principles, even while contradicting Aristotle. Whereas previous theologians such as Basil had rejected the eternity of matter on theological grounds, Thomas offered a rational argument using Aristotelian modes of argumentation. We should also note that Thomas went beyond Aristotle's philosophy, for although Aristotle raised the question of being as such, he emphatically did not come to Thomas's conclusions about the creation of matter. Nonetheless, Thomas set the traditional belief about the creation of matter into a powerful intellectual framework that yielded a philosophical understanding of the traditional belief.

If matter has been created by God, then it follows that the entire universe had a beginning. This was a conclusion that no ancient philosopher, including Aristotle, was prepared to accept. Thomas, with his Christian and Aristotelian commitments, once again had to propose an Aristotelian reason for a thesis contrary to Aristotle's own conclusions. He began with the premise that the will of God is the cause of things. This premise is not an Aristotelian one. To it he joined Aristotle's dictum that an effect is necessary to the extent that its cause is necessary. From this dictum he inferred that the universe is necessary only if its cause (God's willing) is necessary. But Thomas had to reject the proposition that God's willing could be necessitated. Hence it was obvious that the universe's existence is not necessary. In other words, the eternity of the world cannot be proved logically. At the same time, the universe's having a beginning is also not demonstrable by logic. It is logically possible that God has freely willed that the universe exist eternally. Human reason cannot know, by means of logic alone, about those things that God *may* will. As a result, the belief that the world has a beginning rests on revelation alone.[4]

Having settled that all things, even matter, have been created by God and that the universe had a beginning, Thomas turned to another legacy of ancient philosophy, the question of whether the world was created by God directly and immediately or whether it proceeded from God through a series of intermediaries. According to Aristotle, the principal unmoved mover does not exercise efficient and direct causation. Instead, its intrinsic perfection inspires a host of other celestial beings to move the spheres that surround the earth. These spheres, in turn, create the alternation of day and night and the seasons on earth as well as all other mundane motions. The ultimate result is life on earth. Creation, therefore, involves a series of intermediate movers. Since this view conflicts with the Genesis account, Thomas had to find a way of expounding the Christian doctrine and of refuting Aristotle's error while employing Aristotelian principles. Thomas proposed a hypothetical hierarchy of causes, each level encompassing a wider field of reality than the level below it. The higher the cause, the more numerous are the things to which its causation extends. The highest cause would accordingly underlie the totality of reality. From this he concluded that the universal principles of being (i.e., those pertaining to every entity) must proceed directly from the highest cause. For example, because matter is a universal principle, it can be created only by the highest cause and not by lesser beings.[5] Here again Thomas expounded a traditional belief in philosophical terms that, for the medieval thinker, would have been comprehensible. Whereas previously the thesis that God created directly and immediately every kind of creature was a matter of faith, Thomas had transformed it into a matter of philosophical knowledge by using Aristotelian modes of argumentation. Thomas had shown, for those who shared his intellectual framework, not only *that* the traditional belief is true but also *why* it is true in the most rigorous intellectual terms possible in that day.

Another issue raised by Aristotle's philosophy was whether this universe is the only universe. It seemed obvious to medieval people that there must be something beyond the outermost sphere of the universe, even if it were only empty space. But empty space without limits could hold one or more universes. Thomas's approach to this question relies on his typical Aristotelian strategy as augmented by Christian considerations. Aristotle had argued for a principle of teleology in the universe, in contrast to the atomistic philosophers, who attributed all things to the chance conjunction of atoms. In Aristotle's view, it is evident that there is an order in the universe that rests on metaphysical foundations and not on mere chance. Thomas expanded Aristotle's view and argued that the universe's order proves that everything created belongs to one universe. The universe's order implies its unity and oneness. Everything is connected to other things, either as a means to an end or as an end. Besides this, all things are related to God. In short, the teleological order of the universe, whereby all things are connected to each other and to God by relations of purpose, testifies to the fact that this universe encompasses all finite reality. To argue otherwise, as did the ancient atomists, is to ignore the wisdom of God that has ordered all things in the universe teleologically and in a unified way.[6]

Another issue of theological importance was the question of God's governance of the world. This was a controversial issue among ancient philosophers. The Stoics affirmed a doctrine of divine providence; Aristotle and the Epicureans denied it. Thomas was obliged to affirm it but, as everyone recognized, the Aristotelian system that he employed offered few resources for doing so. But, using the Aristotelian view that in nature things usually happen in teleologically appropriate ways, he concluded that the only reasonable explanation for this teleology is that events in nature are directed toward ends. Then, taking a step beyond Aristotle, he asserted that such teleological direction could be interpreted only as governance. To buttress his point, he recalled the reader to his earlier argument that creation is grounded in God's goodness. If that is so, he argued, then it must also be true that each thing has been created with its own goodness (i.e., teleological end or goal). Perfection for natural beings lies in their attaining their ends. God's activity of leading creatures to the attaining of their ends, he concluded, is an act of governance.[7] Consequently, the Epicurean emphasis on chance and denial of providence was mistaken.

This sampling of subjects from Thomas's *Summa Theologiae* illustrates one way in which the doctrine of creation was understood in the context of a Hellenistic philosophy. Certainly not every medieval Christian thinker chose to pursue the task of understanding and, of those who did, some steadfastly resisted adopting the Aristotelian system. Nonetheless, by the end of the thirteenth century, Aristotle's philosophy had become the dominant conceptuality for European intellectuals. Although such attempts at understanding were dependent on biblical and Christian tradition, it is evident to us now that Thomas's understanding of creation was subtly different from the ways in which these subjects were understood in the Bible and in the early centuries of Christianity. Whether Thomas's understanding represented an improvement on biblical views is a matter of debate. By the early sixteenth century Protestant reformers and others were longing for a rejection of Aristotle and a return to the comparatively simple faith of the Bible, at least as regards theological topics. However, developments in the sciences, to which Protestants had to become inured, would lead Christian thinkers, not behind Aristotle to the Bible, but ahead of Aristotle in new and unanticipated directions.

The Age of Modern Science

In this section I examine some of the ways the doctrine of creation was understood in the period of modern science. Anything like a comprehensive treatment of the subject is ruled out because of the volume of scientific results and the quantity of theological responses to it. The exposition must be limited to a brief discussion of the impact of Isaac Newton's (1642–1727) physics and of Charles Darwin's (1809–1882) theory of evolution.

In Newton's day and in the succeeding century, virtually every scientist in Europe thought with theological convictions that were recognizably Christian. Naturally, some held these convictions more fervently and overtly than did others. Nonetheless, it was an era when many scientists carried on their daily work with a self-consciously theological mind-set. They practiced scientific inquiry with religious motivations and concepts, and they practiced religion as scientists. In particular, scientific concepts exercised an influence on theology. For example, when natural laws were portrayed as having been chosen at the universe's beginning by God, then God was simultaneously being defined as the being who originally framed the laws. In a scientific age, it was inevitable that God would come to be thought about in association with scientific concepts and with the problems that scientists found interesting and urgent. The understanding of the doctrine of creation in the age of modern science, then, has largely been the attempt to relate it to the results of natural scientific inquiry and to express it in terms of the problems that have propelled this inquiry.

One of the main philosophical debates of the Newtonian era concerned matter. There were, broadly speaking, three options. The first claimed an ancient heritage, going back at least as far as Aristotle. It was the view that matter has intrinsic properties and the power of action. Theistic exponents of this view, such as Gottfried Wilhelm von Leibniz (1646–1716), could regard these properties as having been endowed on creatures from the beginning of creation.[8] Opposing this view were the two dominant systems of the day, the Newtonian and the mechanistic. Both agreed that the Aristotelian view posed grave problems for belief in God, for the intrinsic properties and activity of matter seemed to render God otiose. There would be no need for an active God if natural phenomena could be explained solely in terms of matter and its potential for action. Newtonians and mechanists disagreed, however, on how and when divine activity appears in the natural world. Mechanists such as René Descartes (1596–1650) pictured God as establishing the laws of the universe in the beginning in such a way that no further action was necessary. Newton, fearful that such an opinion would be as harmful to theism as Aristotle's, argued that, in addition to God's original act of establishing law, God occasionally intervened in the universe to maintain the equilibrium of such things as our solar system. This philosophical issue, then, was heavily loaded with theological assumptions and consequences.

Newton's physics and the accompanying theological convictions had a varied influence on later thinkers. Samuel Clarke (1675–1729), Newton's ablest theological defender and interpreter, emphasized that the principles of Newton's physics required an active God. Nothing in the concept of force implied the direction of the motion resulting from the force. Therefore the original direction of planetary motion must have been established by God. A physical system consisting of matter and force could not have determined the motion that we observe. Further, God was required to impart to matter such nonmechanical properties as gravity, which was a function of the mass of material things and not simply of their surface, as would be the case if the mechanical philosophy were correct. As a result, Clarke grounded the design inherent in natural laws in the personal choice exercised by God in the beginning. Going beyond Newton, he grounded the occasional intrusions of God into the world in God's eternal decree, thereby seeking to safeguard God from any hint of capriciousness.[9] Colin Maclaurin (1698–1746) recognized that Newton's physics established an adequate basis not only for the sciences but for religion and morality as well. Of course, by *religion* he meant natural religion. No one expected Newtonian physics to demonstrate such revealed doctrines as the Trinity. By showing that God is present and active everywhere in the universe, however, and by showing the dependence of all physical forces on God, Newton had laid the basis for the essentials of natural religion and morality.[10]

Although the Newtonians claimed that their approach alone was compatible with belief in an active God, upholders of the mechanist philosophy were as assiduous as the Newtonians in arguing for the theological soundness of their view. Their main challenge was to show that understanding the universe to be a machine does not imply the inactivity of God. Beyond this apologetic purpose, they were eager to exploit the implications of mechanism for theism.[11]

Demonstrating that belief in a mechanistic universe is compatible with belief in an active God was comparatively easy. They needed only to argue convincingly that the laws that Newton had discovered and the forces that matter possesses were imposed on the universe at its beginning in such a way that no further invention by God was required. In other words, they interpreted divine activity as an original act that established once and for all the course of the universe.[12] Although this maneuver might appear to some to diminish the scope of God's activity by relegating it to the distant beginning, mechanists simply insisted that the fact that the universe needed no correcting intervention by God is a testimony to God's perfection. Naturally, they never claimed that God could not intervene in the natural course of things. They asserted only that there was no need for God to do so.

Beyond this defensive need, mechanists believed that their approach contained valuable resources for religious faith. Descartes, for example, believed that this philosophy, with its stark dualism of spirit and matter, was the proper conceptual understanding of the traditional Christian faith in the immortality of the soul and of the unique status accorded to humankind in the first chapter of Genesis.[13] Writers such as Marin Mersenne (1588–1648) and Isaac Watts (1674–1748) interpreted mechanism in terms of the late medieval distinction between the absolute and ordained power of God. That is, the lawfulness of the universe was a reflection not of God's inactivity but of God's freedom and will. The fact that the universe has laws and that everything in the universe occurs as a consequence of those laws is due to God's ordaining power. But the precise character of the laws points to God's absolute freedom, for God could have endowed the universe of matter with different forces and laws.[14] Willem Jacob 's Gravesande (1688–1742) countered the charge of atheism leveled at mechanism by representing the laws of nature as a result of God's wisdom. Mechanism, in his opinion, was conceptually a more simple theory than was Newton's interventionist view, since it required fewer factors to explain the processes of nature.[15] In short, the mechanists asserted that, at least with respect to the natural order, the principal form of God's creative activity was to have established the universe's laws at its beginning.

From today's scientific perspective, these seventeenth- and early eighteenth-century debates seem more than a little unnecessary. At the very least, the history of science has largely made them antiquated. Descartes's dualism of spirit and body is suspicious in the context of contemporary neuroscience. Newton's fervent insistence on the need for God periodically to adjust planetary motions hardly survived the century, for deists adopted his physics but dispensed with his intervening God. If these debates made no lasting scientific contribution, however, they nonetheless serve as excellent illustrations of the tendency for the doctrine of creation to be understood in terms of the ambient conceptual schemes. In spite of their differences, Newtonians and mechanists agreed that the act of creation was primarily a matter of

God's devising and then imposing laws on matter. Although theologians in previous centuries had made use of the concept of natural law, never before had God been defined chiefly in terms of law. Such a picture of God was to be expected in an era whose leading intellectual accomplishment was Newton's *Principia*, with its simple mathematical descriptions of the most universal laws of nature. Of course, this portrait of God and of creation was not calculated to support such distinctively Christian doctrines as the Trinity and salvation, but the emerging conception of God the creator as the bestower of laws was sufficiently similar to the traditional view that assimilating this new conception to the Christian faith seemed natural.

This happy agreement between theology and science was threatened by Darwin's *The Origin of Species*. As is well known, Darwin's conclusions initially met with considerable resistance from both theologians and scientists. The apparently seamless connection between Newton's God and the God of the Christian tradition was replaced by the looming agnosticism of Darwin's thought. Nonetheless, by the end of the nineteenth century, many Christian intellectuals, including many leading theologians, had reached an accommodation with Darwin's biology. The mainstream of Protestant theology provides illustrations of theologians coming to terms with Darwin.[16]

Coming to terms with Darwin, however, meant different things to different people. Broadly speaking, there were three options for Protestant intellectuals who wished to accept at least some aspects of evolutionary biology and achieve intellectual equilibrium with their theology. First, they could accept the theory of evolution to the extent that it did not conflict with their understanding of traditional beliefs. Second, they could reform their understanding of Christian doctrine to make it conform to evolutionary theory while remaining within a Christian intellectual framework. Third, they could jettison the traditional bases of theology and make evolution itself the foundation of their theology.[17] Since the hinge on which the discussion turned was the Bible, these options reflected different strategies for interpreting Scripture.

In general, theologians who wished to accept the theory of evolution at some level could either construe the relevant biblical passages in such a way as to show their agreement with the accepted aspects of evolutionary theory or decide that the Bible was not to be regarded as a source of scientific information. The first strategy allowed believers to maintain most traditional assumptions about the Bible. In particular, it posited a simple identity between Bible and the Word of God, a supporting theory of the Bible's inspiration, and the conviction that the Bible conveys accurate information about whatever subject it mentions. Challenges to this strategy were raised by developments in geology and biology, which suggested both a great age for the earth and a slow process of geological and biological evolution. Those employing the first strategy met these difficulties by invoking secondary strategies such as the notion of accommodation. In Scripture, they averred, God had communicated truth in a form that ancient people could grasp. In other words, the biblical account of creation was true, but it contained the truth in a form simplified for a prescientific audience. Once it was properly elucidated, the biblical account would be seen to be in harmony with the findings of the sciences.[18] The second strategy, the decision that the Bible was not a source of scientific information about the natural world, was simpler than the first but also more radical. It demanded that the interpreter cast aside assumptions about the Bible's inspiration that had been common for centuries, if not millennia. It also forced believers to come to a new understanding of the Bible's purpose. None of these tasks came easily to those schooled in traditional ways of thinking about the Bible. The Darwinian revolution, coming on the heels of the rise of biblical criticism, helped to force unprecedented changes in the interpretation of the Bible.

For those embracing the first strategy, the first order of business was to show the compatibility between orthodox doctrine and the theory of evolution. This was more than an exercise in logic. The representatives of this posture realized that the future of Christianity in a culture increasingly awed by advances in the natural sciences would be dim if people perceived a contradiction between the Christian faith and science.[19] The matter had been forcefully put by Charles Hodge (1797–1878) of Princeton Seminary, who had unequivocally asserted the incompatibility of natural selection with belief in a divine purpose manifested in the natural order. Faced with this ultimatum by one of America's premier theologians, proponents of the first posture had to argue that the theory of evolution was not reducible to the idea of natural selection and could be extracted from any system that appealed to natural selection.[20] Although the prospects for this approach do not seem promising today, it is good to keep in mind that these theologians were not simply altering the theory of evolution by means of ad hoc hypotheses designed to make it fit their theology. On the contrary, the scientific community in the late nineteenth century was undecided about the merits of the idea of natural selection. A majority, it appears, had doubts about it, at least as the sole mechanism of speciation. Theologians adopting this position believed that they could show the agreement between the theory of evolution and their theological convictions without compromising the integrity of either. They went on to assert not only the compatibility of the two but the apologetic value of evolution. The theory of evolution, they argued, supports the claims of theism, for it shows that the lawfulness that we observe in the cosmos generally is observed also in the biological realm. In this apologetic tactic, the Newtonian understanding of God as bestower of law was broadened to include the laws governing the processes of life. Indeed, extending the apologetic vein, some argued that evolution makes sense only if it has transpired under the guidance of some intelligence.[21] Accordingly, the notion of design, seemingly banished from consideration by the theory of evolution, made a comeback as people such as Asa Gray (1810–1888) began to see evolution itself as the object of God's design and the instrument by which God's purpose is fulfilled.[22]

The second strategy was far less conservative than the first. It involved a reduction in the content of traditional belief. For example, as the idea of natural selection came to be understood by nonspecialists, awareness of the brutal side of nature was heightened. Species had died out, life was harsh and competitive, and everywhere there was pain. These facts cannot have evaded the notice of people in previous eras; however, the idea of natural selection seems to have brought the facts into relief, especially against the background of belief in God's providential care for the universe. For theologians adopting the second strategy, divine providence was made less particular. It was no longer a tenet of faith for these theologians that each aspect of the natural world exhibits God's benevolence. While affirming providence in general, they shrank back from claiming to be able to show it for every particular case.[23] Providence also seemed somewhat more remote. Frederick Temple (1821–1902) was led to the belief that providence was an original decree of God relating to the general and evolutionary order of nature—but it was not about God's occasional intervention in the natural world. Providence was connected more with God's original plan for creation than with any daily governance of the world.[24]

These theologians were also induced to abandon the belief that the Bible is a reliable source of scientific information about the world. James McCosh (1811–1894), president of Princeton University, ultimately decided that theology is not tied to specific beliefs about the fixity of species, the age of the cosmos, and the means by which new species arise.[25] These matters would have been of pressing concern to theologians adopting the first strategy, for they believed that the Bible, being the Word of God, must provide accurate information about every subject it addresses. Theologians of the second strategy, however, had come to regard the Bible in quite different terms. They were pushed along in this direction because of the results of biblical criticism, according to which the Bible is a historically conditioned product of an ancient civilization, not the timeless and inspired Word of God. For those who accepted some version of this view, the theory of biological evolution would seem to be just one more instance of a more general and dynamic feature of reality.[26]

Conclusion

The purpose of this chapter has been to show that faith in the creator has always been the subject of understanding, and that understanding occurs when thinking is done by means of concepts drawn from the prevailing modes of human knowledge. The modes of human knowledge that theology must today draw upon are constituted by the natural sciences.

The main contribution of the hermeneutical dimension lies in its philosophical role of working toward the goal of unifying human knowledge. Although apologetics is necessary for understanding, it is not sufficient. We cannot be said to understand the statement "In the beginning God created the heavens and the earth" if we are limited to espousing the regulative dimensions of the doctrine and are assured that they do not contradict well-established scientific theories. Understanding demands that we attempt to provide a better exposition of the faith by means of those scientific theories in the attempt to demonstrate the substantial unity between the convictions of faith on the one hand and the elements of scientific knowledge on the other. The philosophical task of the hermeneutical dimension calls us to fit the doctrine of creation into a unified structure of knowledge that encompasses the other domains of human knowledge. This necessarily remains a constant task, not an accomplishment.

A secondary contribution of the hermeneutical dimension is the help it gives us in understanding the tension between theological conservatism and liberalism in the history of theology. Theological conservatives tend to remain content with the understanding of doctrine characteristic of a previous era. Theological liberals are characterized by an eager willingness to embrace new modes of understanding. For example, in the centuries before Thomas, the standard way of intellectually expressing the Christian faith employed an amalgamation of Platonic and Augustinian ideas. Yet, while some theologians in the thirteenth century were eagerly making use of the Aristotelian philosophy, others of a more conservative temperament were clinging to the Platonic-Augustinian approach of previous centuries. Naturally, this intellectual context was dynamic. Whereas conservatism in the thirteenth century meant resisting Aristotle in favor of a vaguely Platonic philosophy, to be conservative in the sixteenth century meant clinging to Aristotle in the face of modern science. Today's liberals can easily become tomorrow's conservatives.

Apart from these attitudes toward new ways of understanding, both the theologically conservative and the theologically liberal have distinctive problems with which they must contend. Conservatives face the danger of identifying their historically conditioned understanding of the faith with the faith itself. When conservatives succumb to this danger, then they pass over into a fundamentalist mind-set that would identify the Christian faith with a specific and culturally bound way of understanding. This is what happened, for example, in the twentieth century when some Christians insisted on identifying the doctrine of creation with beliefs associated with pre-Darwinian theories of biology. In these cases a transitory moment in the history of human thought has been equated with the Christian faith in a very simplistic manner. Liberals face a different problem, namely, the temptation to compromise the regulative aspect of doctrine in the interests of embracing the new modes of understanding. When theologians fall into this temptation, the result is a loss of concern for tradition, an excessive readiness to assimilate the Christian faith to their intellectual milieu and, in extreme cases, a more or less deliberate stepping outside the boundaries of the Christian faith. Naturally, whether a particular theologian or movement has or has not fallen into this temptation will always be a matter of debate.

4

Creatures' Participation
in the Trinitarian Life of God

In the previous chapter, I asserted three things: (1) Faith is accompanied by an understanding of faith; (2) understanding always draws on cultural modes of thought; and (3) in our intellectual situation today, the most appropriate mode of thought is the natural sciences. In the next three chapters I wish to set forth an understanding of the doctrine of creation that takes seriously the results of modern scientific inquiry. Before setting forth an understanding of the doctrine of creation, however, it is necessary to discuss the relation of creatures to God. The purpose of this chapter is to show that, within the biblical-Christian tradition, an understanding of this relation has slowly emerged according to which creatures may be said to relate to God by participation. We *participate* in the trinitarian life of God.

The Old Testament

The Old Testament speaks about creatures' relation to God with the concepts of wisdom and spirit.[1] In this way it launches the development of trinitarian thought even though it does not provide a fully systematic form for that thought.

The wisdom of God, according to the Old Testament, expresses itself in the orderliness of the created world. This order is variously understood in the Old Testament. It means that the world has been created for habitation and not to be a chaos (Isa 45:18) and that God makes provisions for living beings (Ps 147:8-9). By far the most dominant aspect of wisdom in the created world, however, is the moral order. The creator who established the earth on a secure foundation and who ordered nature also has created a moral order that is nearly lawlike in its workings.

Proverbs 1:24-33 expounds on this theme by enumerating the consequences of not paying heed to wisdom. Those who fail to heed wisdom and conform their lives to it will experience calamity like a whirlwind. Anguish and distress will visit them (v. 27). They will reap the fruit of their own foolishness and suffer from the devices that they have fashioned (v. 31). The remainder of Proverbs articulates in great detail the many forms that these disasters will take in the lives of the foolish and wicked people who refuse wisdom. At the same time, those who follow the path of wisdom reap untold blessings. They will be saved from the wicked (2:12), abide in the land (2:21), enjoy a long life (3:2), earn a good reputation (3:4), obtain material prosperity (3:9-10), and in general will have all the blessings that are possible in human life while avoiding the problems that plague the foolish and wicked.[2]

The important point is that, according to the Old Testament, creatures have a share in God's wisdom. They participate in it. On one hand, participation in wisdom appears in the order of nature—the seasons and rhythms of nature, the earth's provision for life, and so on. On the other hand, wisdom has a special meaning for humans, where it appears as the moral law of cause and effect, a law that humans can participate in to their blessing or resist to their destruction. Naturally we today cannot simply transfer the biblical understanding of wisdom and the world's order to our context. Our understanding of the universe's order is vastly more detailed and precise than is the ancient one. The Bible's view is understandably simplistic. Nonetheless, we are pointed in the right direction if we think of creatures as participating in God's wisdom and, as a result of that participation, as exhibiting features of orderliness.

The other concept that the Old Testament employs to depict creatures' relation to God is spirit. At its most basic level, spirit is the source of life. Genesis 2:7 suggests that the breath or spirit of life is the difference between a living being and a heap of matter. Psalm 104:29-30 and Job 34:14-15 expressly identify this spirit of life with the spirit of God. Life is lent to us by God; the return of spirit to God means our death. The spirit of God is also the basis of renewal, both individual and corporate. In Ps 51:11 God's holy spirit is associated with the moral and spiritual renewal of the individual after sin: "Create in me a clean heart, O God, and put a new and right spirit within me. Do not cast me away from your presence, and do not take your holy spirit from me." Ezekiel 36:25-27 promises that God will place the divine spirit in redeemed Israel, resulting in a new Israel that is quick and willing to obey the law of God. Isaiah 44:3 likens God's pouring the spirit onto redeemed Israel to the pouring of water onto dry and thirsty ground. By receiving the spirit Israel will again sprout like watered trees. The same point is made in Ezekiel 37, in which the prophet sees Israel as corpses whose desiccated bones lie in a valley. He then sees the spirit of God come upon the bones and recreate life by the restoration of flesh and breath. Finally, the spirit of God is associated with special power and gifts: wisdom, understanding, counsel, and might for the purpose of ruling justly (Isaiah 11), skill in arts, crafts, and metal-working (Exod 31:1-5), the ability to solve riddles and interpret dreams (Dan 5:11), unusual strength, courage and other military virtues (Judg 15:14),[3] and prophecy (Joel 2:28-29).[4] Briefly put, spirit, like wisdom, expresses the biblical ideal of human existence and behavior. All of us ought to be wise and to enjoy the full measure of the spirit's gifts. Yet all of us fall short. In one sense, wisdom and spirit are universal, for all beings partake of them. At the same time, creatures enjoy wisdom and the spirit of life only in a measure and for a short time. Among humankind, the time of our enjoying them is marked by the possibility of our misuse of these gifts and of our ignoring their source.

As in the case of wisdom, we cannot simply transfer the Old Testament's concept of spirit into a contemporary view of things. To do so would be to resurrect the specter of vitalism and to posit occult forces that give rise to life. Nonetheless, we will not be doing an injustice to the Old Testament if we interpret life today with the same theological perspective that it does. This means regarding the processes of life, in all their forms, as participating in the spirit of God. Of course, to do so is not to propose a scientific hypothesis that could be capable of empirical testing but to see life from the perspective of the central conviction that there is a transcendent ground to the worldly phenomena that we see around us. In short, like divine wisdom, God's spirit is something in God in which finite beings participate.[5]

The New Testament

The concept of creatures' participation in God in the New Testament is found mainly in Paul's notion of being in Christ and the ideas reflected in John 15 and 17. In 1 Corinthians 12 Paul finds an analogy between the relation of individual Christians to Christ and the relation of the parts of a body to the body itself. The Christian community as a whole is said to be Christ's body, individuals being, as it were, parts of that body (v. 27). Although this passage does not speak directly of participation, the idea lies close to the surface, for it uses an organic metaphor to describe the relation of Christians to the transcendent and lordly Christ. This conviction is expanded in Col 1:18, where Christ is said to be the head of the church, which constitutes his body. Finally Gal 2:20 points to the close connection between the Christian and Christ in a different way. In this passage, Christ is said to live within us. Although this changes the metaphor (Christ being in us rather than we being in Christ), the effect is the same as in 1 Corinthians and Colossians. Each passage indicates the intimate connection between the Christian life and the life of God. This point is reinforced by other passages (such as Rom 8:9-17 and 1 Cor 12:13) that point to the Holy Spirit as the means by which we are incorporated into Christ.

The same ideas recur in John's Gospel. Like Paul, John uses an organic metaphor when, in 15:1-6, the believer is likened to a branch that lives or dies according to its connection with the vine. Just as the branch lives only through its union with the vine, so the believer endures only through abiding in Christ. Also like Paul, John here places the emphasis on the believer's relation to Christ. In the metaphor, the Spirit has little place and the Father is merely the gardener. A more developed account of participation occurs in chapter 17, where Jesus prays that, as the Father is in him and he is in the Father, so may believers collectively be in the Father and the Son (v. 21). Here the life of the believer is represented as a participation in the common life shared by the Father and the Son. Although there is still no mention of the Spirit, John 17 marks an advance by setting participation in the context of the relation of the Father and the Son. A trinitarian approach to participation, which appears incipiently in the Old Testament's notions of God's wisdom and spirit, emerges more clearly here and points toward further developments in the Christian tradition. This participation in God's trinitarian life, however, is viewed in the New Testament strictly in terms of the new creation. Although the New Testament does not deny the Old Testament's recognition of the universal aspect of participation in God, it emphasizes one-sidedly the fact that in Christ a new mode of participation in the Trinity has appeared, a mode that is the fulfillment of the Old Testament's hopes for human wisdom and spiritual life. What is needed today is a theology that does justice both to the Old Testament's sense of the universal aspect of participation in God and the New Testament's insistence on the significance of the new mode of participation available in Christ.

The Christian Tradition

Early Christian thinking about creaturely participation in God focused on the divine wisdom, routinely associated by now, through connection with the Greek concept of *logos*, with God's Word. Athanasius is a representative figure. He affirmed the by-now familiar belief that it is by the Word that the world is ordered. The Word steers (or governs), preserves, and orders all things.[6] In common with both biblical and Greek philosophical thought, the Word is understood to be the principle of order in the universe. Without the Word, the universe would fall into anarchy.[7] With the Word, the universe is like a well-governed and harmonious city whose order testifies to the presence of a single ruler.[8] But the order is not statically conceived. The Word is not merely a structure reflected in the world; it also governs and preserves the universe. To see why the Word is also the sustainer of existence, it is necessary to recall the early Christian teaching that the universe was created from nothing. This teaching had value as an analysis of creaturely being. If creatures are created from nothing by the power of God, then apart from that power they will relapse into nothing. Creaturely existence has an innate tendency toward death and dissolution. These forces are resisted only as the creature continues to participate in the Word.[9] Through the Word, Athanasius averred, God had given to creatures substantial (although not permanent) existence.[10]

Athanasius also taught that the Word gives life to all things and sustains them, showing a tendency to conflate the Old Testament functions of Word and Spirit.[11] As we have seen, in the Old Testament life is a function of the spirit. As Athanasius wrote in a summary statement, "Obeying him . . . things on earth have life and things in the heaven have their order."[12] If life is a function of the Word, then what is the proper role of the Spirit? For the most part, the Spirit appears in Athanasius's writings in connection with the new creation. Whereas the Word has a cosmic function, the Spirit, it seems, does not. The principal function of the Spirit is the deification of redeemed human beings. The eternal Word became human so that humans might be made God.[13] But such deification does not occur simply by virtue of the incarnation. The grace that brings this about is received by participating in the Word "through the Spirit."[14] It is by our participation in the Spirit that we are deified.[15] Athanasius thus does have a notion of our participation in the Spirit, although it pertains mainly and perhaps strictly to our deification. In common with other early theologians, Athanasius did not make room for the role of the Spirit in creation.[16]

Athanasius's special interest is in human participation in the Word. Humans have a share of the divine Word that distinguishes us from other animals. Creation in the image of God means, for Athanasius, that all humans universally participate in the power of the Word. In this way, we are rational beings and are made capable of blessedness.[17] Because of this participation, human life in its created state corresponded in some way to God's life. Had we maintained our participation in the Word through resisting an attachment to corruptible things, we would have remained in this condition. Our participation in the Word would have staved off the corruption that is inherent within us due to our being created from nothing.[18]

Athanasius invoked the cosmological functions of the Word mainly in the context of defending the Christian faith against pagan philosophy. He used it to account for the unity of the world so that he could argue for the unity of God. But there was little systematic development of the role of the Word in creation and even less with respect to the nature of participation. For a far greater degree of systematic articulation we look to Thomas Aquinas, whose work presents us with a much fuller account of participation and of the Word in creation. Thomas represents an advance in thinking conceptually about participation in the trinitarian life of God. Thomas framed the question of creaturely participation in a philosophical scheme much more elaborate than that of Athanasius. His philosophical point of departure is twofold.

First, God relates to creatures as cause to effect. Second, God is being itself. From these premises he argued that all the perfections of being that we find in creatures must be originally in God. Creatures, insofar as they have being, have a share in the perfections of being that exist in God preeminently and which, in the act of creation, pass over into the creatures.[19] For Thomas, if x participates in y, then y is in some sense the cause of x. Creatures, having been created from nothing, do not have a foundation of being in themselves. If they possess being, it must have been caused in them by that which is being itself, just as, he argued, iron becomes heated by fire.[20] Participation, then, is connected to the metaphysics of causation. To say that creatures participate in God is to say that like God creatures have being. Moreover, being implies not just existence but all the modes of being such as life and intelligence. All of these are preeminently in God. Some creatures have a share in a few of these, others in a greater number.

Thomas, however, had to erect a barrier against misunderstanding. If God is being itself and creatures are said to participate in God, then the result seems to be pantheism. In part Thomas had already safeguarded his theology against this problem by defining the relation between God and the world in terms of causation. The world cannot be identified with God, just as the effect cannot be identified with the cause. He nonetheless took the further precaution of arguing that, although creatures are *like* God, they and God do not fall into the same genus or share the same form.[21] Because creatures have their being by participation, there is an analogical relation between them and God. In the act of creation it is not God's own being or form that is communicated to the creatures. Instead, there comes to be a likeness of the creator in the creature.[22] Participation, therefore, does not mean that creatures possess the form of God or the very being of God. Thomas was not completely clear on what it does mean, but he was emphatic on its negative connotation. Just as, he wrote, the atmosphere does not possess its own light and must be illumined by the sun which does inherently possess light, so creatures do not possess their own being but must receive it from God, who is being itself. Just as the atmosphere does not participate in the sun's nature, so creatures, though receiving being from God, do not participate in God's *nature*, although they do participate in being generally.[23]

The diversity of creatures implies that there are various ways in which creatures can participate in God's essence. Each species participates in God in a way that distinguishes it from other species.[24] One philosophical expression of this idea is the notion of God as the exemplary cause of things. *Exemplar* refers to a model used by a builder in the construction of something. According to Thomas, the thoughts of God's mind comprise the original exemplars of all things that were to be created. These exemplars, which are plural only in our estimation (being in God's mind utterly one) comprise God's wisdom, for they are the principle whereby the universe has its order. God's wisdom is God's conception of the universe to be created, the plan that God would follow in creating the diversity of beings.[25]

The notion that one creature's mode of participating in God differs from that of another appears also in Thomas's distinction between the trace and the image of the Trinity in creatures. A trace, he wrote, is found when an effect represents something else only as a cause. For example, smoke is a trace of fire, because fire causes smoke. From an analysis of smoke, however, nothing of the nature of fire can be gathered apart from its capacity to cause smoke. The case is different with the image. Here the effect resembles the cause's form. For instance, a statue of a person represents that person because between them there is a similarity of form. This distinction allowed Thomas to assert that a trace of the Trinity is found in all creatures, since they are all effects of God's causality, but only rational creatures bear the image of the Trinity, since only rational creatures have mind, the structure of which is analogous to the Trinity.[26] Thomas's analysis of the various ways in which creatures participate in God did not go beyond this twofold distinction. He nonetheless pointed the way toward a more refined analysis of the variety of modes of participation in God.

The same notion appears also in his discussion of the way in which the blessed in heaven know the essence of God. Since they are rational, their knowledge of God's essence must involve the intellect.[27] At the same time, the creature's natural intellect is unable to know God's essence.[28] As a result, Thomas argued, the power by which the creature can know the essence of God must come from God. This supernatural intellectual power is a likeness of God, who is intellect itself. Accordingly, this power in the creature is a participation in a likeness of the divine intellect.[29]

With the concept of the divine exemplars, Thomas improved to some extent on the trinitarian understanding of participation in God. The divine wisdom, which is the Word of God and the second person of the Trinity, is, as in Athanasius's thought, the principle of universal order. His argument is that God, in knowing the divine essence, knows every creature. God's self-knowledge is at the same time God's conception of the entire world of creatures. The divine intellect in one eternal act comprehends the divine essence and all creatures and in this act conceives the eternal Word just as a parent begets a child in an act of conception. The result of this one eternal act of intellect is the eternal Word. This Word is the expression of God's eternal knowledge. As a result, the Word expresses God's creative knowledge of the created world.[30] As mentioned, the Word comprises the exemplars that constitute the ideas of God's intellect. The eternal Word, then, is the basis of creaturely existence and distinction. But there does not appear to be a corresponding role for the Spirit in creation.[31] Thomas, drawing on the Platonic and Aristotelian heritage to give philosophical structure to his thought, understandably focused on the Word or Wisdom of God, because these corresponded to the Platonic and Aristotelian emphasis on form. Regrettably, he did not extend the Christian understanding of the Spirit's role in creation.

Thomas contributed to the development of the idea of participation in God in two ways. First, he offered a philosophically more precise account of participation than did other writers such as Athanasius. For Thomas, participation was embedded in a larger metaphysical framework grounded ultimately on the notion of being. Second, he advanced beyond Athanasius in elaborating the notion that creatures participate in the divine being in different ways, depending on their particular modes of being. Further elaboration is nonetheless necessary if a trinitarian doctrine of creation is to be fully articulated; for, in spite of these contributions, Thomas's account of participation is insufficiently trinitarian. Although the role of the Word is quite clear, especially in his exposition of the divine exemplars, his account is unquestionably weak on the function of the Spirit. At most he offered some hints of a fuller explanation. Further, his view of the world's order in relation to the divine exemplars is somewhat static. Each individual in the universe's history corresponds to an idea in God's mind, so that God's knowledge is an exhaustive and unchanging eternal knowledge of the entire course of the universe. Still, it remains focused on individual beings or static essences, whereas we today are more likely to put the emphasis on natural laws and physical processes in which individual entities are embedded and from which they arise.

A further step toward an understanding of participation is found in the theology of Paul Tillich (1886–1965). Previous theologians had focused on the function of the Word in giving order to the universe. Tillich, however, saw that creatures' participation in God was about far more than cosmic order grounded in God's wisdom. He saw that participation in God must concern the trinitarian life of God. Only in this way could justice be done to the other persons of the Trinity. Only in this way could the doctrine of creation be saved from being a *logos-ology* narrowly focused on the Second Person.

The first thing to note is that Tillich generalized the idea of participation. It, along with individualization, is an aspect of the basic ontological structure of self and world. Everything real has elements of selfhood (insofar as it is an individual) and belongs to a world (insofar as it participates in something).[32] Since participation is part of the fundamental structure of reality, all things participate just as all things are individualized in some degree.

God is the principle of participation. According to Tillich, this means that God is, in his words, the ground and aim of every being. More graphically, Tillich expressed this in terms of God's participating in every creature, having community with it and sharing its destiny. At the same time, Tillich was aware of the symbolic character of such talk. God's participation in creatures is God's presence in creatures, but this is a presence that is also an absence. It is not a spatial or a temporal presence, for God is no part of the world of space and time.[33]

To see why God is the principle of participation it is necessary to explore further Tillich's understanding of reality. As noted previously, the fundamental structure of reality is the relation of self (individualization) to world (participation). All finite beings are in some measure individuals and all to some degree participate. Unlike finite beings, however, God is not a being that partakes of the structure of participation and individualization. On the contrary, the structure itself is grounded in God's being. In fact, it may be said that God *is* this structure of being, as long as it is not conceived statically.[34] For this reason it is appropriate to designate God as "being itself."[35] So, whereas as creatures are individualized to some degree, God is perfectly individualized. And, whereas creatures participate in some measure, God is the complete participant. Finally, whereas in creatures there is some tension between individuality and participation (since one seems to come at the expense of the other), God is the perfect harmony of the two.

Finitude means that the individuality and participation of creatures is restricted and that there is always a tension between the two. God is not subject to these limitations, because God is the structure of self and world, individuality and participation.

Another way of expressing finitude is with the language of nonbeing. Creatures' participation in God is restricted because finite beings are as it were mixed with nonbeing. Again, this is a highly picturesque way of speaking, but Tillich's point is similar to that of Athanasius. Creatures are created from nothing and possess an inherent tendency to relapse into a state of nothingness. For Tillich, although finite beings participate in being itself (God, the structure of being), they also participate in the power of nonbeing.[36] In fact, finitude can be defined as that which falls short of complete participation in being itself.

Finite beings, then, participate in the divine life in a limited way. Although the divine life is a perfect unity, the existence of creatures is marked by estrangement and the life of creatures is characterized by ambiguity. This means that finite beings cannot maintain the perfect harmony between the ontological elements that characterizes God. One or the other of the two poles (individualization and participation) will tend to dominate. The self-integration that leads to individualization is countered by disintegration. Life's self-creation is threatened with destruction. The self-transcendence of life, whereby it strives toward God, is countered by the creatures' profanization. Given the nature of finitude, which is a mixture of being and nonbeing, it is impossible to overcome this ambiguity. Finite life in itself is always ambiguous.[37] Only the kingdom of God represents the overcoming of ambiguity.

This incomplete participation of creatures in God explains the meaning of God's transcendence. Because God is being itself, God is not *a* being.[38] Tillich never tired of insisting on this point. Because God is being itself, God transcends every being taken individually and the entire world of finite beings taken collectively. Further, the ontological gap between God and finite beings is absolute, infinite and unbridgeable by the creature. At the same time, this absolute transcendence of God does not prevent the participation of all things in God. Accordingly, being itself has a twofold characteristic. On one hand, it infinitely transcends finite beings because they participate in it in only a limited way. On the other hand, being itself is creative, for all things derive the power of resisting nonbeing by participating in it.[39] Naturally, this characteristic of God is beyond human powers of comprehension. We can only point to it and describe it with symbols, such as "ground of being."

The clearest instance of creaturely participation in God as the power of resisting nonbeing is human salvation. Tillich referred to this as our participation in the "new being."[40] In humankind's historical condition we exist in estrangement from God. As a result of this estrangement we experience the negative and destructive consequences of being separated from the ground of our being. The Christian message, however, is that God, in Jesus Christ, has taken on this estrangement and its destruction by participating in human being. Those who then reciprocally participate in that divine act (i.e., those who are "in Christ," to use Paul's phrase) experience the power of the new being. The cross of Christ, then, is God's act of taking negativity into the divine being and overcoming it. Of course, this overcoming of nonbeing is an eternal act in God's life. God does not first overcome nonbeing in the cross. The cross is, however, the historical manifestation of God's eternal victory over nonbeing.[41] Our participation in the new being, which is God's participation in human estrangement and suffering, brings about the transformation by which our self-destruction in sin is overcome.[42]

In what sense is Tillich's account of participation a trinitarian theology? The doctrine of the Trinity comes into consideration with Tillich's further analysis of the structures of being. As noted previously, the fundamental ontological structure of being is that of self and world. The principal elements of this structure are the pairs individualization and participation, dynamics and form, and freedom and destiny. Individuality, dynamics, and freedom are represented in religious literature as God's power and mysterious depth. Participation, form, and destiny are represented in religion as the *logos*, as that by which God is revealed, and as the element of meaning within God. God, then, unites these two polar elements—power and meaning, the mysterious depth and the *logos*. However, God is not only being itself (the structure of being) but also Spirit.[43] Spirit, for Tillich, is the fulfillment of being. It is the perfect and harmonious union of the two aspects of being.[44] Consequently, in discussing God we must use three sets of terms, the first denoting the element of power and depth, the second denoting the element of form and meaning, and the third denoting

God as Spirit. These are the trinitarian principles.[45] Being, therefore, fulfilled as Spirit, has a trinitarian structure. As finite beings participate in being, they participate in the trinitarian life of God.

Some, however, participate more fully than others. All beings participate in the basic structure of self and world, with the concomitant ontological elements. Yet organic beings are self-preserving and self-increasing, something that cannot be said of inorganic beings. Organic beings represent a greater actualization of participation than inorganic beings. Within the organic realm, animals are distinguished by having an inner awareness, signifying a still greater degree of actualization.[46] The apex of participation is human being, for in humankind the inner awareness of animal being emerges into the dimension of spirit. So far as we know, only humans live in the dimension of spirit.[47] Only in humans are the structures of being fulfilled, although not without ambiguity. The spiritual dimension of human being takes the forms of religion, morality, and culture.

Tillich's theology signals an advance on that of Thomas, at least with respect to the idea of creaturely participation in God. First, the conception of participation has been expanded and made more central in the system of theology. Second, he gave more attention to articulating the various ways in which creatures participate in God, depending on their modes of being. Third, Tillich clarified the language used in connection with participation. Thomas had spoken somewhat vaguely of creaturely participation in God's likeness in order to avoid pantheistic implications. Tillich improved on this analysis with a more rigorous philosophical conception of participation that he joined to a theory about the symbolic nature of theological language. Finally, his presentation is more solidly trinitarian than is Thomas's, especially with regard to the Spirit. Indeed, God as Spirit is the fulcrum on which Tillich's analysis rests.

But Tillich's theology of participation is not above improvement. First, a better account of the Trinity is needed. Tillich's understanding of the Trinity follows the tradition of German idealism in seeing the Spirit as the central member of the Trinity. The Spirit is the principle of unity within the Trinity, providing balance for the first two members.[48] Consequently, the Spirit is the completion of God's trinitarian life, the first two members being as it were the elements out of which the unity of the Trinity arises. In this view, it is the first two persons who are coordinated with each other, with the third person, the Spirit, uniting the coordinated pair. The problem is that such a view corresponds poorly with the biblical representation of the trinitarian persons. In the Bible it is the Son and the Spirit who are coordinated with each other and the Father who is their source. A contemporary trinitarian theology of the creator must take this into account. Second, a fuller analysis is needed of the various ways in which finite being participates in God's trinitarian life. Tillich himself, for example, pointed out the importance of the inorganic realm;[49] however, his own treatment is inadequate. An analysis based on contemporary science is required. Finally, Tillich's theology of finite being tends to put too much emphasis on the life and structure of individual entities. A contemporary account should devote more attention to the transindividual forces, laws, and other structures that largely determine the nature and behavior of individual entities.

The Trinitarian Life of God

The theological task today is to build on the tradition of reflection on participation. In particular, theology today that wishes to be Christian must give an account of participation that is thoroughly trinitarian. Theology today must also describe the universal participation of creatures in God while also making it clear how each sort of creature participates in God in distinctive ways. Finally, theology today must show how universal participation (the participation of *all* creatures in God) is related to but also distinct from participation (as the New Testament represents it) as the result of redemption. This calls for an understanding of the relation between the created world and the kingdom of God.

A trinitarian understanding of participation begins with the fact that the trinitarian life of God is a life that embraces identity and difference. Identity points to the oneness of God in the midst of this trinitarian life. To speak of Father, Son, and Holy Spirit is to speak of the one God. Nothing that is affirmed about the distinction of persons compromises this oneness. The distinction of persons does not compromise the identity—indeed, it is necessary for God's identity. This is because the identity of the triune God is not simple and undifferentiated but rather an identity that embraces and is constituted by difference. This identity does not maintain itself by excluding all that is different but rather gathers together difference. The identity of the triune God is not something in addition to the distinctions of the persons but is, on the contrary, the identity of these distinct persons with each other. Further, the unity of God's identity is not additive—the trinitarian persons are not parts. They do not constitute the one God when added together. Instead each is God. Yet the three together are not three gods but the three ways in which the one divine life is.

The participation of the universe in the trinitarian life means that the dialectics of identity and difference appears in creatures. Naturally, this dialectics does not appear in creatures in precisely the way in which we find it in God, for the world of creatures is finite, not infinite. Identity and difference appear in various forms in the world of creatures. Creatures participate in the life of God in ways that are appropriate to their modes of being. To discern the variety of ways of participation, it is necessary to listen to natural sciences, for the forms that finite being takes cannot be deduced from the concept of creation or the triune creator. Although the universe, as a participant in the divine life, must show forth identity and difference, the forms that identity and difference take are, it seems, contingent. They can be learned only empirically through the discipline of scientific inquiry.[50]

Investigation of the created world, however, discloses as well that the universe's participation in the trinitarian life of God is not complete. Creatures do not exist as God does. Their existence is attended by all manner of limitations that show forth their distance from God. If the participation of creatures in God were complete, then creatures would transcend the limitations of the universe and would be divine. The theological term denoting the ensemble of limitations is *finitude*. To be finite is to be limited and conditioned by something else. It is to lack self-determination, at least in some respects. The finitude of creatures is reflected in the fact that they are all parts of a universal causal nexus. Each entity affects and is affected by other entities in its spatial and temporal proximity. The entire universe is this nexus in which entities condition and are conditioned by each other. Theologically considered, this means that the universe and its components are quite different from God, who should be thought of as self-determining and unconditioned. It also means that there is built into the universe a principle of limitation. For there to be a universe there must be causal connections by which entities condition one another. Without these connections there would be no universe—only fragmentary, isolated bits of material reality, lacking the wholeness of a world-system. The existence of a universe, then, implies the finitude of its members.

A theology of participation must not end with the finitude of creatures. The gospel is the message that in the midst of human finitude and sin, God's kingdom has appeared. This kingdom does not overcome the effects of finitude; creatures remain creatures and are not transformed into divinity. The kingdom of God, however, does represent the overcoming of the distortions of finitude under the condition of sin. The consequences of this overcoming for the cosmos can only be guessed at. Its significance for human existence is the subject of the New Testament.

PART TWO

UNDERSTANDING THE UNIVERSE
IN A TRINITARIAN WAY

5

Persistence and Change in Time

At the end of chapter 4 I argued that the life of the Trinity is a life of identity and difference. I also argued that the same dialectics of identity and difference shows itself in the created world by virtue of the world's participation in the trinitarian life of God. To understand the world in a trinitarian way, therefore, is to think about the world dialectically and in terms of identity and difference. The purpose of this chapter and the following three chapters is to offer a theological interpretation of the world as it is disclosed to us by contemporary science, using the concepts of identity and difference as these appear under the various conditions of finite being.

One condition under which finite being appears is temporality. In the form of temporality, identity and difference appear as persistence and change. A temporal entity or a state or process has some identity insofar as it remains the same in time. Insofar as its identity is interrupted or changed, difference appears, although in every temporal process something persists during change. The extent of change and persistence varies greatly in the universe. In some cases change is minimal and persistence prevails. In other cases, change is continuous and dramatic. Nonetheless, everything in the universe shows forth the dialectics of identity and difference in its temporality.

The Physical Universe

The world of elementary particles gives us an extraordinary and paradoxical picture of persistence and change. On one hand, the particles are characterized by persistence, to the near total exclusion of change. While they subsist, they are in effect changeless. Their few properties, such as rest mass, charge, and spin, are mathematically determinate and remain constant as long as the particles endure. They do experience comparatively superficial modes of change, such as change of location. These superficial forms of change, however, do not affect their fundamental properties. On the other hand, quantum-physical analysis reveals a world in which rapid and dramatic change is the norm and persistence is short-lived. A neutron, for example, decays into its constituents when one of its down quarks is transformed into an up quark via the weak interaction, a process that yields (ultimately) a proton, an electron, and an antineutrino. A muon decays into either an electron or a positron plus a neutrino and an antineutrino. This illustrates the point that, except for electrons, neutrinos and their antiparticles (all of which appear to be changeless), subatomic particles exist in highly dynamic states of exceedingly short duration. For the most part, change takes the form of transformation into another particle. Another and even more dramatic form of change pertains to particles and their antiparticles. An encounter between an electron and a positron, for example, results in their annihilation and the transformation of their entire mass into two gamma rays. Conversely, a photon raised to a highly energetic state will emit an electron-positron pair out of, so to speak, the excess energy. The features of persistence and change that we find in subatomic particles hold true for atoms and molecules as well. An atom persists unchanged unless it is transformed (via transmutation) into another sort of atom.[1] Molecules for the most part remain the same, unless through chemical interactions they are either dismembered into constituent parts (atoms, radicals, and so on) or incorporated into a larger molecule.[2]

The world of particles, then, shows us persistence and change. Particles persist, if only briefly, without change until they are utterly transformed into another sort of particle or are annihilated. At any rate, we do not observe what we may call *development*—the process in which the entity persists not *until* it changes but *while* it changes. In development something remains the same even while it changes in significant ways. The development of an embryo is an example. Here there is remarkable change over the course of time, but there is no doubt that it is the same embryo that is developing. The world of particles does not exhibit development in this sense. Particles do not develop. They either persist unchanged, or they are transformed into a different sort of particle, or they are annihilated.

Although the world of quantum phenomena is marked by frequent, rapid, and dramatic change, there is another consideration that reveals the significance of persistence. If we consider not particles but the processes in which particles take part, then we get a greater sense of persistence at the subatomic level. Take, for example, the decay of a neutron. This process itself remains strikingly persistent throughout the world of particles. The same is true of annihilation. Although the particles in each case may show little persistence, the processes themselves persist without change. The encounter between an electron and a positron will invariably result in annihilation and the production of two gamma rays. Likewise, neutrons decay in the described manner with statistical regularity. In these and other physical processes we find the physical universe exhibiting the sort of persistence that embraces change, and we find processes of change that are remarkably persistent. This persistence is due, it seems, to the various conservation laws. In electron-positron annihilation, for example, both the momenta of the particles and their mass-energy are conserved and expressed in the momenta and energy of the resulting gamma rays. Conservation laws describe the invariance of processes such as decay and annihilation and the laws themselves persist unchanged over time.

In the case of very large composites, whether planets and suns or solar systems and galaxies, the dialectics of persistence and change appears in a new form. These sorts of entities change over time in ways in which particles, atoms, and molecules do not. As noted, these latter entities remain substantially the same as long as they endure. Change for them means ceasing to be, either through annihilation or transformation into something else. Very large composites, however, have the capacity to change while remaining recognizably the same. A star, for example, experiences a considerable degree of material change (e.g., transmutation of its atomic constituents or ejection of gases into space) and other sorts of change (e.g., size) in the course of its existence while remaining the same star. It begins when the gravitational field associated with dust and gas draws them together and compresses them to the point that nuclear reaction occurs. The star then enters a stable period, but one that is still subject to important sorts of alteration, with changes in the star's surface and developments in its interior. At length, the end of nuclear processes brings about predictable results in the star's death. The point is that the star, unlike particles, atoms, and molecules, does not remain simply identical with itself over time. Its identity is such that, while remaining the same star, it undergoes much change. Its identity persists in spite of the fact that its atomic constituents change. Over the course of its existence its hydrogen atoms fuse and become helium and, later, heavier elements. Nonetheless, the star has a persistence that endures in the midst of these changes. This is quite unlike a particle or atom, a change in whose constituent parts means a transformation into something different. In the case of very large composites, then, we find not only change but development, the persistence of identity in the midst of change over time.

Finally, let us consider the universe as a whole. It is no exaggeration to say that one of the discoveries of twentieth-century physics was that the universe as such is a historical entity. We are justified in speaking of an evolutionary history of the universe—of the universe's becoming. Prior to the twentieth century the universe was regarded as something static. Although it was recognized that there are dynamic processes within the universe, it was only with the rise of twentieth-century cosmology that belief that the universe as such is dynamic became prominent. In the current understanding, the size of the universe has grown dramatically over the course of its history. This growth will turn out to be considerably greater if the inflationary model of the universe proves to be correct. In this latter case, the actual universe will be unimaginably larger than the part of the universe that is visible, even with the most powerful telescopes. At the same time and as a direct result of the increased volume of the universe, the average amount of energy within a given volume of space has decreased. The universe has gone from a state of extraordinarily high energy-density to a state of minimal energy-density. In the earliest moments of the universe's history, this decrease in energy per unit-volume resulted in the differentiation of the four fundamental interactions out of an originally undifferentiated condition in which there was a single sort of high-energy interaction between particles. Now, in its place we have the familiar distinctions between gravity, electro-magnetism, and the weak and strong interactions. With the decrease in energy-density has also come the bonding together of particles to form the composite entities that constitute the familiar matter of experience. Lower energy allowed quarks to form stable nucleons and then nucleons and electrons to form stable atoms. At length, through the nuclear reactions of stars, large and heavy atoms were created, making possible the formation of planets with the elements that make life as we know it possible. In this way, the universe of daily experience—a universe of enduring elements capable of forming molecules—has come into being through a temporal and dynamic process.

In all these ways and more, the universe shows itself to be a dynamic temporal process. But in what sense does it manifest persistence and identity? What justifies our saying that it is the *same* universe that undergoes these changes? What is the basis of the universe's persistence over time? It is natural in this connection to think of the lawlike character of the universe and its processes. For example, if we think of the universe as the sum total of matter-energy, the law of the conservation of energy tells us that, although the universe's matter and energy may undergo various transformations, the total quantity remains fixed. Energy may be transformed from one form to another (for instance, from kinetic energy to heat) and matter may be transformed into energy (as in nuclear reactions and annihilation), but the universe forms a closed system into which no new matter-energy enters and from which none is lost. In this way, the universe, in spite of its evolutionary character, maintains material continuity over time. Other regularities, such as those pertaining to the strength of fields (for instance, Newton's well-known equations for gravity), bring it about that the behavior of particles is predictable and orderly. In other words, these regularities mean that the *same*, that is, the identical, processes recur throughout the history of the universe. If we represent the universe as the sum total of all these processes, then the sameness of these processes over time means the identity of the universe in its history, in addition to its substantial continuity as a totality of matter and energy.

The Biological World

The biological world is, so to speak, the physical universe raised to a higher degree of complexity and organization. This means two things. First, the biological world depends utterly on the characteristics of the physical universe. It requires the stability of atomic structure, the variety of chemical compounds, the sun as the ultimate source of energy, and more. There could be no biological life without a physical universe. Second, the biological world cannot be explained only in terms of physical and chemical processes. Life arises out of the organization of physical structures. Because of this organization, the living world is characterized by properties that are not simply latent in the properties of the physical universe, except insofar as they are a further development of the capacity for complex structure that we find in the physical universe.

With an increase in organizational complexity comes a more complicated exhibition of persistence and change in temporality. Above all, we note the overwhelming importance of time in the biological world in contrast to its relative unimportance in the microcosmic aspects of the physical world. Many physical processes are indifferent to time in the sense that they can be reversed. This is not true of all physical processes, as the principle of entropy reminds us. Nonetheless, there is a manifest difference when we come to living beings, for here practically *no* processes are reversible.[3] Cells, for example, come to be by a process of division. Because the cell is not just a collection of chemical parts but embodies a distinctive and complex organization of those parts, it is practically impossible that two cells that had previously resulted from the division of a parent cell could merge together to reform the parent cell. The point can be seen even more clearly in the case of a multicellular organism such as a mammal. The possibility of its reverting to the condition of a fertilized egg does not strike us as feasible. The same is true of the evolution of a species. Since evolution is a function of genetic mutation and adaptation to a dynamic environment, the possibility of evolution reversing itself seems quite remote. Finally, time in the sense of timing is crucial for life. In the development of an organism, for example, it is vital that genes be expressed not only in a specific location but also at a specific time. There are critical moments in development when a gene's failure to be expressed may result in death or debility. On a larger scale, the emergence of a given species (for instance, *Homo sapiens*) depends utterly on the prior emergence of other orders and species (hominids, primates, and so on). In short, in biological processes the directionality of time is essential and irreversible.

The dialectics of identity and difference is manifest at every level of the biological world. At the most basic level, that of the cell, we see this dialectics in the temporal rhythm between the unity of the parent cell and the plurality of the daughter cells. The process begins with a single cell, which (in mitosis) then divides, each resulting cell being genetically identical to the parent cell but materially different from it. In cell division, identity is maintained through numerical multiplication and differentiation. The same is true of multicellular organisms, except that in organisms with specialized systems (such as the circulatory system or the neural system) the cells of such systems are no longer differentiated merely by the fact that each is materially different from the organism's other cells. In this case cells are differentiated also by the fact that cells in one system have their genes expressed in ways that differ from the ways in which genes are expressed in cells of different systems. There is still genetic identity within the organism, for all cells have resulted by division from the original parent cell. The structure and function of cells, however, are now differentiated on the basis of the varied expression of genes. Because of the persistence of genetic identity in the midst of both material differentiation and the varied expression of genes, it is appropriate to affirm that biological beings *develop* in a way in which physical beings do not. Physical beings change but, at least at the level of particles, when atoms and molecules change it means the cessation of existence—the loss of identity. Only on the scale of large composite entities (such as stars and galaxies) is there change over time that does not bring a loss of identity. But even if we speak of development in the case of stars and galaxies, we must qualify our meaning, for planets, stars, solar systems, and galaxies come to be largely because of gravitational forces. Cells and organisms, however, develop according to genetic instructions that guide the developmental process in ways that are specified in advance.

Genes, however, do not completely account for development. Development depends also on environmental contingencies and, in the case of some animals, on learning. Through imitation and communication such organisms are able to develop behaviors that are not specifically programmed by genetics. This capacity significantly enlarges the possibilities for differentiation, even though the identity of the species is not further compromised by this increased differentiation.

The evolution of species illustrates the same point. A species (or population) may be considered to be something identical over time. *Identity* here does not mean absolute sameness. For one thing, there is plenty of genetic diversity within a population at any given time. For another, the population's genetic identity will change over time. It is nonetheless appropriate to speak of species enduring in an identifiable way for centuries or even more. In some cases contemporary representatives of species are essentially identical with their ancestors, there having been no environmental changes that would favor significant genetic changes. It is in this sense that we may speak of a population being something identical. At the same time, as noted, this identity is not static. Over the course of time, the population remains identifiably the same while experiencing genetic changes. In some cases and under certain circumstances, these changes will be sufficient to bring about the existence of a new population, i.e., a population reproductively isolated from the original. Here the process of genetic diversification has superseded the boundaries of the original population. Identity with difference (a single population with genetic diversity) has now become two identities (i.e., two populations), each with its own genetic diversity.

Human Existence

Human social being is historical existence. But this historical existence presupposes the time characteristic of inorganic and organic being. Historical time does not contradict these other sorts of time. It presupposes and builds on them. It is impossible to imagine how human beings could have historical time apart from our participation in the time of physical reality and the time of biological reality. Just as the biological world is grounded in the physical universe, so human existence and human time are grounded in the biological and the physical. Just as the biological represents the physical raised to a higher degree of complexity, so human existence is the biological world raised to yet a higher degree of complexity. This means that, just as the time of biological entities and processes differs from the time of physical entities and processes, so the time of human existence has distinctive traits.

This difference shows itself in the relation between human time and physical and biological time. Each of these times has a historical aspect, for time in the form of history, whether in the physical, biological, or human worlds, is marked to some extent by unrepeatability, contingency, and particularity. Physical entities such as galaxies, biological entities such as cells, and human beings all share these characteristics. Human historicity, however, goes far beyond these three characteristics. A way of getting at this difference is to consider the nature of the past and the future.

In the physical world, the past and the future resemble one another to a considerable extent. As noted above there is plenty of dynamic change if we consider any given particle or system, but when we examine the larger features of the physical universe we observe a world in which the deterministic laws of classical physics seem to rule, a world in which the future is the outcome of the past. The future and the past are alike, just the result of physical laws operating on the fixed amount of matter-energy in the universe. The situation is different in the biological world, where the elevated degree of contingency means that the future may be quite different from the past. But even in the biological world the future is largely the effect of the past. At the most basic level, the development of an embryo proceeds along the lines indicated by its genetic heritage, except as contingent external factors intrude. The same is true on the larger scale of populations. Apart from the effect of the environment and random genetic changes, future generations would largely resemble past generations. In other words, even in the biological world there is a tendency toward a somewhat static repetition of the past into the future.[4]

In human historical time, however, the future is more than just the outcome of the past and the past is more than just the cause of the future. In human existence, the past is something that is *remembered*. It is not simply what happened prior to the present but something that has an effect on us and becomes significant for us. There is nothing necessary about this. It is possible for the past to be merely that which happened before and which inexorably works an effect on us without our knowledge or our consent. In this case the present is the repetition of the past. But such is not historical time in its distinctively human form. In historical existence, the past becomes not causative but instead authoritative, because it has become something that we have appropriated and allowed to shape us. This is the concept of tradition: the past that has become ours—that into which we have fitted ourselves.[5] The past as remembered—tradition—is a past that has been passed through a sieve. The remembered past is not the sum total of things that have happened. It is instead a past composed of events that have been selected and interpreted. It is because of this process of selection and interpretation that the past becomes for us authoritative and not merely causal. Physically and biologically considered, human beings are the caused result of all that has gone before. As historical beings, however, it is only the past as it becomes tradition that assumes historical importance.

The implication of this is that history does not unfold organically or genetically. For example, the development of nation-states from the Middle Ages to the modern period can hardly be described as organic.

The same is true of the development of governmental forms, of the history of art and of science, and of many other developments. For this reason, it is problematic to describe human history as a teleological process, although there may be teleological processes within history. At any rate, history does not develop organically in the manner of an embryo.[6]

Likewise, in human historical time, the future is something that is *envisioned*. It is not merely an outcome. It is instead the object of intentional activity. The future is for us something produced by action. As with the past, it is not a matter of necessity that the future be such. It is possible for our future to be simply an outcome, a result of forces in the past moving through the present. Our future can be something fixed and determined, but this would not be the future in its distinctively human form. The future of human historicity is an ideal state that we project and toward which we strive with purposeful action. In this sense, the future is not latent in the past. It is not the inexorable outworking of the past but something created, both in our intentions and in our actions. Finally, the future is also not merely contingent, some state that will occur through who knows what factors. The future is not an accident, although its shape is obviously affected by contingent events. On the contrary, the future is principally the object of intentional human action. To be sure, the future is not unrelated to the past, considered as tradition. Our image of the future may well be given in the past as tradition. Our past may and perhaps should indicate how we should envision the future and work to actualize it. But it is still the past as selected and interpreted and appropriated that will do this for us.

This means that human existence has an ideal and futural character. By this I mean that, in considering human existence, the future is as important as the past. Human existence is lived not only from the past but also from the future. But, as noted, the future is a sort of ideal concept of what we may be, whether individually or collectively. As a result, we must not think of human nature apart from the concept of the future. Since the future is something not yet accomplished, human nature is also something not yet accomplished; it is underway. The future is that from which human nature occurs and is worked on and onto which it is projected. But we should not think that the future lacks efficacy just because it is ideal, as though it were only a thought. The future is that ideal (or those ideals) of human existence for the sake of which we act. As a result, the future is the basis of human freedom. To the extent that we lack a future (in the sense described here) and to the extent that the future is simply the outworking of the past, to that extent we find ourselves doomed to a repetition of a past that we find oppressive. Freedom is the quality of human actions that are performed for the sake of a future that in some significant way transcends the present and the past.[7] Consequently, human freedom takes its meaning from the fact that human nature is a matter of the future that is itself the object of human activity.

This discussion of the past and the future is important for understanding the distinctive way in which humans, in their temporality, participate in the dialectics of persistence and change. I refer not to human beings in their organic existence but in those features of temporality that are distinctively human. With respect to our organic existence, human beings exhibit the same features of persistence and change that we find in the biological world. As organic beings we develop in just the way in which other biological entities, especially primates, develop, once allowance is made for the greater role that learning plays in human development. The human species likewise has come about because of the same genetic and environmental factors that have given rise to all other species. But our subject now is the ways in which humans, because of our participation in the trinitarian life of God, exhibit persistence and change according to their particularly human mode of being. In short, I am here concerned not with merely physical or biological forms of persistence and change but instead with human culture. To grasp this point, it will be helpful to consider human temporality in terms of dialogue and narrative.

Human culture is more than just economic activity and social behavior and organization. Culture designates, in part, the fact that for us the activities and structures of human life are objects of reflection. Although humans, as primates, invariably have some social organization and activities, it is a matter of human culture that social organization and economic activity are the sorts of things that we reflect upon. But reflecting upon does not merely mean that we reproduce these phenomena in our thinking as an image in a mirror reproduces something. Reflection instead means that these phenomena are scrutinized and evaluated. They become objects of philosophical inquiry and normative judgment as we ask about the best form of government or the nature of justice or the fairest distribution of social goods.

Human culture and philosophical inquiry have a history. The ideals by which we think about our lives are not eternal realities that fell ready-made from heaven into the human mind. They are instead the subject of a dialogue that began long ago in humankind's past. The dialogue is about ideas set forth in books. It is like a stream that has brought, from far away, a current into which we enter. In entering we become participants in the dialogue, assimilating those parts of the current that we can and in turn passing on to the future the heritage of the dialogue and whatever contribution to it that we have made. Above all, by entering into this dialogue we accede to its shaping effect and take on ourselves the burden of shaping future generations. We establish ourselves as partners in a dialogue with the future and thereby enter the human community.

Wherein lies persistence? First, in the books and other artifacts in which this dialogue has been lodged. But we have to look deeper, for these books and artifacts have continued existence only because we and previous generations have regarded them and the dialogue and culture they bear as something valuable. The deeper source of persistence lies in the nature of human historicity. In particular, it lies in the human capacity and will to gather the past and the future and to hold them together in the present. This points us to the narrative quality of human existence. *Narrative* means that human existence has a story-like quality. In other words, we seek to interpret human existence (whether individual, local, or universal) as a meaningful whole. But such an interpretation requires that we prevent the past and the future from receding into irrelevance. Instead they must be gathered so that together they might give us a present that is a part of a meaningful whole. Persistence in human existence, then, means that we intentionally construct a life-story, whether for ourselves as individuals or for our community and nation or for the human race as a whole. We construct it by gathering together the past (in the form of tradition) and the future (as an ideal of human existence projected before us). Because of this gathering, human culture endures as a historical and on-going dialog. Without this gathering, human existence would be reduced to the immediate present, a present without connection to any larger historical whole and to any social ideals.

Human culture is ineradicably historical. This historical character accounts for the particular nature of change within human temporality. But "history" is not simply the sum total of what has happened in the past; it is our interpretation of a past that has become significant for us. The past exists only as it is rescued by memory, by assuming institutional form, and by inquiry. This rescuing is part of the process of gathering together. It is not the empirical fact that things change (one empire succeeding another, one idea supplanting another) that gives us history. History is a matter of interpretation, and interpretation inevitably means that our *understanding* of the past changes. Events that in the present seem of great importance may fade into obscurity in the future. Conversely, seemingly minor occurrences in the present may loom large to future generations. Not only is the past subject to interpretation, but the future also comes into consideration, for our understanding of the past can never be separated from our picture of the future, that is, from our ideal of human existence as it is projected before us. As this ideal changes in the course of time, so our understanding of the past and of its importance for us changes. Interpretation thus implies that the ways in which we today understand history differ from the ways in which it has been understood in the past. It also implies that our understanding today will likely differ from future modes of understanding.

With respect to what is distinctively human, then, we again find persistence and change. They appear in the form of historicity, which is the specifically human form of temporality. In historical existence, past and future are gathered together as in a narrative so that the dialogue of culture—the dialogue that makes us human—can take place. At the same time this gathering together implies acts of interpretation. Experience shows that interpretation of history changes over time, sometimes subtly, sometimes dramatically.

Under the Conditions of Finitude

To say that entities and processes in the created world are finite is to say that their participation in the trinitarian life of God is not complete. Because of their participation, they exhibit the dialectics of identity and difference; they do not do so, however, in an unrestricted way. Their participation is limited by the conditions under which created beings exist, including the subject of this chapter, the condition of temporality.

At the heart of temporality is the relation of before and after. Each temporal entity or process persists in the transition from before to after. But experience shows that each *before* is also an *after* in relation to a previous before. Each after is also before subsequent moments. If we trace the sequence of befores and afters, we are led to the beginning and the end of each entity or process. The fact that things have beginnings and endings, resulting from their temporality, is a measure of their finitude. For each thing, the dialectics of persistence and change itself endures for a limited stretch of time.

To be sure, there is great variety in the sorts of beginnings of things. Each galaxy had a definite beginning that depended on the formation of stars. Stars, in turn, did not exist in the universe until there were hydrogen nuclei (protons) and neutrons that could fuse to form helium. Protons and neutrons, being composite entities, first came into being when the ambient temperature of the universe fell below 10^{13} degrees Kelvin, allowing quarks to bond together. But what about quarks (and electrons, also needed in the formation of atoms)? Do they have a beginning? The answer to this question is not currently available. Although it is the subject of considerable speculation and modeling, the energy required to answer the question experimentally is prohibitive. Current theory nonetheless suggests that in the earliest moments of the universe, the energy level was such that elementary particles of many sorts may have come into and gone out of existence in extraordinarily short stretches of time.

The question, then, is not so much whether particular classes of particles had a beginning but whether the universe as such had a beginning. But this question as posed is ambiguous. It may mean, Was there a *time* before the universe existed? Or, Was there a beginning of the universe's temporal duration? Since time seems to be a condition of the finite creation, there is no reason to think that there was a stretch of time before our universe existed. At the same time, it appears that there was a beginning of the universe's time, at least if big bang cosmology is correct. It may have been the case that the temporal aspect of the universe—its time-dimension—came to be at a certain moment in the past. Prior to this moment, there was no time; after this moment the universe was expanding and developing in the ways described by big bang cosmology. But this leaves us with the question of whether the universe existed before the emergence of its temporal dimension. Recent speculations about the primordial state of the universe suggest that, prior to the universe's expansion, it existed in the form of an energy-filled vacuum, from which emerged—and into which merged—elementary particles, just as according to quantum theory a host of virtual and temporary particles surrounds any given physical event. If this view is correct, then the universe would have existed primordially outside of time but with spatial dimensions. As we can see, the question about how long it existed in this state before expansion began is ill-posed. There was, in this view, no before and no after. Or, a bit more exactly, the temporal duration of the universe is finite, having had a definite beginning. This temporal duration, however, is not a complete measure of the universe. This temporal duration has taken place within a more primordial spatial extension that, in some significant sense, lies outside time. To be sure, this view is far from well-established. But if it or something like it is correct, then it would still be true to say that *our* universe along with its temporal dimension had a beginning and in this way shows forth finitude.[8]

Not only the beginning but also the end of things exhibits finitude. As noted above, in the case of some elementary particles, the end appears as annihilation, as in the encounter of a particle with an antiparticle. Although it is just as true to think of this as the particle's transformation from matter to energy, it is nonetheless the end of that particle's existence as particle. In the case of larger composites, such as atoms and molecules, the end comes either through decomposition or by being assimilated into a larger atomic unit. Through transmutation, an atom of a given element may decompose into another element. After transmutation, it is no longer the same element. Likewise, the chemical-electrical bonds that hold a molecule together may dissolve, leaving the constituent atoms. Or the molecule may become embedded in a larger molecule, thus bringing its existence to an end, at least as an autonomous unit.

When we look more globally at the universe, it becomes more difficult to speak about endings. The laws of conservation suggest that, although there may be many beginnings and endings within the universe, the regularity of physical processes itself does not come to an end. Annihilation of a particle may bring about the end of that particle but from the perspective of conservation, there has been only transformation from one state to another, a transformation preceded by others and followed by others. If conservation laws are truly laws, then the total amount of mass-energy in the universe is constant in spite of innumerable momentary transformations.

Does the physical universe as a whole have an end? Like the question of the universe's beginning, this question does not have an answer. As is well known, contemporary physics suggests three possible outcomes for the universe. In one, the amount of matter in the universe will be sufficient to cause the universe eventually to contract and return to its primordial state. In this case, its end would be identical to its beginning. In another outcome, the amount of matter would be such that the universe would continue to expand at its present rate. In this case, the universe would continue to exist indefinitely, although not in a state that would permit life as we know it. This is because in this indefinite future the stars will, in this view, have all gone through their natural cycles and their nuclear processes will have been exhausted. The universe's energy will then exist in a state of total equilibrium. The same result occurs in the third possibility, in which the amount of matter in the universe is just the right amount to ensure that the universe neither contracts into its primordial state nor expands indefinitely. In this case, the rate of the universe's expansion slows and approaches (without ever quite reaching) zero. In each possibility, it is meaningful to speak of the universe's ending, although with different meanings of *ending*.

It is easier to grasp beginnings and endings in the biological world. Every cell, for instance, has a definite beginning in cellular division. Every organism comes to be from a process of cellular division. Every species has identifiable antecedents in some other population from which it has become reproductively isolated. The fact that organisms and species have beginnings is a measure of their finitude. Their persistence in time is limited. The same is true of life on earth as such. Although there is no theory explaining the origin of life on earth that has won general acceptance and has experimental support, there can be no doubt that life did indeed have a beginning, even if it had nonorganic antecedents.

Life comes to an end in the biological death of organisms and in the extinction of species. At the same time, from a more global perspective perhaps we could say that, although individuals die and species become extinct, the processes of life are carried on. From this global perspective, the important thing is that the individual's genetic heritage is transmitted to future generations. Once that is done, the individual's death is inevitable and salutary. It clears a space for the next generation to live in and its decomposition provides the nutrients that other organisms need to thrive. From this perspective, death is no calamity but is instead a necessary part of a cycle that endures. This does not seem to be the case with species. As reproductively isolated, a species is not in a position to contribute its genes to some larger living world. As occupying an environmental niche, it is not competing with other species, so its extinction does not necessarily contribute to the well-being of other species. And yet, it seems clear that every species comes to an end just as every organism comes to an end. It might be thought that cells are, through division, potentially immortal. The practical realities of biology, however, suggest that no form of biological life can truly be immortal. Even if we overlook catastrophic events, such as collisions with comets and asteroids, that have destroyed huge numbers of species in the past, there is still the fact that some day in the future the nuclear processes in our sun will come to an end. As the amount of hydrogen available for fusion is exhausted and the fusion of helium into carbon and oxygen occurs, our sun will expand to such an extent that the earth will be encompassed and destroyed. So, there is an absolute end in sight for all life on earth—not only individual organisms and species but for all the processes of life.

Biological entities are thus also finite. Their life depends on their maintaining unity of structure and function, but this unity can be compromised in numerous ways. The components of a cell or organism, for example, may malfunction in illness. The extreme case of this is death. Just as particles can pass out of existence through annihilation, so cells and organisms come to their end in death. Naturally, there are important differences between organic death and the annihilation of particles. For one thing, not all particles are annihilated. Indeed, it appears that most particles subsist through the history of the universe without annihilation. The end of existence is for them a mere possibility that is only infrequently actualized. For organic beings, however, it is different. Although a cell is potentially everlasting by virtue of the fact that replication could go on indefinitely, the eventual end of organic existence is a virtual certainty. This certainty is due in part to the nature of organic life, in which one entity flourishes at the expense of others, where the ongoing process of life presupposes death. But it may also be due to cellular mechanisms that wear out in time and are not susceptible to the organism's ability to repair itself. At any rate, finitude in the form of cessation of existence is for organic beings practically certain. And, while we human beings may someday alter our genetic composition in such a way as to eliminate the wearing out of cells, it is highly unlikely that we can control the environment to such an extent as to eliminate human death altogether. Further, unlike the annihilation of a particle, organic death is utterly the end. The direction of time, therefore, is decisive for living beings and for the nature of organic death. The annihilation of a particle is an instantaneous event in which the particle's mass is converted into energy. Organic death, however, is a process that takes time, even if the length of time is comparatively short. Just as the life of an organism occupies a certain length of time, so does its death. Once again we can see the way in which time enters into organic being and is a vital consideration in its understanding. A third difference is that annihilation is a transformation in which the particle's mass is converted into energy. Death, however, is not this sort of transformation but a process that results in the organism being decomposed into its inorganic constituents. In spite of these differences, however, we are justified in noting the similarities between annihilation and death. In each case the individual entities of the universe are subject to limitations to such an extent that their nonexistence is a possibility and, in the case of the organic, a certainty.

Human existence is not exempt from finitude, and yet we have found it more difficult to accept the inevitability of the death of human beings. In a certain sense, human death is just another occasion of organic death, but humans are not merely organic beings. Although distinctively human activities such as cognition have an unmistakable and profound organic and chemical basis, it is difficult to avoid the conclusion that with the appearance of human beings genuinely novel properties have emerged. With humans, conceptual thinking and the entertaining of values becomes significant. This is an aspect of our existence as cultural beings. It is for this reason that human death, although connected in obvious ways to organic death, is more. Let us say that human death is an event of meaning. What I mean by this is that humans, as the sort of beings who seek to understand through acts of interpretation, treat the event of death not merely as an organic happening but also as an event that is to be understood. Human death has significance for humans that animal death does not have for animals and that plant death does not have for plants.[9]

Death functions especially as an event of meaning because of the fact that human beings are aware not only of the fact and inevitability of death but of the inevitability of their own death. Death thus becomes the ultimate event. With birth, it forms a bookend of human life. But it has a significance that birth does not have. As the temporally ultimate event of one's life, death brings our story, as it were, to an end. Birth constitutes the possibility of having a story, but it is death that determines what, if any, significance our story has had.

Finally, human death is an event of meaning because of its meaninglessness. As noted above, human life has a narrative quality. We try to construct our lives so that they form meaningful wholes. We interpret events with this interest in mind. The good and bad of life are interpretively drawn into the ongoing narrative of our lives. Death, however, is not merely the closing event of the narrative; it is also experienced in anticipation as a disruptive event. That is why untimely deaths bring with them such anguish. For example, when a child dies we feel that death has arrived too soon—in advance of its natural time. It has not allowed the child's narrative to be formed, but has instead interrupted the child's effort to construct a meaningful totality of life. But even when death is not untimely, when one dies at "a ripe old age," we still feel a sense of interruption, of disruption. We feel that there is in fact no natural termination of life, that life could go on and on, just as a narrative can be continued indefinitely without loss of coherence and with an increase in richness. Death, then, although in one sense the closing act of life that brings all things to a close and allows for a sense of totality and completion, is in another sense a disruptive force that brings unnecessarily to an end something that need not be brought to an end.

Is human death evil? Implicit in the previous arguments has been the opinion that the ending of physical entities and of biological life is not evil but is instead a reflection of finitude. To the extent that we regard human death as simply an organic event, we cannot think of it as evil. Since with the rise of human beings there comes to be in the universe new properties, however, a deeper understanding of human death is both necessary and possible. As an event of meaning, especially in its meaningless character, death may very well be experienced as a great evil. By disrupting the course of life, by prematurely and unnecessarily ending the construction of one's narrative, by gashing open human life and leaving the survivors with the ragged edges of loss, death is indeed a great evil. It stops cold what we regard as the highest development of finite reality—the capacity to know and to love and to engage in other distinctively human activities.

But death is a great evil for another reason, which is connected to the fact that with the appearance of human beings in the universe we find the development of morality. Because of morality and the character of human choice required for morality, human death is often more than merely a natural event. It is often a moral event. It is a moral event when one individual kills another and it is a moral event when a social community is responsible for death. Because human death is often a moral event, it will sometimes be a moral evil, as when death occurs unjustly.

It is for reasons such as these that human death is the chief manifestation of our finitude and of the fact that our participation in God is not so complete that we have unconditioned existence. Like every other entity in the universe, we are subject to limitations. Our lives are conditioned by factors outside our control and even the construction of meaning is subject to disruption and contingent factors.

The finitude of our temporality shows itself not only in our death but in the human propensity to distort our relation to the past and the future. I mentioned above that, in the human world, time takes the form of history. Because of our historicity there is an open-ended character to human nature. This character, however, is subject to finitude. For instance, our history, which can serve as a positive ingredient in the ongoing construction of human being, can also weigh oppressively on us as a nagging legacy that must at all costs be repeated. Alternatively, our culture may fall into a state of collective forgetfulness in which the past is dismissed in favor of a rootless and superficial present that has no future. To be human, however, is not only to have a history but also to have a future that guides our action in the present. Yet the future, which can be an unlimited horizon of hope, is often constrained by the narrow limitations of the present. In periods of cultural pessimism, the future may appear as a conclusion or as something fated. In either case, it does not evoke hopeful action. Instead it discourages hope and plunges us into despair.

Human existence is oriented toward the future—a teleological process in that it aims at an ideal. This means that human being involves not only development but also striving and decision. All this is a way of expressing the fact that human being is created out of nothing. Although our true and authentic being lies in the future as a task to be accomplished, the futurity of our authentic being causes anxiety. Hence the temptation to turn our back on our future orientation and become preoccupied with the past or the present. In these latter cases, we abandon the task of becoming authentically human.

Beyond forgetfulness and despair lies the possibility of an immoral use of the past and future. Under the conditions of sin, the past and the future become things to be manufactured and manipulated in just the way in which truth is manufactured through propaganda and the natural environment manipulated through thoughtless technology. The past and the future are no longer sources of power for the liberation of humankind. They are now objects of power as we employ them to our own ends. No longer does the past speak to us with wisdom in a voice demanding to be heard. Instead it is we in our everlasting present who determine the past and the future. It is not even we collectively but those who aggrandize power to themselves and attain thereby the capacity for determining our past and our future. At the hands of political forces the past becomes a plastic thing capable of assuming any number of shapes as the needs of the day demand. The future likewise becomes what we want it to be. Through careful use of media images, advertising and control of educational curricula, it is possible for humankind to be thoroughly misled about the past and to be just as misled about the future and its prospect. The same manipulative efforts can bring it about that we see ourselves, not as contributing to the ongoing human project, but instead as helpless effects of forces beyond our control, whether those forces bears the names of abstractions (e.g., communism) or people (e.g., Jews). Humankind, always ready to surrender its freedom and its responsibility and its possibilities, grasps with eager desire any excuse to see ourselves as under the domination of sinister forces, the revelation of which depends on political systems posing as saviors.

Finally, even when the past is acknowledged and the future is open, we must still acknowledge the limitations of human freedom. In spite of popular and often theological convictions to the contrary, it cannot be the case that humans are endowed with absolute freedom. Our participation in inorganic and organic structures argues against it, as does our participation in human communities and structures. Although humans undoubtedly exercise choice, our choice is always between limited alternatives, and they are always conditioned by what we have been—by our history. We choose as we do because of the sorts of persons that we have become. This is not to deny the possibility of our making dramatic changes in our lives, for our present life is not simply the sum total of our history. To believe otherwise would be to deny the interpretive nature of our existence, whereby we construct ourselves from the history available to us. Nonetheless, even a radically changed person has changed for reasons that make sense to that person in the context of that person's total life. For these reasons, it is evident that human freedom, while real, is quite limited.

The Kingdom of God and Identity and Difference in Time: Eschatological Existence

The kingdom of God is God's response to the distortions of finite existence. It is not the end or the overcoming of finitude. Creatures always remain creatures, even in the kingdom of God. This means that they retain the essential features of finitude. In the kingdom of God, however, the distorting effects of sin are being overcome.

What does this mean for the temporal existence of human beings? The kingdom of God does not destroy or alter the temporal structure of human existence. Even in the kingdom, human existence is marked by persistence and change. Identity amid difference remains a task to be accomplished. The past still appears in the form of tradition and as that which is effective in the present through our remembrance of it. The future remains as an ideal projection of our existence and as a practical task. What is different in the kingdom of God is the character of our past and our future.

To be in the kingdom of God is to receive a new past. Although each human person has a distinctive past constituted by his or her unique history, and even though each human community has its own past formed out of its memory, it is also true that humankind shares a collective past that bears continually on the present of the entire human race. This past we all have inherited, and we appropriate it in the construction of our self-identity. This past is the past of sin, a past marked by our failure to be mindful of God and by our acts of inhumanity. This past is the power of sin that channels our lives in harmful and self-destructive paths. But to be in God's kingdom means that we receive a new past with which to constitute our present. This new past is the history of God's salvation, the history of God's grace and of people's faithful and obedient response to that grace. This past casts itself forward into our present in the form of God's promise of a new creation. But this past is not, as it were, natural to us. We have not made it; God offers it to us, and we can appropriate it only through decision. By this decision we allow the past that God offers to us to overcome the power of the sinful past that humankind has made for itself. We enter into a new tradition, one marked by faithful obedience and mindfulness and love. We thereby gain a new identity as the power of this new past begins to bring about a new humanity within us.

To be in the kingdom of God is also to receive a new future. Too often, the future that we project and which guides our present simply carries on the sinful and inhumane tendencies of the past. Instead of the future being the field of new possibilities of developing our humanity by continually heeding the voice of God, it becomes for us another opportunity for alienation and self-destruction—a repetition of our past. To be in the kingdom of God, however, is to be presented with a future created by the God who makes all things new. Unlike the everyday futures that we make for ourselves, the future of God's kingdom is constituted not by our own conceptions but by God. Of course, as the future, it remains a task. The future of God's kingdom is not a state of affairs already determined and just waiting to happen in the course of time. It remains to be accomplished, and it is accomplished not by human striving to actualize an ideal image of human existence but by faithful obedience to God's command. Further, the future of God's kingdom is not simply an event or series of events that has not yet happened. Like our humanly constructed future, it confronts us as a possibility, in particular as judgment and as promise. As judgment, the future of God's kingdom confronts us with God's condemnation of every human attempt at actualizing the future without heeding the command of God and at making the future conform to the past of our sin. The kingdom of God is thus God's no to all human striving done oblivious to the will of God and to the way of righteousness shown to us in the kingdom. At the same time, this future comes to us as a promise made by the God who makes all things new. This promise is God's yes, the yes of the new creation.

The kingdom of God is God's response to human distortion of temporality. In our sin we are heedless of God's grace and ignorant of our having inherited humankind's common sinful past. Although we are complicit in that past insofar as we unthinkingly appropriate it and allow it to determine our identity, we remain ignorant of its power over us. Determined by the past and hence without an open future, we fall into a hopeless if unconscious despair, in which we exist without God, our future utterly and sadly limited to merely human possibilities. To us in this condition God's kingdom appears, giving us a new past and a new future. With it comes the admonition to remember both the sinful past that the kingdom overcomes and also the new past of God's grace that we have been given. With it additionally comes the command to live henceforth entirely oriented to the future that God is providing, a future of possibilities that transcend those that we conceive by extrapolating from our past.

The kingdom of God is also God's response to the phenomenon of death. The biblical metaphor for this response is eternal life. Eternal life is not the unending continuation of human existence but must be thought of as a present reality, just as the future is to be thought of as that which presses on the present as the domain of the possible. Eternal life is a life conducted in the face of the future of God's kingdom and in the power of that future. It is the overcoming of death not only in its organic form but also as an event of meaning. In the kingdom of God, we receive our identity through receiving a new past and a new future. As a result, death is not the decisive event of our narrated lives. It remains *an* event, but not the event that determines the meaning of our lives. Through eternal life, human existence is set in a context that transcends the significance of death. This is true also in cases where death seems meaningless. Even here our lives transcend the limits imposed by death, for the narrative of one's life is no longer dominated by untimely or unfortunate death. It is instead narrated according to its place in the kingdom of God.

Does eternal life also mean victory over the organic aspect of death? This is the question of immortality. Faith in the God who makes all things new compels us to acknowledge the victory of the kingdom of God over death even in its organic form. But it is exceedingly difficult for us to gain a clear picture of what such a victory entails. Does it mean the survival of the individual person as an individual? A re-creation of the universe? Or something else? It is impossible to know. The Bible presents us with striking images that are suggestive but incapable of being incorporated into a theoretical account. Nonetheless, our incapacity to form a concrete picture does not nullify confidence that the kingdom of the God who makes all things new is already present, overcoming death in all of its aspects.

The same combination of confidence and modesty should rule our understanding of the significance of the kingdom of God for the cosmos as a whole. The Bible speaks about a new heaven and a new earth, but again this does not furnish the sort of information that can establish a theory. Moreover, if it is difficult to picture the victory of the kingdom of God over organic death, it is all the more difficult for us to conceive of the implications of the kingdom for the entire universe. The temptation will always be to imagine a universe that corresponds to a condition best suited for human beings. For example, we may imagine a world without death (at least animal death), but it is difficult to conceive of a universe with biological life in which one sort of animal does not live off other sorts, either as predators or as parasites. Or we may imagine a universe that is not material at all but a purely spiritual reality. At any rate, faith in God and in the new creation does not require a firm and accurate picture of the ultimate consequences of the kingdom of God. It requires only that we conduct our present lives with the confidence that the God who is already at work overcoming death and the distorting effects of sin will continue that work into the future. This confidence implies that the new creation will be effective in the cosmos in ways that are analogous (but not identical) to the effects of the new creation on human existence.

6

Generic and Individual Features

The Physical Universe

In addition to persistence and change in time, entities within the physical universe demonstrate their participation in the trinitarian life of God in the relation between generic and individual features. This relation rests on the fact that physical entities possess (or perhaps are identical to) identifiable and universal physical properties. These properties are the basis of the periodic table of elements and also the classification of biological entities according to kingdom, phylum, class, order, family, genus, and species. They allow physical and biological entities to be categorized into natural groups and in this way establish the foundation of scientific knowledge. The main point is that each entity shares properties with every other member of its class. To the extent that each entity shares these generic features, to that extent it is identical to every other member of its class. At the same time, in many cases there are properties that distinguish entities as something particular and as different from the other members of its class. In this interplay of generic sameness and individualizing difference, we see once again the participation of creatures in God's trinitarian life of identity and difference. In its generic sameness, each thing exhibits identity with other entities; in its individualizing features, it exhibits difference from those entities.

Naturally, identity and difference in the form of the generic and the individual assume more or less importance in relation to each other according to the physical entities that we consider. At the sub-atomic level, the identity of generic sameness overwhelms any tendency toward individuality and difference. Each electron is qualitatively indistinguishable from every other, except in sofaras it exists in a higher or lower energy state. Each electron is characterized by the same properties, such as rest mass, charge, and spin, and each possesses the same mathematical values for these properties that every other electron possesses. The same is true of the other elementary particles and of nucleons as well. Every proton is identical to every other proton. None has intrinsic characteristics that would permit us to distinguish it qualitatively from other protons. However, as we ascend to the larger scale of atoms, the dominance of the generic over the particular begins to recede. At this level it is meaningful to distinguish two atoms in the same class in the case of isotopes. For instance, hydrogen exists in three isotopes, depending on whether the single proton is paired with two, one, or no neutrons. Further, the difference between two isotopes is not merely a quantitative difference in weight, for the differences in atomic weight are correlated with differences in the ways in which the isotopes behave (in radioactive decay, for example). Here, in the qualitative difference between two isotopes of the same atom, we can see a difference that allows us to distinguish one from the other as something particular. Of course, the extent of this difference is not very great. After all, every deuterium atom is identical to every other deuterium atom. There are individualizing differences within the class of hydrogen atoms but still overwhelming generic sameness within the sub-class of (for example) deuterium atoms.

What is true of atoms is true of molecules and other physical realities as well. In each case, we can speak of a generic sameness or identity with other members of the class and of some measure of differentiation within the class. However, the further we proceed on the scale of size, the more variation there is within a given class of entities. Simple molecules are identical with one another, except to the extent that different isotopes of atoms are incorporated into the molecules. But the matter is different with large and complex molecules. There is, for example, a generic sameness that describes every DNA molecule. They are all composed of the same bases (thymine, adenine, guanine, and cytosine), with thymine always pairing with adenine and guanine always pairing with cytosine. To this extent, every DNA molecule is the same as every other. However, this generic sameness is accompanied by enormous diversity in the sequence of these pairs. From the perspective of sequence, no two DNA molecules are alike; each can be said to be an individual in the sense that its sequence of bases is unique. The same is true of physical entities at the largest scale: all galaxies are generically identical with each other with respect to their material composition, being just collections of stellar systems, gas, and dust held together by gravitational forces. However, this generic and somewhat abstract identity stands alongside a concrete diversity of considerable richness. Galaxies differ from one another in size, shape, age, and other respects; even though each galaxy falls into one of a few types of generic categories, it is not stretching language too far to say that each galaxy has individual features that make it unique. Stars could likewise be considered generically identical to one another on the basis of their chemical composition and internal processes. Beyond this sort of generic identity, however, there is considerable and significant difference. Whether each star is chemically and physically unique is difficult to say; given the enormous number of stars, it seems mathematically possible that two stars could be composed of the same number and types of atoms and molecules. However, as a practical matter we are justified in stating that each star is materially unique. And even though, like galaxies, stars exhibit generic features that enable us to place each star in one of a few categories (based upon each star's mass), it seems evident that the details of each star's origin and development will cause it to differ from other stars of similar mass. Large entities of the physical universe, then, from molecules to galaxies, exhibit considerable diversity. The generic identity that characterizes elementary particles here gives way to a richer and more complex identity, one that includes significant if limited differences within each class. Generic sameness is no longer total, with every entity in a class being just another copy of the type; at this level we find genuine diversity within classes of entities. Unlike elementary particles, each of which is an illustration of its class and where only the class is unique, very large molecules such as DNA and entities such as galaxies and stars show real uniqueness.

What of the universe in its entirety? Does it also exhibit generic sameness? Is it unique? The answers to these questions depend on the vexing cosmological question of whether ours is the sole universe or whether it is one of many. Recent cosmological speculation has suggested the possibility that, if our universe emerged as a fluctuation of energy in the primordial vacuum, then other universes may have as well. In that case, it makes sense to raise these questions; however, at present the matter is wholly speculative. Comparison of our universe with others, even if they exist, is impossible in the current and all foreseeable states of knowledge. At the same time, if there are other universes, the conviction that all finite reality participates in the trinitarian life of God compels the belief that these universes exhibit some aspects of generic sameness in comparison with each other and also a measure of individualizing difference.

The Biological World

Like the physical universe, the biological world exhibits the relation between generic identity and individualizing differences. Each biological entity has formal qualities that permit us to classify it taxonomically. Mammals, for example, all have some important properties in common, such as the four-chambered heart and hair. At the same time, each biological entity is in some sense an individual with differentiating features. In contrast to particles, atoms, and even molecules, biological entities possess a genuine degree of individuality. Here authentic uniqueness appears alongside generic sameness.

The cell illustrates these points. On one hand, each cell shares important generic similarities with every other cell. For instance, every cell has a wall, genetic material, and cytoplasm. Every cell is capable of replication. Every cell engages in metabolic processes. These are important generic features; they represent a sort of minimal list of features for any possible cell. On the other hand, having learned this much we are still far from grasping all the important features of any given cell. Whereas in the physical universe a knowledge of the generic features is (at the sub-atomic level) virtually the whole of our knowledge or at least (in the cases of larger physical entities) the principal part of our knowledge, in the biological world knowledge of these generic aspects does not begin to give us complete knowledge. Knowing, for example, the generic aspects of the cell tells us nothing about that cell's function within a larger system of cells. It also gives us little specific information about the internal organization of the cell or about the ways in which it interacts with its environment. All of these aspects—function, internal organization, interaction with the environment, and more—depend on the particularities of each type of cell.

Of course, this is not to claim that every cell is *absolutely* unique. In a human body, for instance, every somatic cell is genetically identical to every other somatic cell. In this way, cells exhibit generic sameness. Nonetheless, this generic identity occurs alongside profound differences in cell functioning within the body. Through the mechanisms of cell expression, cells come to be differentiated in function, so that liver cells, neurons and skin cells, in spite of their genetic identity, perform in varied ways.

What is true of the cell is true as well of the organism. On one hand, every member of a species shares with the other members important generic features that define what it means to be a member of that species. On the other hand, each organism is distinct from every other member of its species. First, it is genetically distinct and in fact unique (except in the case of identical siblings). Second, most organisms develop particular and individualizing features due to their interaction with their environment. An abundance or lack of food, water, energy and other essentials can importantly modify the organism's functioning and well being. Third, at least with some sorts of animals (such as primates), each organism has a particular life history of experiences and learning that contribute to its degree of individuality. Again, this is not to claim that each organism is absolutely unique. It is only to indicate that in the biological world, in comparison to the physical universe, there is a far greater development of individuality.

As with the physical universe, it is impossible (given the current state of knowledge) to answer the question of whether the biological world in its totality exhibits a generic similarity to other biological worlds, for so far as we know there are no other biological worlds. It is certainly very difficult for us to conceive of a world in which life is not grounded in chemical processes, in which the fundamental unit of life is not the cell, and in which reproduction does not occur by means of genetic transmission. We can only assume that, if there are other worlds of life, they must have roughly the same structures as ours. On that assumption, and with the theological conviction that all finite beings participate in the trinitarian life of God, it is reasonable to suppose that the same relation of the generic and the individual subsists in any possible biological world, even if the precise structures differ markedly from ours.

Human Existence

The question of generic identity and particularity takes a distinctive form in human existence, for while assuming the importance of biological factors (such as genetic inheritance) we also consider the effect of human society and culture on our identity. I have argued in this chapter that in the biological world real uniqueness occurs, at least with respect to the genetic constitution of each biological organism and also in the particular learning-histories of animals such as primates. Human beings have at least this sort of uniqueness and individuality. The question now is whether we are truly unique with respect to the distinctively human features of our existence. To what extent is each of us identical with and different from other members of our social communities? To what extent is each of us an individual? To what extent is the formative effect of human societies so dominant that only cultures and societies are unique, persons being just more or less identical instantiations of societies?

The answers to these questions are available, by analogy, in the biological world in the example of identical twins. Here, where genetic identity is complete, an individualizing tendency is at work at a very young age, the siblings' development taking a unique path according to their respective physical and learning environments. By analogy, the tendency toward generic identity that comes to us from a given society's formative pressures does not fully cancel out the particular life histories that contribute to our identity and that affect our uniqueness as individuals in those features that make us distinctively human.

Humans, in the distinctive sphere of human existence, exhibit sameness. By that I mean that, within a given society, there is widespread similarity of language, beliefs, values, practices, and so on. This similarity arises from the fact that we are acculturated in and through social communities. The formative effect of these communities can be quite dominating in the shaping of a person's beliefs, values, and behavior. Military training gives us an example of the way in which indoctrination and regimentation can bring about an extraordinary degree of cultural uniformity in large numbers. The loose network of university communities provides another example, this time associated with a different set of attitudes, beliefs, and practices. There is a general tendency for members of a society to act and think alike. However, even with these sorts of regimentation, individuality appears. People do behave and believe differently from one another in the military as well as in the academic world. In spite of the indoctrination of beliefs and values, military service is, for example, compatible with a wide range of worldviews. A military unit may contain people of various religious and political opinions. In short, even in a military culture, in which uniformity is highly sought after, the individual person is more than just an example of a type. Even here, there is a significant degree of individualizing difference in ways that are distinctively human. The same is true all the more in other social communities such as the family and voluntary associations. In each case it is legitimate to speak of a common culture that is inculcated and which provides the individual with a measure of generic cultural identity. But even the most efficient mechanisms of acculturation do not completely overcome the individualizing tendencies operative on each of us. Naturally, we should not imagine that these individualizing tendencies are due to some hidden and personal essence that each of us possesses and that prevails in spite of all socializing efforts. We should instead understand that individuality is rooted in the variety of social networks of which we are members, in the particular life histories that distinguish each of us from others, and in the capacity we possess to diverge intentionally from the beliefs and practices of our communities. Only in a totalitarian community of perfect efficiency would all of our social networks be conformed to a single acculturating regime and thus be able to determine (at a practical level) the life histories and decision-making of each individual. In such a social condition, human individuality and uniqueness would be minimal and generic identity would completely rule.

It should not be thought that for human beings generic identity is evil, as though individuality without this sort of identity were the highest good. Although its maximization in totalitarian societies is evil insofar as it quashes individuality, the identity that comes from participation in a community is a condition of being human. For example, language is an utterly social phenomenon. Not only does it exist in the interactions between human beings, it exists before any given individual and has an undoubted formative effect on each of us. Language is something into which we are born and that nurtures us in our becoming human. Without one's participation in language it is difficult to see how one could exist as a human, for without a language one would have no access to the symbolic realm of meanings. Even if a purely private language were possible, one's capacity to create such a language would still presuppose that one had already learned a social language such as English. Another example is found in beliefs and values. It might be thought that an individual human being could discover and hold certain beliefs and values and become convinced of their validity strictly without participation in a community. Reflection on actual human practice, however, shows this to be unlikely. Scientific inquiry, for example, is a thoroughly communal endeavor. Scientists are trained according to community standards and are initiated into the scientific community by the personal intervention of those who are already scientists. Their inquiry depends on the work of the larger scientific community and requires a large degree of trust in that community. Finally, the validation of one's scientific work assumes the competency of the community. What is true of scientific knowledge is true of beliefs and values in general. Ubiquitous features of human existence such as beliefs and values are unthinkable apart from the formative effects of social communities.

Like everything else, then, human persons participate in the trinitarian life of God and its dialectics of identity and difference. In human existence the possibilities for individualization emerge with greater strength than in the physical universe and biological world. At the same time, generic identity rests on distinctively human grounds, such as shared values and beliefs, which are formed by the various communities that we inhabit.

Under the Conditions of Finitude

Under the condition of finitude any ideal balance between generic and individual features is unattainable. On the contrary, the tendency of entities to exhibit generic features generally means that these entities fall short of complete individuality in some measure. At the same time, at least at the level of human existence, there is often, in response to socializing pressure, a tendency to elevate individuality to the status of a principle and to abstract the individual from social relations and even from social responsibility. When this happens proper individuality is lost and the human person becomes an emaciated version of authentic human existence.

The finitude of the physical universe reveals itself in the defining properties of its entities and processes. As already noted, particles especially are characterized by a massive degree of generic sameness. Each is identical with every other member of its class. One class differs from another one with respect to a few, highly quantitative features such as mass and electric charge. Of course, this analysis does not imply that this enormous degree of generic sameness is in any way evil.

On the contrary, it is a condition of the universe's existence that particles are interchangeable. A physical universe in which every particle is qualitatively different from every other particle, a universe in which particles do not fall into natural classes can hardly be imagined. A universe in which each particle within a class were as different as one human being is from another would be quite unstable. This observation is another way of stating that finitude is not evil. It is not an evil that in particles the generic has almost completely won out over the individual. It is instead a reflection of the finite character of the physical universe's participation in God. Even at the level of large objects such as stars, where properties are more complex and where a rudimentary form of individuality appears, generic identity rules rather severely. In spite of their individuality, each star is substantially like all other stars, being composed mainly of hydrogen and helium and undergoing the same nuclear processes. While it is true that each star has a particular origin, life-cycle and end, stars nonetheless fall into a few categories (based on a quantitative factor, the stars' masses) and the course of any star's life is fairly predictable once its mass is known. Defining properties in the physical universe thus contrast with defining properties of entities in the biological world and of human beings, in which we observe the possibility of greater individuality. The physical universe thus exhibits vestiges of the Trinity's dialectics of identity and difference, but only in an exceedingly remote way.

Biological entities also show the effects of finite participation in God. In comparison with the physical universe, the biological world shows a heightened measure of individuality and the appearance of authentic uniqueness. However, this individuality is always qualified and partial. In spite of the genetic particularity of each biological being, for the vast majority of living things similarities with other members of the population far outweigh any individualizing properties. These individualizing properties are not negligible but in many cases are not the most scientifically important properties. By this I mean that the object of study for most living things is the population, not the individual. This is true even in the case of the study of human beings in their biological and perhaps even their social existence. In mammals and other animals with highly adapted responses to the environment and where genuine learning occurs, behavior is nonetheless often quite stereotypical, with minimal differences from one animal to another. The same must be said of humans, whose behavior and thought exhibit the same tendency toward generic sameness that we observe in the rest of the biological world.

The rule of the generic in the biological world is not, of course, evil. As with the physical universe, it is most likely necessary for the existence of biological organization. Although a world in which every organism is literally unique is conceivable, it is difficult to imagine how such a world could evolve beyond the cellular level, for organs and systems require that numerous cells possess the same structure and function and be able to function together as an aggregate. Sexual reproduction is also difficult to imagine under these circumstances. If the biological world is to develop highly organized beings, it seems necessary that cells fall into generic categories. Likewise, the behavior of living things develops over time into certain routine paths that prove efficient and that tend to be repeated because of their efficiency. The sustaining of life is built upon the repetition of such behavior; a high degree of individuality, i.e., behavior that diverges from the routine and biologically efficient paths, would likely prove fatal. At the same time, it is evident from human history that behavioral conformity is not an unmixed blessing and can be disastrous. In summary, individuality in the biological world is quite limited and is limited for the very good biological reason that life requires high levels of genetic, functional, and behavioral conformity.

The relation between the generic and the individual in the sphere of human existence is characterized by the fact that human beings in our social and cultural existence show a greater degree of individuality than do other members of the biological world. Two tendencies are at work. First, the generic features of distinctively human existence result from our participation in communities of all sorts. As noted above, language, beliefs, and values are all social realties that have an essential and formative effect on our development as human beings. These are realities that are largely common to all within a society. As a result, the relation between the generic and the individual is effectively the relation between the community and the individual. Second, the potential for humans to develop in the direction of individuality implies a contrasting tendency to distinguish ourselves from the societies of which we are a part. This insight finds expression in the view, articulated by developmental psychologists, that the psychological task of adolescence is to develop an identity and to become a person in one's own right. More broadly, the quest for individuality is the attempt to actualize one's artistic, cognitive, social, and other capacities. These two tendencies (exhibiting generic social features and becoming an individual) are contrasting but not necessarily opposed. Under ideal conditions, the quest for individuality would culminate in an embracing of the beliefs, values, and practices of those communities that we inhabit. Authentic individuality would be discovered in and through the community. In turn, society would nurture authentic individuality and would, in fact, be composed of persons whose potential as individuals would be fully actualized. In fact, however, human society and individuality take place under the condition of finitude. We inhabit multiple societies; the beliefs, values, and practices of one may conflict with another, with the result that the quest for individuality means either deciding between conflicting communities or psychologically denying the conflict or living a life divided by the conflict or (in extreme cases) withdrawing from human community. There can be no truly generic, i.e., universal, human features until there is a single, all-embracing community in which the beliefs, values and practices of all other communities find their fulfillment. At the same time, the quest for individuality always remains incomplete. Even apart from mental illnesses that compromise one's identity, there are the everyday maladies and shortcomings that prevent the full integration of our experience into a harmonious whole and that prevent the full realization of our capacities. As a result, our lives are psychologically divided, with conflicts between one feeling and another and between feeling and thought. We are also socially divided, with conflict between one moral commitment and another. Thus we fall short of authentic individuality.

The relation between the generic and the individual subsists not only under the condition of finitude but also under the condition of sin. There it takes on a decidedly moral aspect. On one hand, political, religious, and other institutions that bring about cultural identity may strive to make their members conform to a standard in such a way that individuality is effaced. This tendency is characteristic of so-called religious cults but can be found to some degree in all institutional cultures. The armed forces once again furnish an example. Here every effort is made to erase individual differences and achieve a uniformity of appearance, values, and behavior. Totalitarian regimes represent the attempt to achieve this sort of uniformity on a massive scale, enforced by all the powers of the state. Popular culture reflects our anxiety about this institutional tendency, with books such as *The Organization Man* and *1984* depicting societies, actual and hypothetical, in which individuality is extinguished. However, uniformity often does not need overt enforcement. Public opinion, peer pressure, and other forms of socialization bring it about that most people in a society conform reasonably well to general expectations. At the same time, we find reactions to the generic sameness of social life. Such reactions consist in the elevation of individuality to the status of highest good. In our culture, the beat poets of the 1950s, the counter-cultural movements of the 1960s, and the contemporary quest for spirituality outside the bounds of religious institutions represent recent manifestations of this quest for individuality. In this tendency, the generic identity provided by membership in an institution or other corporate entity is felt to be stifling and every effort is made to escape its enervating effects. The more that communities and institution, use their power to enforce conformity, the more we are driven to resist by separating ourselves from those communities and institutions and to seek individuality in isolation from them.

These two tendencies are rooted in the fact that humans participate in the trinitarian life of God under the condition of sin. Because of our participation in God, we like every other finite entity show both generic features and individualizing tendencies, but under the conditions of sin these qualities come into harmful conflict. The more one tendency is emphasized, the more the other tendency is felt to be something that must be pursued, even at the price of losing balance. The result is either a bland social conformity enforced, if necessary, coercively or an abstract individualism. Conformity is bland when a society is intolerant of diversity and when social or political pressures are such as to cause the great majority to shun expressions of individuality. Abstract individualism is the assertion of individuality in isolation from one's membership in community. In these cases the individual is represented as existing without social connections. It is possible for a society to be characterized by both bland conformity and abstract individuality simultaneously. This happens when, as in our current culture, there is a publicly endorsed and widespread commitment to abstract individuality that masks an actual and equally widespread conformity. Hence the paradox of a society that celebrates rugged individualism but is at the same time socialized to a high degree in fairly circumscribed ways.

The Kingdom of God

We can consider the kingdom of God and its historical anticipation, the church, in terms of the generic and the individual. The kingdom of God is the Christian symbol for the ideal community in which the generic aspects of human existence become truly universal without threatening the quest for authentic individuality. In the kingdom of God, generic identity is conceived of in terms of Jesus Christ. To be in the kingdom means to be in the process of becoming conformed to the image of God, Jesus Christ. In the eschatological kingdom, all humankind comes to have the qualities of Jesus Christ. Yet the kingdom is not the end of individuality. On the contrary, as the New Testament's teaching about spiritual gifts shows, the unity that God seeks is a unity fully consistent with individual diversity.

However, this ideal harmony of the generic and the individual is an eschatological reality. It is present in the world but does not completely rule in human affairs. It remains a task set before us as something to be striven after in the church. The church pursues the generic identity found in the kingdom by urging humankind to become conformed to Jesus Christ. In particular, this means holding to the doctrinal rule of faith, practicing the disciplines of the Christian life in common with other members of the kingdom, and, above all, practicing love of neighbor. In this way, members of the church come to have an identity grounded in their similarity one to another and, above all, to Jesus Christ. However, this generic identity is tolerant of considerable diversity and individuality outside the rule of faith and the essential practices of the faith. Opinions on a wide range of subjects, modes of worship, political views, ethnic and national customs, and many other aspects of human life are matters of liberty. The generic identity found within the church does not extend to these things.

The kingdom of God is God's response to the distortions of sin. The church is called to be an anticipation of that kingdom under the condition of sin. As such, when it is true to its calling it stands for and promises human community that fosters identity but that also allows for real individuality in its members. It stands for a community of free individuals whose freedom is fully harmonious with the integrity and formative role of the entire community. In short, it stands for the perfect balance of identity grounded in sameness and difference in the form of authentic individuality. As such, it stands against political totalitarianism in all forms. At the same time, it stands against the abstract individualism that totalitarian regimes evoke as well as the obverse of such individualism, bland conformism. Although the fullness of the kingdom lies in the future, the church trusts that this future is God's future, a future that is already becoming present in spite of sin.

7

Part-Whole Relations

In previous chapters I have shown how the temporal structure of persistence and change and the relation of the generic and individuality are forms that identity and difference assume in the finite world. In this chapter I will focus on another form of identity and difference, the part-whole structure of the created world. Of course, it must be kept in mind that the part-whole structure is no more a direct image of the Trinity than are the temporal structure of persistence and change and the relation of the generic and individuality. The divine Trinity is not a whole composed of parts just as it is not a temporal entity that persists amid changes or something generic shared by individuals. Instead we should think of whole-part relations as one of the ways in which the trinitarian life of identity and difference appears in creatures that subsist under the conditions of finitude.

Unlike persistence and change, part-whole relations are not about the dialectics of identity and difference under the condition of time. Unlike the relation between the generic and individuality, they are not based on class membership. Instead, in part-whole relations, identity and difference appear as the unity of the whole in contrast to the diversity of constituent parts insofar as things exhibit internal organization. In this relation, identity appears as the unity of the whole while difference appears as the diversity of the constituent parts.

The Physical Universe

Not everything in the universe exhibits internal structure. In the world of elementary particles there are, according to contemporary theory, a handful of particles that are fundamental and without parts.

These fall into two classes, quarks and leptons. These correspond to the classical idea of the atom in that they are the basic elements of matter incapable of further division. The electron appears to be such in a preeminent way, for it is not only fundamental but also stable. Because of the conservation laws of energy and charge, it does not decay into other particles. It is otherwise with the other elementary particles. A negative muon, for example, decays spontaneously into an electron and a neutrino-antineutrino pair. A down quark becomes an up quark during neutron decay. Nonetheless, it is best not to think of these as composite *entities*, for at this level of reality, the distinction between matter and energy is somewhat arbitrary. From the quantum theoretical point of view, these processes of decay are better thought of as changes in energy levels, not as the transformation of one thing into another.

Beyond these elementary particles, however, everything in the universe and the universe itself shows internal structure. Nucleons and atoms illustrate this. By virtue of the so-called strong interaction, quarks bind together to form mesons (particles composed of two quarks) and hadrons (particles composed of three quarks). Already at this level of physical reality we can see the structure of whole and part. Of interest is the nature of the composite wholes. They are not like a collection of three pencils lying on a table. In such a collection, subtracting one of the pencils or adding a fourth changes the collection only quantitatively. The pencils do not interact with each other. They relate to one another only in their spatial orientation. Things are different in atomic and sub-atomic wholes. Nucleons (protons and neutrons), for example, are not simply a collection of three quarks. They are instead three quarks bound together in a way that new properties are brought into being. Most notably, a nucleon's mass is, it appears, far more than the masses of three separate quarks. Most of the nucleon's mass derives from the kinetic energy of the constituent quarks and from their potential energy in the bound state. Atomic structure follows the same pattern, although with a greater degree of differentiation among the constituent parts. Like nucleons, every atom is an organized whole with constituent parts. The greater differentiation among its constituents lies in two respects. First, whereas the constituents of nucleons are all quarks, although admittedly with different charges, the differences among atomic constituents (nucleons and electrons) are more pronounced. There is, for example, considerable difference in mass between nucleons and electrons. Further, nucleons are themselves composite entities, whereas electrons are indivisible. Additionally, whereas every nucleon is composed of three quarks, atomic structure shows a much greater variation, from the hydrogen atom (one proton in its nucleus) to the heaviest elements with scores of nucleons. Admittedly, this variation is essentially quantitative, since it is simply a matter of adding nucleons and electrons. Yet this purely quantitative variation is responsible for the entire range of chemical differences shown by atoms. As a result, whereas every proton is just like every other proton, every atom is not like every other atom. In atomic structure, then, we can see the same organization of whole and part that we observe in nucleons, except that the parts exhibit a greater degree of differentiation. This in turn makes the unity and variety of the atomic whole more complex than that possessed by nucleons. It also makes the unity more unstable, with atoms of heavier nuclei being increasingly susceptible to transmutation through radiation. In summary: in the part-whole structure of physical reality we can see identity taking shape as the wholeness of composite entities. We can also see difference appearing as the differentiation of parts within these composite entities. In this way, physical realities, even on the smallest scales, exhibit the same dialectics of identity and difference that characterizes the life of the Trinity.

The part-whole organization found in nucleons and atoms recurs on larger scales. Two of the more familar are molecules and galaxies. In each case, due to a fundamental interaction entities come together to form a complex organized whole with distinctive properties that did not pre-exist in the constituents. In the case of molecules and larger composite entities, the basis of the whole-part relation differs from nucleonic and atomic structure. In nucleons, the unity of the parts results from the so-called strong interaction. Atomic unity between nucleons results from the residual effects of the strong interaction. In molecules, however, the responsible interaction is electromagnetic. In the case of stars, solar systems, and galaxies, the responsible interaction is gravity. Nonetheless, the same pattern of whole and part is evident in every aspect of the physical universe. As in the case of nucleons and atoms, molecules, stars, and galaxies are not physical things in addition to their constituent parts. They are not physical things that exist apart from their parts. They are instead those constituent parts organized in a certain way as a result of some fundamental physical interaction.

Because of this organization, molecules, stars, and galaxies enter into distinctive physical processes into which their constituents do not enter prior to or apart from their participation in the organized whole. The nuclear processes of a sun, for instance, do not naturally occur apart from the concentration of hydrogen and helium atoms that constitutes the star. The chemical properties of a molecule are not simply equivalent to the chemical properties of its constituent atoms. That is, metaphysically considered, a molecule is a collection of atoms. It is not itself a physical thing that exists apart from those atoms. Nonetheless, a molecule is not just a heap of atoms. It is a collection of specific atoms that, by virtue of the electromagnetic interaction, come to be structured in a definite way. Because of this physical structure, chemical processes take place between one molecule and another that would not occur between the constituent atoms in their separateness. The same is true of galaxies. They are not physical things that exist in their own right apart from the stellar systems that compose them. They are instead structured assemblies of stars.

The relation of whole and part that characterizes the entities of the physical universe characterizes as well the universe as such. Just as a molecule or a star is a functional unity and not just a loose collection, so the universe has its own unity and is a totality in its own right. As a result, we are justified in speaking of the unity of the entire universe, even though the portion of the universe that we have experienced directly is quite small. There are untold galaxies of stars that we never have and never will observe. There are portions of the universe that will forever lie beyond our experience. Nonetheless, the universe is a unity. It is a unity in spite of the variety of entities that inhabit it and in spite of the diversity of processes that transpire in it. The universe's unity, therefore, like that of other physical entities, is of the same sort that characterizes the Trinity. It is not an undifferentiated unity that excludes difference. It is also not a reality apart from or prior to the plurality of things that compose it—the universe is not itself a thing. At the same time, the universe is more than just a collection of things. It is the ensemble of entities and processes that are unified by the lawful order that the universe exhibits. The plurality of things that compose the universe is genuine yet it does not overcome the unity. Because of the universe's lawlike order, the entities and processes of the universe may be thought of as so many different embodiments of the universe's order. It is not just that they are the universe's constituent parts; we may also think of them as being the universe in the form of particularity and differentiation. This fundamental unity and order of the universe is why the natural laws of physics are so powerfully explanatory and are able to subsume quite different phenomena under simple laws.

The unity of the universe lies in its order as described by natural laws. It is by virtue of this order that we can be confident that the same sorts of entities and processes that we are aware of locally exist also in the portions of the universe that we do not observe. This same order convinces us that the laws that we employ today to describe and predict physical processes were at work billions of years ago and will still be at work billions of years hence. It is because of this order that the universe, composed of innumerable entities, is one single world-system, embracing fields and particles, matter and energy, space and time. Because of this order, the universe, as a *universe*, is a unity that embraces a plurality.

This order is described mathematically and conceptually in the laws of nature. It is because of its lawlike character that the universe is an ordered whole and not a chaotic collection of matter and energy. Even though there are dymanic processes in this world, they are extraordinarily predictable and regular and are describable by laws. Temporal processes are a predictable aspect of the lawlike features of the physical universe. Our sense of the deep-seated lawlike character of the universe is reinforced by the principle of invariance, which states that the laws of the universe are the same regardless of the frame of reference in which we choose to perform experiments. The universality of law extends not only to all possible events in space-time but even to all frames of reference in which measurements may be made. Furthermore, the descriptive laws formulated in the physical sciences are mathematically precise and simple, i.e., they are able to subsume huge ranges of phenomena under mathematical formulas of comparative brevity. It was this subsuming power of laws that enabled Isaac Newton to account for such diverse phenomena as planetary orbits and the daily tides by means of one comparatively simple formula. It is this massive degree of lawfulness and predictability that has enabled physics and chemistry to attain their astounding success. It is true that the twentieth century witnessed an important amendment to the notion of law in the guise of quantum field theory. Previously laws were regarded as yielding completely deterministic predictions of particular events. However, quantum theory forced scientists to acknowledge that, while laws are reliably predictable in the world of large objects and in cases of statistically large numbers of particles, laws do not possess predictive certainty in the case of particular events at the quantum level, i.e., at the level of particles. Nonetheless, even the odd nature of quantum phenomena does not negate the lawlike character of the universe. It is true that these phenomena do not obey *deterministic* laws; however they still obey laws of probability. In short, the properties and behavior of all things are completely law-bound, even if our conception of law has undergone modification in the last century.

It is another question how far the rule of law extends. With respect to the physical universe, it seems that natural laws are both universal in extent and also immutable. Their universality means that nothing in the universe occurs outside the framework of the order described by those laws. Their immutability means that this order does not change over the course of time. However, we may ask whether lawlike order is as helpful a concept in other sorts of scientific inquiry as it is in physics. For example, although genetics can be explicated in terms of probability laws, the concept of law does not seem particularly helpful in biology generally. Even less has the concept of law been useful in the human sciences. Certainly biological entities and human beings do not violate physical laws. On the contrary, they presuppose them. Life depends on chemical processes such as metabolism. If these processes did not have an extraordinarily high degree of regularity, it is likely that life could not have come about. At the same time, the importance of contingency in the biological and human spheres and the irreducibly unique nature of cells, organisms, and especially human beings means that scientific knowledge in these areas will not be able to make significant use of law without further amendment and enrichment of the concept of law. It may turn out that there are laws of biology and human being that can be made as mathematically precise as are those of physics. Or it could be that biological processes and human behavior merely rest on physical laws without being completely capable of being described by more specific laws. But even if there are no laws peculiar to biology and human behavior, these domains will still be characterized by a massive degree of order and regularity. It is such order and regularity that brings about the unity of the biological world and such unity as we find in human society. At any rate, law is one of the fundamental forms, if not *the* fundamental form, that the unity of the universe takes. The stability of the universe and the possibility of organized structures depend on this unity. However, to say that it is fundamental does not imply that it is the only significant form of unity. It implies only that all entities, processes, and events in the universe are built upon laws of nature.

In short, the physical universe in its entirety exhibits the dialectics of whole and part, just as do the entities within it. From the small scale to the large, there is part-whole organization. Physical realities, except at the smallest level, are all composite beings. New properties and forms of unity arise as individual entities become related to one another as parts in a larger structural organization. In the unity of organization and in the diversity of parts within it we see the participation of the universe and all of its members in the trinitarian life of God.

The Biological World

When we turn our attention to biological entities, we observe the same dialectics of whole and part. The cell exemplifies this. Each cell is a unified whole that consists in constituent parts. Moreover, the parts—nucleus, protoplasm, organelles, and cell wall—differ appreciably from one another. The cell's unity, accordingly, is the unity of differentiated components. In this respect, the cell differs from the elementary particles of the physical world. They possess unity at the expense of internal differentiation. Even atoms and molecules, which like cells are composed of parts, have (in comparison with cells) an exceedingly simple relation of whole and parts. Their parts are relatively homogeneous. The atoms that compose a molecule may differ from one another but this difference is, qualitatively considered, far less than the difference between, for example, a cell's DNA and its mitochondria. Whereas the atoms within a molecule differ according to atomic weight and electrical properties, DNA, mitochondria, and the other components of a cell differ in a great many other ways, including structure and function. Although the difference in organizational complexity and function between a molecule and a cell is a relative one, it is nonetheless considerable. As a result, the unity of a cell is of a more complex sort than the sorts of unities that we find in the physical universe.

The whole-part relation that characterizes the cell permits us to speak, in a qualified sense, of a physiological sense of teleology. The wholeness of the cell is not a thing or entity in addition to the nucleus, the organelles, the cytoplasm, and the cell wall. The cell can be analytically described in terms of its parts without physical remainder. The cell does not exist apart from these parts. At the same time, the parts apart from each other—apart from their organization—lack structure and could not perform their functions. The parts function only in relation to the whole that is constituted by the parts. We must think of the cell, then, as the organization of constituent parts, an organization that brings about the emergence of functions (such as metabolism and reproduction) of which the parts are individually incapable. This organization also brings into being a unity of behavior marked by a complexity far exceeding that of non-living entities. To speak of teleology is to say that the parts of a cell, in their organizational unity, contribute to functions that do not exist outside that unity.

The relation of whole and part is found as well in other types of entity in the living world. Just as in the physical universe, so here there are composite entities. In each case, the composite is a unified whole composed of parts that differ from each other in structure and function. These composites include organs (e.g., the liver), systems (e.g., the circulatory and nervous systems), organisms, and, in the case of some animals, societies (e.g., baboon troops and the human family). Biological composites are similar, in some respects, to physical composites such as galaxies and stars. Like them, each part of the composite is a member of the same class. For example, every member of a baboon troop is a baboon just as every part of a star is an atom. Every part of the liver is a liver cell. But there are also important differences from physical composites, especially in the ways in which the parts within a composite relate to one another. Stars and galaxies are held together by gravity. For this reason, they have comparatively simple forms of organization. But within an organ we find more complicated relations and organization. Spatial relations and gravity play important roles but chemical interactions are perhaps even more significant, as the emergent activities such as cell division and metabolism are chemically, not physically, driven. In the case of animal societies, the relations and organization may be even more complex. Here we must take into account the capacity of members of the society to communicate with each other and to interpret events in their environment.

Although (like all biological processes) communication and interpretation are built on a physical basis, they are more than simply an exchange of atoms or energy. On the contrary, they are newly emergent functions that exist only at a certain level of structural organization and complexity.

All that I have noted about biological entities and composites applies to human beings. Both individual human beings and also human societies exhibit the dialectics of whole and part. Human life in all its aspects is rooted in both the physical universe and the biological world. Individual human beings possess a unity of biological function similar to that of other organisms. We are integrated wholes composed of highly differentiated parts. Human society, like other animal societies, shows forth the dialectics of whole and part, even if it does so in a far more complex way.

Like the physical universe, the biological world in its totality can be considered a whole possessing its own component parts. That is, it has its own unity and is not merely a collection of entities and processes disconnected from each other. Also like the physical universe, the wholeness of the biological world rests upon laws. First of all, it is built upon the laws that describe the regular processes of the physical world at the sub-atomic, atomic, and chemical levels. However, the more complex nature of living beings and the greater role of contingency in living processes means that law has a significance in biology other than its significance in chemistry and physics. Perhaps we can speak of a fundamental law of biology to the effect that all life is a function of cells. However, this law does not have the mathematical character of physical laws. Furthermore, it may not be universal, for there may be life in the universe that does not have a cellular basis. For this reason, the hypothetical-deductive model of scientific inquiry is less useful in biology than it is in physics. It is mainly in genetics, with its close relation to chemistry, that natural law assumes great importance. Elsewhere in biology, law must be supplemented with other concepts if we are to attain a complete understanding. What is critical, however, is the universal application of these supplementary conceptions—the fact that they accurately describe universal biological phenomena, even if they do not have the predictive value of mathematically articulated laws. Such universality supplies the wholeness and unity of the biological world in its totality.

There is, for example, a structural order in the cell that consists in the internal organization of its constituent parts into ordered unity. This structural order is not readily reducible to a mathematical model, as atomic structure has been modeled in quantum physics. There is also a functional order in organisms, consisting in their tendency to maintain a relatively constant internal environment (e.g., temperature). Each of these sorts of order demands its own distinctive sort of explanation. None can be expressed with mathematically precise laws in the manner of physics. The variety of order here is a testimony to a vast increase in complexity as we move from the physical universe to the living world and to the consequent need to broaden the scope of scientific explanation.

In spite of the fact that the biological world is not fully explicable in terms of laws (at least in the sense that 'law' has in physics), it has a unity and wholeness of its own. Of course, unlike the physical universe it is not an utterly self-contained unity, for such external events as weather, the moon's effects on tides, energy from the sun, and collisions between the earth and asteroids have a considerable impact on the biological world. Nonetheless, we are justified in thinking of the biological world as a system of interconnected parts. The whole system is, in a measure, self-regulating, at least in the sense that the various parts can affect one another in dramatic ways. Changes in a local environment, for example, may profoundly affect populations of living beings in a way that radiates into other adjacent environments. The food chain provides another example. Loss of crops through disease or pests can have a devastating effect on human and animal populations. Its unity is also grounded in the pervasive effect of selection mechanisms, whereby every population adapts to its environment. The unity of the biological world, then, is not simply the unity of a law-governed system. It is instead a more complex unity. It is the unity of a system characterized by persistent and diverse processes, from embryological development and metabolism to migration and reproduction. These processes bring the plurality of biological entities into the unity of the biological world and justify our considering it, analogously to the physical universe, a whole with component parts. In this way, not only each biological entity but the total system of the biological world exhibits identity and difference by virtue of its participation in the trinitarian life of God.

Human Existence

A human being, as a biological organism, is a whole with component parts. In what sense is a human person, in its distinctively human features, a whole with component parts? There is no question that the human personality is internally diverse. Ancient philosophers analyzed the soul into two or three aspects such as reason, emotions, and desires. Sigmund Freud offered a more sophisticated theory in which largely unconscious and unrealistic drives (the id) were in conflict with a somewhat unconscious and just as unrealistic inner moral authority (the superego). The human ego emerged as the principle of realism attempting to mediate between the two. Even if one does not accept the details of Freud's view or that of the ancient philosophers, it still seems evident that the human personality has a certain complexity about it. The question is whether, amid this complexity, the personality has a wholeness.

In view of the historical nature of human existence (discussed in chapter five), it is best to say that the wholeness of the personality is not something that comes to us ready-made upon birth. It is instead a task whose completion lies always before us. It is the task of integrating every aspect of our lives into a harmony. The personality is, in its natural condition, the site of conflicting tendencies. The open-ended nature of this task is a consequence of two facts. First, with respect to the constitution of our personaltiy, the conflicting tendencies within the personality are not easily harmonized and perhaps cannot be completely harmonized. Second, with respect to our conscious beliefs and values, our experience has a dynamic quality. As we pass through life, there is a continual addition of experiential material needing to be integrated into the structures of our beliefs and values. For this reason, children, who have the least experience, have in some ways the most harmonious world-views. Adults, with a longer and more complex history of experience, will inevitably struggle to fit beliefs and values together in such way as to do justice to the full range of lived experience.

Consideration of the human personality leads us to our social existence and the existence of our communities. This is because beliefs and values are not arrived at through solitary reflection but are instead largely mediated to us by the social communities in which we dwell.

As in the physical universe and biological world, there are composite realities in human existence. These composites are our communities, including the family, the nation, and voluntary associations of all sorts. We may also speak of the entire human community as a composite, although at present such a community is more an ideal than a reality. The difference between human and non-human composites is that, whereas physical composites such as atoms, molecules, stars, and galaxies are constituted by physical forces and biological composites are constituted by chemical bonds, human communities are bound together in other ways (although human community, like all things human, remains rooted in the physical universe and biological world). At one level, human composite realities are held together by the same factors by which animal societies are held together. These include kinship relations, various sorts of communication, and organization based on sexual and nurturing behavior. This is to be expected, given the fact that human existence is grounded in the biological and, more proximately, primate world. But at another level, in human composite realities new bonding factors come into play that are distinctively human. By this I mean that such things as shared commitment to values and beliefs. The family, for instance, is constituted by factors (such as care of the young) that we share, in some ways, with primates. But it has also become the vehicle for the transmission of human culture, of ideals, and of values. The same is true all the more of other types of human composite realities. Nations and voluntary associations exist for purposes that go far beyond those of animal societies. Their existence is founded on distinctively human bases, such as law and other forms of consent. In all these cases, human beings are brought together into social groupings on the basis of things that are peculiar to human existence. However, like the existence of the person, the unity of human communities is not guaranteed. On the contrary, it remains a task set before us that must be worked at continually.

The significance of human composites is the same as that of physical and biological composites. As physical and biological wholes condition the functioning of their constituent parts, so human composites give shape to and condition the life of individuals (although individuals in turn exercise a formative influence on their communities). Since human being is not completely determined by physical or biological realities and since individuals are not fully self-determining, social composites play an important role in shaping the contours of human life. In other words, we cannot understand the character of human life apart from the social networks in which we participate. Our life as individuals is largely given to us by the societies of which we are a part. Naturally the direction of influence is not one way. Social composites, although pre-existing any given individual, nonetheless exist only as long as there are individuals participating in them. Still, from the perspective of the individual, social composites have an incalculable effect in determining the shape of social relations, of ideas and values, of behavior, and of likes and dislikes. This is not to say that our lives are completely determined by our participation in social composites. Some features are undoubtedly determined or at least conditioned by biological factors. Beyond this, we are able, at least to some extent, to rise above the conditioning that we receive from our social involvement. Ideas and behavior instilled in us by family and nation can be balanced or even eradicated by those learned in other social contexts. Whether our initial social conditioning as children can ever be completely overcome remains an open question.

The effect of social formation on a society's members appears in the symbolic order of religions and cultures. Morality, for example, is not merely an elaborate form of behavior regulated by social norms. It is also connected to systems of meaning and values. The symbolic order consists of myths and other forms of story that inform people about what is valuable and about the meaning of things. These myths includes stories of the people's founding and their destiny and the images that shape their activities. The systems of meaning associated with the symbolic orders give us power or at least a sense of power over the unknown and establish social order by explaining matters such as family, gender, and customs. According to this view, both myths in the traditional sense, as well as modern stories such as that of the American West and that of modern science, function as the bases of symbolic orders. The symbolic order includes icons as well, which point beyond themselves to what is held to be ultimate in the system. For example, in a scientific and technological culture, Albert Einstein and Carl Sagan have become icons that symbolize for people certain values. In Marxist thought and especially in the political systems that allied with it the symbol of the proletariat functioned in much the same way. Andy Warhol pointed out the iconic value in our society of Marilyn Monroe and Elvis Presley. The symbolic order, in short, is an interpretation of reality that informs us of our place in reality and explains the significance of what we find in reality. It is an integral component of the social composite of which each of us is a part.

Under the Conditions of Finitude

The part-whole nature of the created world universe shows us not only creatures' participation in the trinitarian life of God but also the finite character of that participation. With respect to the structure of created beings, this finitude is most evident in the fact that the entities of the universe, which are wholes composed of parts, are subject to decomposition and dissolution. The wholeness of entities is eventually lost through their coming apart. For example, under the conditions of extraordinarily high energy, the strong force, which binds quarks together to form nucleons and whose residual effect binds nucleons together to form atoms, is overcome. Under these conditions, which obtained in the earliest moments of the universe, matter resolves itself into a state in which material substance in the customary sense of the word does not exist. Molecules and even atoms cannot exist. But even apart from this extreme condition it is possible for atomic composites to decompose. This occurs in the apparently spontaneous decay of a neutron into a proton, an electron, and an anti-neutrino.[1] It also occurs in the case of radiation, when for example a large atom spontaneously ejects two protons and two neutrons, beginning a cascade of events that results in a transmutation from the original element to another. More familiarly, molecules are subject to decomposition as well. Of course, the reason for molecular decomposition differs from that of atomic decomposition, being the result of the breaking of chemical bonds due to familiar sources of energy such as heat and to the effect of enzymes and other catalysts. Nonetheless, the result is the same: entities that are composite are reduced to their constituent units, with the composite whole ceasing to exist and with its emergent functions ceasing. The same process is at work in composite entities in the large scale structure of the universe. Stars, for example, are composed of innumerable smaller atomic units by gravity. When the helium that is fused to form heavier elements is exhausted, the motion of atoms toward the surface of the sun can no longer overcome the gravitational attraction within the star. The star collapses under its own weight and, if the mass is great enough, the compression of atoms in the collapse causes a massive explosion (a nova) that brings the star as a composite entity to an end. Any planets in the vicinity likewise come to an end, their constituents caught up in the explosive energy of the nova and distributed in the surrounding space. In short, the part-whole nature of the universe establishes the condition for finitude in the form of the cessation of existence.

Organic composites such as systems, organs and societies also participate in finitude. While they do not die in the same sense in which organisms die, they are susceptible to cessation of function and loss of organization whereby the integrity of the composite is lost. Sometimes this happens through physical trauma. The unity of the nervous system can be lost through physical damage whereby the neural pathways are severed from one another. The heart's unity of function can be lost by physical injury. The animal body can be torn apart by physical force. More subtly, integrity can be lost through disease and other forms of invasion. In the case of the human mind, unity can be lost through chemical imbalances and other organic maladies. In every case, the organization that characterizes the composite is lost. As this organization is lost, the cells that compose the composite and that in turn depend on it in various ways die.

Finitude appears also in the part-whole relations that characterize human existence. If we consider the individual person as a psychological whole that strives for an ideal unity of constituent parts, then the finitude of the person shows itself in the failure to attain this ideal unity. This failure marks every one of us. Our lives are fragmented and compartmentalized. We fail to resolve the inner conflicts that plague us psychologically and we fail to integrate our moral obligations with our behaviors. In itself, such failure is not evil although it is quite destructive. Human existence is such that, due to no fault of ours, we may not have the means of resolving psychological conflicts. Conflict between moral obligation and behavior may be due, not to moral failure, but instead to intractable contradictions between one moral obligation and another. It is characteristic of the finitude of human existence that our moral obligations are not easily harmonized and perhaps cannot all be harmonized with one another. At any rate, the historical character of human existence means that the wholeness of the person is a task that lies before us. At the same time, this task always remains to some extent unfinished. In pathological cases such as psychosis and

Alzheimer's disease, the narrative unity of the person is disrupted to an extreme degree. In these cases the temporal continuity of the person is interrupted by behaviors, beliefs, and feelings that diverge so dramatically from the person's normal life that the individual seems to have become a different person or in some ways not a person at all. Even if medical science eventually discovers cures for these disorders, the human person will still be limited and conditioned by other factors, even if it will then be the efficacy of the medical regimen necessary to restore mental health.

It is important, in this context, to note that organic disorders are not the result of sin, either original sin or the actual sins of individuals. They can certainly be exacerbated by sin and immoral acts; however, the disorders themselves are a result of our finitude and that of the entire physical and organic world. It is true that in the Bible sickness and other misfortune is often represented as arising from the will of God.[2] However, this representation is part of the Bible's, and especially of the Old Testament's, tendency to see God as the cause of all things, from the hardening of Pharaoh's heart to disasters of all sorts. It is very difficult today to maintain this belief. Not only does it seemingly implicate God in evil but it also compromises our sense of the relative autonomy of the natural world—the sense that the universe operates according to laws and not by the direct action of God. Although we may, for theological reasons, affirm that God operates in the universe through the laws and may wish to hold that God *can* operate directly and apart from the laws, the Bible's affirmation that all, or nearly all, events are the direct and immediate result of God's action is best regarded as part of an ancient and (for us) incredible world-view. Accordingly, we should think of organic disorders and their effects on human being as a consequence of the finitude inherent in all organic beings. However, this is not to say that theological considerations are irrelevant to an understanding of organic disorders. Although neither God nor human sin directly causes these disorders, it must be pointed out that under the conditions of sin, we have learned to induce the effects of organic disorders through the abuse of alcohol and other drugs. We have also managed to create anxiety, paranoia, eating disorders, and hysteria through other means such as political terrorism and oppression and the manipulation of public media. Modern inattention to physical health has increased rates of debilitating stroke and heart disease. In these ways and others, humankind under the condition of sin has contributed to and even created organic disorders, compounding our natural limitations.

The composite social realities of human existence are likewise subject to dissolution. Families, communities, associations, and nations can all fall apart. Families can be destroyed, not only through physical dislocation of its members but in other ways as well. A family can cease to exist even when people are living together if the bonds that bring individuals together are destroyed. Political systems likewise can degenerate into chaos. Nations can be dissolved. Of course, the causes of these events are different from the dissolution of organic composites, but the pattern is the same. A complex whole composed of individuals loses its coherence and the constituent members slowly die as the supporting network on which they depended withers. In this way, for example, the Roman empire slowly crumbled, leaving in its shadow the disintegration of society and law. More recently, the collapse of the Soviet Union, although not without benefit to world politics, has not been an unmixed blessing to the people formerly under its rule.

Because human existence has emerged into the moral sphere, the limitations of our part-whole relations take on a moral aspect as well. For one thing, we must regard the unity of personality for which the individual strives not only as a condition of human social existence but also as a moral obligation. This is because of its teleological character. This unity of personality is something intrinsically good. As an aspect of the fulfillment of our nature, it is a goal toward which we are drawn and which we pursue by intentional action. At the same time, failure to attain this goal is often due to a refusal or even incapacity to act in morally appropriate ways. Personal unity implies, for example, that we are able to delay the gratification of our desires. However, such delay requires the exertion of moral seriousness. Often we do not exert ourselves thus or do so inadequately, with the result that we do not attain to the unity of personality. Unity also implies that all aspects of our lives are connected with all other aspects. In particular, it means that we bring everything in our lives under the test of moral probity. However, we often allow our lives to fall into the disunity of compartmentalization, in which we shield certain parts of ourselves from the scrutiny of moral seriousness.

There is also a moral dimension of the composite social realities of human existence. Because humans are intrinsically social beings, social community as such is intrinsically good. It is one of the conditions of human existence and of its good. But communities like all composite realities inevitably tend toward dissolution. Sometimes this is due to extraneous circumstances beyond human control, as when disease or physical dislocation disrupts the life of a family. But probably more common is the dissolution of human society through the destructive effects of human misdeeds. In some cases these effects come from failing to act as we ought. Each of us is obligated to contribute, in various ways, to the well-being of the communities of which we are members. Yet for selfish reasons we often do not, preferring to allow others to shoulder the burden. But each such refusal to accept responsibility detracts from the community's existence. Too much of this can destroy a community. In other cases these effects come from overt acts that, directly or indirectly, aim at the destruction of the community. Crime and political corruption fall into this category. In these cases individuals and collections of individuals aim, whether consciously or not, at the destruction of the community. Communities are also destroyed by the political and economic action of other communities. While there is no law that requires one community to support another, it is not too much of a stretch to extend the individual's responsibility toward other individuals to one community's obligation toward other communities. Yet we generally fail to acknowledge the force of such obligations. As a result, communities in human history have persistently proven destructive to one another. In these ways, the finitude of human social composites presents us with a moral side.

The community can also exhibit its moral limitations in its relation to its members. Through family and nation we transmit values and ideals and support the task of fashioning human existence. Through ignorance, misfortune, and malice, however, communities of all sorts can be instruments, not of human welfare, but of destruction. Families can stunt our emotional and cognitive development. National policies can hinder our well-being. Voluntary organizations can fail to nurture human fellowship and to provide the sustenance for which they have been created. The state can exercise its power to distort and manipulate education and other formative institutions. When this happens, although the form of community remains, true community has been diminished or destroyed. As the desiccated body of a dead animal still retains the outward form of organizational structure but lacks the processes of life, so a community that destructively turns on its members may remain as a political entity long after human community has disappeared. Particularly demonic is the way in which the community can multiply the misdeeds of individuals. It is not just that communities and institutions can be used by individuals to achieve evil ends. The greater malady is that communities can further evil in a way that transcends the particular acts of individual members of the aggregate. The classical example of this is the way in which the extermination of Jews and others was efficiently made a part of the German nation between 1933 and 1945. Death became an integral part of the national life. Although the number of actual killers was relatively small, the entire nation was involved, with a great number of people participating in small and seemingly unrecognizable ways. Individuals could plausibly protest their lack of involvement in the process, for the entire nation functioned in a way that transcended the sum total of individual acts. We may also speak here about the impersonalization of communities. This occurs when, for example, the government, especially in its bureaucratic form, is regarded as identical with the nation. Nameless, faceless government becomes a subject of action that seems to be beyond the control of any individual or groups of individuals. In our time, the finitude of political communities has manifested itself in two tendencies—totalitarian government and the concept of the abstract individual. Totalitarian government occurs when the aggregate usurps the legitimate functions of the individual. The reaction to totalitarianism is the affirmation of abstract individualism by modern democratic societies. This individualism is abstract because in it human good is regarded as independent of anything except autonomy and self-actualization. In other words, this is the individual abstracted from the communities that shape us, a situation that arises when the political community appears as a threat to human well-being.

The symbolic order of religion and culture is also beset by the limitations of finitude. Human systems of value and meaning are inherently limited. Each such system purports to be an understanding of reality, but the plurality of these systems indicates the vanity of this claim. In view of this fact, a modern addendum to the symbolic order has arisen, one that makes a virtue of necessity by recognizing the fact of religious and cultural pluralism and proclaiming tolerance to be the chief value. Whether this modern liberal myth will endure is a question; however, it rests on a genuine insight, namely that all symbolic systems, in spite of whatever claims to truth they make, inevitably fall short, either by conflicting with reality in the case of manifestly false claims or by the death of the social system with which they are associated. However, all such systems of meaning and value tend to make claims to totality. The sciences claim to be able to bring about the completion of human knowledge, at least in certain areas. Marxist thought claimed to be the ultimate philosophy and to pave the way toward the ultimate form of political life. Such claims are also well known in religions.[3] But such totality is purchased at the expense of exclusion. Scientific knowledge is attained only by excluding from itself any aspect of reality that cannot be brought under its method. For some scientists, such a procedure indicates its finite character; for others it means that what is not analyzable by the method is either unreal or unimportant. The exclusion of certain aspects of reality from a system of meaning and value, from religion and culture, means that these systems make themselves finite. They can sustain their claim to be whole and the totality only by excluding what does not fit. But by the act of excluding they limit themselves by creating something that lies outside the system and that stands opposed to the system. Even if that which lies outside is labeled unreal, it still announces the limitation of the system from which it is excluded. The truly unlimited system would account for everything and nothing would stand outside it.

We can discern the finitude of systems of meaning and value also if we attend to the nature of symbols. Symbols point to something. However, the very fact of pointing shows that what is being pointed to is in a sense unavailable. The designation of something through the symbol means that the symbol is necessary and that the thing symbolized is not completely with us. At the same time, the symbol, by its function of pointing, manifests its own limitations, for every symbol is sooner or later revealed to be a symbol, that is, a *mere* symbol. It is not the thing itself. It substitutes for the thing itself but in so doing it proclaims its own inability to bring the thing symbolized to complete presence with us.

Systems of meaning and value are subject not only to the limitations of finitude but also to the distortions of sin. As such, they are the objects of misuse by humankind and institutions for the purpose of dominating and oppressing and justifying their domination of others. History is replete with examples of religion and culture being employed in the service of political domination. But there is another way in which religion and culture exist under the conditions of sin, namely by impeding the knowledge of God. Ideally, every activity in a culture would inculcate the knowledge of God. Every symbolic system of value and meaning would bring us into the knowledge of God and sustain us there. However, under the conditions of sin, religion and culture to some extent drive us away from the knowledge of God. The most overt form of this is secularism, in which the religious dimension of culture is discounted, intellectually by the cultural elite and practically by the masses. Here the quest for human autonomy from God and for self-actualization becomes the highest value. But religion and culture may also and less overtly impede the knowledge of God by forgetting their role as mediators of the knowledge of God and by making the systems of meaning and value not ways of mediating the knowledge of God but substitutes for the knowledge of God. This is the significance of the Bible's condemnation of pagan religion and its idolatry. The problem is not with using visible and tangible objects to depict the divine. The problem is that the representations may lose their symbolic character of designating and may become the object of worship as such.

The Kingdom of God

The kingdom of God is a future reality. It is the future that God wills for creation. Yet it is also a present reality. It has come to us in the life and ministry of Jesus Christ and has entered human history as an effective power. We experience the kingdom as the presence of a powerful future into which we are summoned to enter.

Even though the kingdom is God's kingdom, those who are in it participate, in a finite way, in the trinitarian life of God. As a result, their participation in the kingdom partakes of the same structure of part-whole relations that characterizes their participation in the physical universe, the biological world, and in human social existence.

In other words, the kingdom of God has the same internal structure of part and whole that is found throughout the universe. The New Testament presents a variety of images that convey this structure. Paul, for example, portrayed Christ as a corporate entity of which individual Christians are members (Rom 12:4-5 and 1 Cor 12:12-27). He also regarded Christ as another Adam who is the founder of a humanity. However, whereas Adam was the founder of humanity in its social existence, Christ has founded a new humanity that is oriented toward God (1 Cor 15:45-49). Here the kingdom is portrayed as a new race of people, who are related organically to Christ as the original humanity is related to Adam. Along the same lines, Ephesians represents the church collectively as a new human being, as God's household, and as a holy temple (2:15-21), images that strongly underline the part-whole character of the kingdom of God.

If we think of the kingdom of God as a composite whole analogous to the other composites described in this chapter, then we gain some insight into the issue of Christian identity. A composite whole is composed of its constituent parts; however, those parts are not really parts until they are joined together in the composite whole. Before their union they are disconnected from each other. In being united, they gain a new identity and take part in a new reality. In the same way, those who participate in the kingdom of God have gained a new identity by virtue of being united with others in the kingdom. Before this union, they were unconnected to other members of the kingdom. They found their identity in other ways. In the kingdom, however, their identity is shaped by their participation and by the mutual relations between the members. In this way they become newly created.

The kingdom of God is God's kingdom. It is not a human creation. There is a human institution that is, as it were, an anticipation of the kingdom of God. This is the church. Like other composite realities, the church is not something that exists apart from its members. On the contrary, it is a reality that occurs in their union. Yet like other composites, it has its own unity amid the plurality of its members. Like other composites, its unity is a matter of its structural organization. In this case, its organization arises out of the reciprocal relations of its members. However, the church, as a human institution, is subject to the limitations of finitude and the distortions of sin. The church may become disintegrated. Historically speaking, it has been disunited more than it has been united. It may also demand uniformity and excessive conformity among its members and it may adopt totalitarian measures. The church is not exempt from any of the limitations that beset other human communities. At the same time, the church is an anticipation of the kingdom. Its members are called to live on the basis of God's future. As such, the church possesses the possibility, perhaps only rarely realized, of conforming itself, as a community, to the image of God, Jesus Christ.

8

The Relatedness of All Things

In previous chapters I have drawn attention to temporal relations, to the relation of the generic and the individual, and to part-whole relations in the universe. I have argued that these relations reflect the participation of creatures in the trinitarian life of God. In this chapter, I wish to extend this analysis in the direction of greater generality by showing that relationality as such, as it occurs in the world of creatures, shows the dialectics of identity and difference and, accordingly, reflects the participation of creatures in God.

The general notion of relationality may not be intuitively obvious. The Christian tradition labored long and hard to come to this insight with regard to the Trinity. It confronted two persistent tendencies in human thought. One is the tendency toward a nominalistic identification of being with individuality. This is the view that each real thing is something particular; universal properties are regarded as abstractions from particular things. The other tendency identifies being with universality. Plato's philosophy exemplifies this tendency. Here particular things are regarded as deficient in being in comparison to the universal forms of reality. These two tendencies appear occasionally in trinitarian thinking. The nominalistic tendency is more common and appears whenever the trinitarian persons are regarded as individually existent beings. The result of such thinking is a practical tritheism, for each person is thought of as a divine being. It also appears whenever God is represented as a monad, i.e., as an individually existent being without internal differentiation. In this case the divine nature is regarded as the truly existent being, the persons being merely historical names or appearances of the divine nature. Deism and Unitarianism are historically instructive examples of this latter tendency. The

second, Platonic, tendency is much less frequent in trinitarian thinking, but occurs whenever the relation between the trinitarian persons
and the divine nature is likened to the relation of an individual to its
species. In this tendency, the persons share a common nature or
essence, which is thought of as more real than the persons. The problem with this tendency is its conception of the divine nature as something generic. Inevitably, in such thinking, the common nature will
come to be regarded as a metaphysical reality in its own right in addition to the three persons.

Trinitarian thought has resisted these two tendencies and has
insisted that the divine persons do not exist apart from each other and
that the divine essence is not a common nature but is instead the com-
munion of the persons—their being with one another. None of the
persons is a substantial entity that could exist without the others. They
are not 'beings' in the commonsense of the term, for each exists only in
and through its relations with the others. Indeed, the doctrine of the
Trinity suggests that the commonsense meaning of 'being' (with
respect to God) needs modifying. Being is neither simply particular
nor universal but is also inherently relational. Accordingly, we should
think of the divine nature as the relatedness of the persons. It is not
what all the persons have in common, for such a view presupposes that
each person is an entity with its own defining properties, some of
which it shares with the other persons. Instead we should think of the
divine nature as the three persons in their differences and in their
togetherness. Admittedly it is difficult not to think of divine nature or
essence as generic features that the persons share. Nonetheless, this is
the implication of trinitarian thinking. The doctrine of the Trinity
makes sense only if we think of divine nature in this way. In turn, such
a way of thinking can yield dividends in our conception of creatures.

If we express these results of trinitarian thinking in terms of identity
and difference, then we will say that the identity of each trinitarian
person is constituted by that person's relations to the other persons.
Each person is known only through a knowledge of that person's relations. In this way, identity presupposes the sort of difference on which
relatedness rests. The persons, therefore, are not to be thought of as
individual beings, each with an identity knowable in itself. On the contrary, the persons have their identity only through their relation to and
difference from the others. This means that we can think of the persons only by virtue of their relations to one another and that we can-

not conceive their existence apart from those relations. For instance, the Father is not the Father without being related to the Son. The Son is not the Son without being related to the Father. For this reason Thomas Aquinas defined the trinitarian persons as subsistent relations.[1]

This review of trinitarian thinking points us toward a conclusion. If creatures participate in the trinitarian life of God, then they will also exhibit relational existence in ways appropriate to finite entities and processes. The being of creatures will have to be conceived as a matter of relatedness. Creatures, accordingly, are not to be thought of as individually existent entities essentially unaffected by their relations with other entities. On the contrary, like the trinitarian persons, each creature to some extent is what it is through the ensemble of relations in which it participates and which constitutes its essence. The remainder of this chapter is devoted to showing how we might think about creatures in the physical universe, in the biological world and about human existence in terms of trinitarian relationality.

The Physical Universe

It is common, outside of scientific circles, to think of particles, atoms, and large-scale physical entities as though they can be simply and exhaustively described in the language of "things." That is, it is common to accord a privileged metaphysical status to the concept of material substance. On this view, one material substance may enter into relations with other material substances; however, such relatedness is not usually thought to affect the defining properties of the related substances. However, trinitarian thought provides us with a more refined conception of relatedness. Relatedness means more than the mere fact that substances stand in some relation to one another. It means additionally that one thing can be conceived only in conjunction with other things to which it is related. If this is true, then considering an individual thing in conceptual isolation from other things results in an abstraction. Our conception in such cases is abstract because it considers the individual thing apart from those other things to which it is essentially related and apart from the relatedness that provides its defining properties. This lesson is supported by the development of twentieth century physics, according to which the concepts of material substance and of the individual thing have no privileged status. Substances and things, in the common conception of them, are not metaphysical first principles.

Take, for instance, particles. While it is not completely illegitimate to think of particles as bits of matter, there is no scientific justification for thinking of them in such a way exclusively. In certain experimental conditions, it is appropriate to treat the nucleus of an atom as a material thing—for example, if we were interested in the behavior of the atom's electrons. In this case, the size of the atom (including its electron cloud) relative to the size of the nucleus and the energy levels relevant to electron behavior mean that the nucleus can be safely considered within this experimental context as a mass of material substance. At this level of analysis, the significant feature of the atom is its electro-magnetic properties. Here, whereas the nucleus can be considered a bit of matter, the electron appears as a measurable fluctuation of energy within the electro-magnetic field of the atom. If however we are interested in a much smaller scale of size and, correspondingly, in a much higher level of particle energy, then the nucleus no longer appears as a bit of matter but instead, like particles, as a quantum of energy within a field. This helps us to see why two particles of the same class are indistinguishable. It is not just that they are two material things with identical properties. It is that particles can be considered quanta of energy within a field. It is meaningless to distinguish one quantum of energy from another, as we do in the case of large physical things.

Another way of stating this point is to note that all particles have wavelike properties. Some particles, such as photons, can easily be regarded, not as material things—hard bits of matter—but as waves within an oscillating field. In the case of the photon, the field is an electro-magnetic field. In such a field between two charged particles, there will be an exchange of virtual photons (in contrast to "free" photons that are emitted and appear to us in the form of light waves). Likewise, between quarks there is a force-field, which is quantized in the form of gluons. This field, particularized as gluons, constitutes the attraction between quarks and results in their bonding together to form nucleons. The same principles hold for the weak interaction (which appears in neutron decay) and, presumably, in the theoretically predicted gravitational force-field. In each case, the particles (that is, bosons) that are associated with fields and that convey forces exhibit wavelike properties that enable us to regard them as waves within the oscillating fields.

The situation is more complicated in the cases of other particles, which (unlike bosons) are more easily thought of as material things with such thinglike properties as spatial dimension. Such particles include baryons (neutrons and protons), which have a definite size and are not, like field-particles, massless and dimensionless geometric points. Yet, massive particles such as baryons and electrons also exhibit wavelike features, even though physicists have not yet detected a corresponding field, of which the particles would be quantized energy and whose oscillation would constitute the wavelike aspect of each particle. The wave-properties of these particles is a peculiar notion, for it raises the question of how such particles can have wave-properties without there being something that is waving (i.e., oscillating). However, in spite of its peculiarity, it appears to be true that these particles have these wave-features. As a result, we must think of even massive particles not merely in terms of material substance but also in terms of energy and field.

If this is true, then we are compelled to modify our conception of material reality and its properties. Perhaps the most surprising result is experimental uncertainty about some of the fundamental properties of particles. In the usual conception, a material thing occupies a definite space—it is in one place at a given moment and that place is identifiable and distinct from every other place. Further, such a thing must have a definite mass and velocity (momentum). However, the wavelike nature of particles suggests that they can also be thought of as, so to speak, distributed throughout space just as a wave is distributed. A wave (for a simple example, a sound wave) exists in every part of an enclosed space. By analogy, a particle, in its wave-features, exists in every part of space—at least until an act of measurement or observation occurs. In the event of measurement, the particle in its familiar material form appears, located in a definite place with a definite mass and velocity. It appears that the event of measurement confers on the wave the features that we associate with particles. What is the wave-particle before the event of measurement? We do not know. It could be literally a wave that has not yet collapsed into the familiar particle of experimental measurement or it could be a particle of whose location and momentum we are ignorant because we cannot predict them. Contemporary physics is far from possessing a satisfactory interpretation of this phenomenon. There is as yet no agreed-on way to translate the demands of quantum theory into a realistic account of the physical events.

Whatever the interpretive outcome, however, our conception of material substance must be dramatically altered. If the particle, prior to measurement, truly is a wave, then somehow the event of measurement confers upon it the property of being spatially localized, whereas prior to measurement it is not spatially localized. If instead, prior to measurement, it is still a particle, but one whose location and momentum cannot be predicted, then its location and momentum at any given instant can be thought of only as statistical probabilities. Either account has dramatic results for our understanding of physical reality at the smallest scale. Interpreting particles realistically as waves is probably beyond our imaginative capacity. But even the probabilistic interpretation is difficult to fit within the customary notion of material substance. The location of an electron, for example, within an atom can be probabilistically predicted on the basis of quantum theory. The predictions yield the familiar picture of the electron as a particle orbiting the atom. However, there are statistically nontrivial probabilities that the electron could, at any given instant, be found (upon measurement) to be outside the atom altogether. Hence the phenomenon of quantum tunneling, in which a particle or larger entity (e.g., a helium nucleus) is able to escape a potential energy barrier, even though such a particle lacks the energy to overcome the barrier. There is a statistical possibility of the particle appearing on the other side of the barrier without, so to speak, having physically traversed the intervening space. In such cases we must speak of a radical physical discontinuity between instants of the particle's history. Such discontinuity is very difficult to conceive if the particle is a material substance in the customary sense. If the location of the particle is a matter of statistical probability and if it is statistically possible for the particle to appear from one instant to another in widely separated regions, then we can no longer think of the particle as a material thing that is identical with itself from one moment to another because of its material continuity.

Yet even if we no longer think of physical particles as material things with a continuous existence, we could nonetheless regard the physical universe as a whole as exhibiting continuity through causal relations. In this view, particles may be ephemeral but the causal structure of the universe remains unchanging over time. However, the quantum physical conception of causation forces us to amend this view and to realize that causation at the smallest physical scale has a very different meaning from its meaning in the observable world. In the familiar world of large objects, causation is experienced daily in familiar ways. Two colliding objects cause noise and motion. Stepping on the brake pedal causes the car to slow to a stop. But in the world of particles the concept of causation requires refinement. An instance is afforded by radioactivity, in which certain atoms exhibit spontaneous decay. Although the rate of decay in a sample of these atoms is mathematically precise, there appears to be no cause that explains why one atom and not another decays at a particular moment and why it decays at just *this* moment. The element americium-241, for example, transmutes into neptunium-237 by ejecting an alpha particle (a helium nucleus). Although the rate of such transmutation can be predicted with great statistical accuracy, no cause can be determined for why *this* particular americium-241 atom ejects an alpha particle and not some other americium-241 atom. Although causation retains its usefulness in the world of large entities and in statistical averages of particle-behavior, its applicability in particular cases at the level of particles is nil.[2]

The idea of entanglement is an even more dramatic illustration of the odd nature of causation in the world of particles. Causation in the physical world is popularly represented as the interaction of billiard balls on a table. As one collides into other, it causes the other to accelerate. However, this customary notion of causality is inappropriate in our attempts to understand the quantum world. According to general relativity theory, the speed of light is the ultimate velocity at which information can be transmitted between two systems (for example, between two particles). According to this notion, two systems can affect one another causally only if transmission of information is possible. Hence, causal relations are limited by the possibility of information-transmission. Any effect of one system on the other should be constrained by the velocity of light. However, there are good theoretical reasons and experimental grounds for holding that two such systems may be entangled and may affect one another *instantaneously* if the two systems represent two parts of what was originally one system. In the standard illustration, two particles with spin are emitted from an atom with no spin. Because of the conservation of angular momentum, the spin of one particle (spin up) must be opposite that of the other (spin down). On the basis of quantum theory and the principle of uncertainty, the spin of the particles is undetermined until a measurement of the spin is made, just as the location and momentum of a particle are undetermined until measurement. However, once the measurement is made on one particle, the spin of the other particle is instantaneously determined (according to the law of conservation) even though there has been no measurement on the second particle. The determination of the second particle's spin cannot have been a causal effect of determining the spin of the first particle, for that determination occurred *simultaneously* with the determination of the first particle's spin. Even at a short distance, information traveling at the velocity of light would not be transmitted instantaneously. This is a very peculiar and unexpected phenomenon; however, it appears to be correct. Particles originally in a single system that are separated retain, as it were, their connectedness even over vast spatial intervals in a way that does not depend on light signals or any other form of communication.

The point of this analysis is that matter, as commonly conceived, is not a metaphysical first principle. Instead particles may be considered to have the traditional attributes of material substance only under certain experimental conditions. Under other experimental conditions, the particle features of the thing will recede in importance and be replaced by its wave features. Philosophically considered, the result is that we can think of particles only in relation to fields and to the energy of fields. Matter is not a primordial starting point for our understanding of the universe; it instead results conceptually (at least at the level of particles) from a certain way of approaching physical reality experimentally.

Admittedly, this point is more difficult to accept for larger entities. It is difficult enough to accept the suggestion that particles may plausibly be represented as quanta of energy. But the large objects of our experience do not resemble energy quanta. On the contrary they possess all the features that we customarily attribute to material substance. Quantum field theory seems, to say the least, extraordinarily implausible as an analysis of these large entities. However, the special theory of relativity, although quite different from quantum theory, like quantum theory leads us to conclude that matter can be understood only in relation to something else.[3] The critical idea is that of rest energy. This sort of energy was unknown in the classical physics of Newton, which knew only of kinetic, potential, and other sorts of energy. Relativity theory, however, posits an energy (equivalent to the product of mass and the square of the speed of light) possessed by entities in virtue of their mass and quite apart from their velocity. The simplest illustration of rest mass is the annihilation of a pi-meson (pion) into two massless photons. In this event, the total mass of the particle is instantaneously converted into energy in the form of photons. The energy of the resulting photons is precisely equal to the rest energy of the pi-meson. Other, less dramatic examples of the notion of rest energy follow from the familiar processes of nuclear reaction. As is well known, in nuclear fission tremendous amounts of energy are released. What is not as widely known is that the reduction in the atom's energy is accompanied by a reduction in its mass, about 1/10 of one percent of the mass being converted into energy. The situation is more striking in the case of nuclear fusion, where, as atoms are joined together, about 1 percent of the mass is converted into energy. As with quantum field theory, relativity theory leads us to the conclusion that, metaphysically considered, matter is not primordial in the sense that it is an ultimate reality in terms of which all else must be explained. On the contrary, modern physics shows us that matter can be correctly conceptualized only in association with energy. Of course, we must not fall into the opposite error of arguing that energy is more primordial than matter. The point is that matter and energy are two forms, so to speak, of the fundamental reality of which the physical universe is composed.

The consequence of these considerations is that it is a conceptual mistake to think of the universe simply as a collection of material things. An adequate conception of material things necessarily must take into account other physical realities, such as field and energy. This, in turn, has consequences for our understanding of the way identity is manifested in the physical universe. This identity must not be understood in such a way that individual physical entities are regarded as metaphysically absolute. The enduring lesson of quantum field theory and relativity theory is that neither physical entities (whether particles or the large objects of experience) nor matter as such is metaphysically ultimate or primordial. This is true in spite of the fact that some particles, such as photons, are virtually everlasting and unchanging. The fact that some particles are extraordinarily long-lived and stable does not mean that they are metaphysical first principles. On the contrary, they and all other physical entities can be conceived fully only in conjunction with such concepts as waves, fields, and energy. Of course, this is not to deny that there are individual things such as particles. Physical things do have essential properties and are individual things in some sense. But the results of modern physics show us that we must broaden our conception of physical reality. We can form an adequate concept of physical entities only in relation to other central physical concepts. If we wish to think of particle, we must also think of wave and field. If we wish to think about matter, then we must also think of energy. As with the Trinity, one thing can be known only in relation to something else.

The consequences of modern physics for our understanding of identity are not exhausted by these considerations of particles and matter. The general point that one sort of physical reality can be understood only in relation to another holds good also with respect to space and time. Until the advent of the special theory of relativity, space and time were regarded as two distinct sorts of reality, each with its own individual properties and essence. It was the achievement of relativity theory to show that space and time are two distinguishable aspects of a single space-time. Consequently, space and time are essentially related to each other in spite of the fact that in our phenomenal experience they appear separated. That is why two observers in different frames of reference will disagree about the spatial and temporal aspects of an event. For example, if one is moving relative to the other or if they are widely separated in space, they may disagree about whether two events are simultaneous. Such instances tempt us to assume that the judgment of one observer was in error or, more drastically, that judgments about space and time are matters of subjective perspective. On the contrary, relativity theory argues that the spatial and temporal properties of things are in fact variable and relative to each other. Imagine, for example, an accelerating object with an attached clock. Observation will show that its length diminishes along the axis of acceleration and that its time (as measured by the attached clock) slows down. The proper conclusion, according to general relativity theory, is that the accelerating object (like all objects) is moving at a constant rate through space-time; however, as it accelerates (according to the observer's frame of reference), it increases the rate of its spacelike motion and consequently must decrease the rate of its timelike motion. For this reason, photons, which traverse space-time at the maximum rate with respect to space (the speed of light), show no timelike motion. In other words, they exhibit none of the temporal features characteristic of entities whose velocity is less than the speed of light and which, as a result, do possess some timelike motion. According to the insights of relativity theory, then, space and time can be thought of only together. Measurement of spatial length and temporal duration will show that the shortening (or increasing) of length is accompanied by the slowing down (or speeding up) of time. An increase of movement through space (through an acceleration in velocity) is accompanied by a slowing down of something's time. A decrease of movement through space (through deceleration) implies a quickening of the thing's time. The measurements of spatial extension and temporal extension are thus inversely related. The only thing that is constant is the rate of motion through space-time.

Finally, the general theory of relativity shows that space-time must be thought of in connection with matter-energy. Prior to this theory, space and time were regarded not only as separate realities but as absolute realities. By this was meant that their properties were unchanging and were independent of the amount and distribution of matter in the universe of space and time. According to relativity theory, however, space-time has a geometric shape that depends entirely on the amount and distribution of matter. Matter in effect curves space-time and the amount of such curvature is a function of the amount of matter. Such bending results in the familiar elliptical trajectory of the earth's orbit around the sun. The earth travels through a region of space-time that has been curved into an elliptical shape by the presence of the sun's mass. If the sun were to disappear, the surrounding space-time would be, as it were, flattened and the earth would then travel in a straight line (apart from the small gravitational influence of nearby planets and other massive objects) as a result of moving in a straightened space-time. In order to think concretely about space-time, then, we must consider the effect of mass upon it. At the same time, we can think of matter-energy only together with the conception of space-time. Whether we have regard to the particle-form or the wave-form, there could hardly be matter-energy that was not extended in space-time. Of course, the space-time of matter-energy need not have the enormous size of our universe in its present state. If big bang cosmology is correct, then the primordial space-time was unimaginably small. Yet some degree of extensiveness is required for a universe of matter-energy. A universe consisting of only two particles would still be characterized by a space-time interval between them. We reach the same conclusion even if we attend to the wave-like aspect of particles, for the field in which the wave is propagated must necessarily, in order to be a field, be extended spatially if not also temporally. Consequently, just as space-time can be conceived only in relation to matter-energy, matter-energy can be conceived only in relation to space-time.

The results of twentieth-century physics compel us to qualify our assessment of physical realities. The conceptual interconnections between particle and wave, between matter and energy, between space and time, and between matter-energy and space-time suggest that we must think of physical substances in ways that recognize the fundamental interconnectedness of these realities. We do not understand them rightly until we understand them in their conceptual relations to each other. To understand, for instance, the concept of matter it is not enough to enumerate some commonsense physical properties of matter. It is necessary to arrive at a more comprehensive conception (such as matter-energy) that embraces both the concept of matter in its customary form and also the related concept of energy, which (in usual ways of understanding) differs from matter. Understanding, then, consists in conceiving one thing in relation to another, thus comprehending identity through difference.

The Biological World

The part-whole structure of the biological world implies that living beings are likewise essentially relational in character. In the biological world, relatedness appears in two main forms, environmental space and behavioral relations.

Just as we cannot think, for example, of particles without also thinking of fields and waves, so we cannot rightly think of organisms and biological processes without thinking of them together with the environmental spaces they inhabit. This space may be as small as the immediate cellular neighborhood of a given cell and as large as the entire biological world, considered as a single ecological system. In every case, living beings of all sorts depend essentially on the character of their environmental space. At the same time, the relation of dependence is not one way, for the environment depends as well on organisms. On one hand, the environment of a given organism is itself largely composed of other organisms. A cell's environmental space includes not only the physical medium in which it is located but also other cells and other organisms in its proximity that can have some effect on it. On the other hand, organisms have an effect on their environment, even in its inorganic aspects. Ants and other insects, for example, contribute to the creation of soil by decomposing organic materials. Beavers build dams, affecting the course of rivers. Most dramatically, human beings use considerable amounts of environmental resources, both organic and inorganic, and in the course of doing so have significantly changed the character of our environmental space. Environment and organism, then, must be thought together if each is to be understood concretely.

It is important to note that the environmental space of living beings differs in significant respects from the space of physical entities. In the living world we are far from the space-time of the theory of general relativity. Whereas physical space and physical time are two aspects of the same space-time reality, biological space, as the site of relations between organisms, differs markedly from biological time. Further, particles are, essentially, spaceless geometric points, whereas living beings occupy space. Particles are *in* space but organisms *take up* space. A cell is the clearest example, for it possesses an internal space bound by its wall. The environmental space of organisms differs in other ways as well from the physical space of particles. Whereas the space of particles and other physical entities is undifferentiated, the environmental space of organisms is sharply differentiated. By undifferentiated I mean that changing spatial location does not affect the fundamental properties of particles (such as mass, charge, and spin). Of course, a change of location may affect a particle's behavior. The effect of an electro-magnetic field on a charged particle gives us an illustration of this. Nonetheless, a particle retains its essential characteristics whether it is in one part of the universe or another. The case is different with living beings. Their space, the environment, is crucial not only to their existence but also, as the theory of evolution explains, to their genetic composition. For particles, changes in spatial location have essentially quantitative effects (such as being accelerated or moving to a different energy state), as these particles interact with other particles and with fields of various strengths. But environmental space exerts not only quantitative effects on organisms (such as the size of a population that the environment will support) but also other effects. This is because the environment is filled with objects that the living being experiences, even if its experience is rudimentary. It finds itself attracted to or repulsed by these objects, not merely because of physical forces, but (at least in the case of some animals) also because of drives and complex physiological reactions such as the "fight or flight" response. In short, for living beings space is filled with meaningful objects that are experienced as beneficial or harmful to their well-being. Additionally, populations of organisms opportunistically fill niches. This is in contrast to a particle or atom, which may, in its history, find itself in any number of spatial locations and in any number of part-whole relations. It may be in empty space or in the interior of a star or in the pages of the book you are reading. Organisms, on the contrary, inhabit a comparatively narrow sort of space. They are largely tied to their environmental niche and may not survive outside it. At the same time, environmental niches are far more susceptible to change than is the space of particles and other physical entities. The latter often remains relatively unchanged for millions of years, whereas the environment of organisms can change dramatically in a short time and, in the case of catastrophic events, can be utterly destroyed. In summary, organisms are more essentially related to their environmental space than physical entities are to their spaces. At the same time, organisms have a substantial impact on their environmental space. As a result, just as organisms and their environmental space cannot be physically separated, so they cannot be conceptually separated in our thinking. In order to come to an adequate conception, both must be thought together.

The other form of organic relatedness pertains to the activity of living beings and their behavior toward one another. Because organisms relate to one another and to their environments behaviorally, we can understand a given organism or population only insofar as we also consider the other organisms or populations with which it interacts in its environment. As with spatial relations, there are important differences between the behavior of physical entities and of biological organisms. The behavior of particles and other physical entities is completely determined (allowing for quantum uncertainty) by their environment. An electron, for example, entering an electro-magnetic field will be affected in utterly predictable ways. However, in the biological world it is appropriate to speak of behavior being not simply caused by the environment but also occurring in response to the environment. This is a relative difference. The claim is not that organisms make decisions whereas physical beings do not but instead that the behavioral relations among organisms and their environment is far more complex than are the causal relations among physical entities and processes (even though the former is grounded in the latter). The word traditionally used to describe the complex character of biological behavior is *teleology*. This term has undeservedly fallen out of favor due to its association with the teleological argument for God's existence. In this argument, the order of the universe in its various forms is adduced as evidence for the existence of an intelligent creator. But it is possible to rescue the term from this untoward use if we note simply that organisms, especially animals, engage in behaviors in response to their environment that are important for their well-being. For example, some animals store food for the winter. Others, such as ants and bees, display highly organized and differentiated behaviors for the well-being of the community. Some primates, including human beings, use tools to manipulate their environments.

Of course, such behavior varies in degree of complexity. At the level of cells, organs, and systems, processes are dominated by chemical reactions. These remain fundamental for all living systems and more complex biological activity. Even the most overtly purposive human activity still presupposes and makes use of these chemical processes. But at the level of animals and animal societies other factors enter in and behavior becomes more complex. Perhaps the most strikingly distinct mode of behavior in the living world is communication, in which animals emit signals that change the behavior of other animals. The environment is also a factor. Animals receive and interpret signals from their environment that lead to changes in behavior. Finally, at least among some animals there is learning. Although most of the information needed by the young is received in the form of DNA, some information is transmitted through teaching. All this testifies to the astounding increase in complexity in the universe's transition from the physical world to the living world. As a result, behavior in the biological world is much more complex than in the physical universe. These considerations lead us to the conclusion that, in order to think adequately about organisms, it is necessary to think holistically about their relatedness to other organisms and to their environments, a relatedness reflected in the reciprocal effects of behavior.

Human Existence

Preliminary Remarks

The relatedness of human existence is continuous with the relatedness that we find in the physical universe and the biological world. We participate in all the forms of physical and biological relatedness previously discussed. The distinctively human forms of relatedness are grounded in and presuppose the physical and biological forms. Just as the biological world is grounded in the physical universe, so human existence is grounded in the biological and physical. To a certain extent, and perhaps completely, the distinctively human forms of relatedness result from the development of characteristics found in animals.

The essential relationality of human being implies that we do not exist autonomously in the form of disconnected entities. Our being is relational in ways that are analogous to the relatedness of physical and biological beings. We are what we are in and through the relations that shape us and that we in turn shape. It is necessary to belabor this point because there is a persistent tendency in our culture to represent human beings as morally and metaphysically autonomous entities. Naturally, there are prudential reasons for insisting on a measure of autonomy for human beings. Doing so is a safeguard against the totalitarian inclinations of communities. Doing so also rightly emphasizes the need to accept responsibility for our actions. Hence a political theory that recognizes the legitimate political autonomy of human persons has an important role to play in the practical life of humankind. The principle of autonomy, however, does not represent the whole truth and, when unduly emphasized without balance, can be positively harmful. My remarks in chapter six about abstract individualism were directed to this point.

Like realities in the physical universe and biological world, human beings are relational beings through and through. Human relatedness in its distinctive form results from the degree of organizational complexity that characterizes human life. This complexity is greater than that of other beings, with the result that our relatedness is more complex than that of physical and biological beings. It allows us to have a greater range of response to our environment and more adaptive modes of behavior to that environment, keeping in mind that our environment is itself more complex. It includes not simply our physical surroundings but also the world of thought and values that language and human community make possible. In this more complex form of relatedness, we can see more clearly (even if still remotely) the relational life of the Trinity.

The Relatedness of the Individual in Relation to Other Individuals

I am here concerned with the relatedness of the human person toward other human persons. Such relatedness goes beyond the sorts of physical and biological relatedness that I have discussed in the preceding sections. It goes beyond, for example, the dependence of one person on another for physical well-being. Human relatedness rests on the fact that human beings become persons only in relation to other human persons. Personhood is essentially a social phenomenon. Because we are constituted as persons by our relations to other persons, the quality and character of those relations is critical for our development as human beings. In trinitarian language, we come to possess an identity as human persons only in relation to someone or something else. It is only as we confront something other than our own selves that we are enabled to become persons. There is no self without some other to which we are related. As in the biological world, we find human relatedness in the forms of space and of behavior.

Space is an important form of and condition of human relatedness. But human space is not identical with physical or even biological space. Space for us is the place of encounter between persons. This space is filled with the presence and the absence of other persons. Although it is odd to speak of space being filled by an absence, this is something we have all experienced. The absence of someone we love fills our personal space as much or more than the presence of other persons. But personal space is also yielded space. We allow others their space and thus recognize their personhood. We understand ourselves to be in a limited space in the sense that we acknowledge that others are in our space only as we are also in their space. Human space is the in-between of persons. Having a limited space—sharing space with others—is one of the things that constitute us as persons.

As the space of personal and social encounter, human space is not simply a matter of physical size or distance. Certainly the immediate space of personal encounter is usually constituted by physical proximity. This is why we feel our lives diminished when someone we love is physically absent or uncomfortable when someone enters our personal space. At the same time, the space of personal encounter is larger than our immediate personal space. It is an ideal field of all possible personal interactions. Thus we can be personally and meaningfully related to human persons whom we do not see and perhaps have never seen. In principle, the entire human race could form a single moral and communicative community, each person having a significant formative influence on all others. If this occurred, every person would inhabit a common, universal space of personal encounter.

Our experience of space in its distinctively human form testifies to our participation in God's trinitarian life, for our space is an inherently interpersonal space. It is not the space of autonomous individuals whose spaces coalesce only accidentally. It is instead a space that is shared and in which human persons find themselves related. In this remote way, it reminds us of the life of the Trinity.

As is true of animals, behavior is a second form that human relatedness takes. Human behavior is grounded in our biological existence. Distinctive functions of human being such as cognition and purposive activity presuppose certain morphological and organic conditions. These include having an erect posture, linguistic capability, an opposable thumb, a certain degree of brain capacity and development, and social organization. It is difficult to see how distinctively human functions could have arisen without these physical attributes. Consequently, whatever we think of the human spirit, it does not denote an immaterial substance that is the true human self and that has a merely tenuous link to the body.

Perhaps this is a good place to address a potential critique. The thesis that human behavior is grounded in our biological existence seems to call into question the account of human creation that we find in Genesis, according to which humans have been created in the image of God (Gen. 1:26-27). As is well known, this idea of creation in the image of God has been the source of considerable speculation in the history of Christian thought. In general, interpreters have proceeded on the assumption that the image of God is to be identified with something in humans that distinguishes us from all other creatures. Naturally enough, the distinguishing characteristic was usually thought to be human rationality. But this line of interpretation has been questioned by modern biblical scholarship, which has tried to take the immediate context of these verses into account. Doing so, we notice that creation in the image of God is associated with the command to humans to have dominion over all of the rest of creation. This juxtaposition of ideas suggests that to be created in the image of God means to rule over the earth as God rules over the universe. This interpretation is reinforced by Ps 8:6-8, which states that humans, created a bit lower on the cosmic scale than the deities composing the heavenly council, exercise dominion over the earth. Once again we have the juxtaposition of two ideas: humankind created similar to God and dominion. Accordingly, it is best not to understand creation in the image of God as denoting some distinctive and inherent property of humans. Instead it points to a distinctive function, namely dominion.[4] The Bible, then, while acknowledging that humankind occupies a distinctive place in the created world, does not ground this in human nature. In this way it shows no tendency to claim that we are not a part of the created order of things.

We relate to our social environment through such behaviors as learning, communication, and thinking. Each of these behaviors has antecedents in other animals and is not exclusively human. Humans, however, have enlarged the scope of these capacities and in so doing have changed the character of our social environment. We have learned how to learn, that is, we have learned about learning. Even if the techniques of teaching how to learn have not been perfected, at least the cognitive processes involved in learning have been made the subject of social inquiry and experimentation. Not only does learning have a formative effect on individuals and societies, but individuals and societies in turn exercise an influence on the process and content of learning. In this way, the relational nature of learning has been expanded far beyond what we find among other animals.

Likewise, some animals, notably primates and some other mammals, engage in verbal communication with each other and thus live socially. Humans, however, have taken communication to new heights, even to the point of creating artificial languages such as computer programs that allow our communicative activity to attain otherwise impossible achievements. As a result, human society has developed in ways that diverge importantly from the societies of other primates. Already we have developed societies that encompass vast numbers of people. But these societies are not only extensive; they are also complex. They encompass not only people but also complex forms of social organization. We can even envision the day when the development of communication will bring it about that there is a single human society, encompassing every or nearly every human being in existence.

Finally, some animals display the rudiments of cognitive processes. But the social and relational character of human cognition far surpasses that of even the most highly developed animals. The sciences are a testimony to this development. The sciences depend on rapid and efficient communication. By means of this communication, a society of knowledge has come into being that has made knowledge-acquisition more efficient than could ever have been envisioned. In this respect, scientific inquiry provides us an example of the social nature of experiences and of knowledge and an illustration of the relational nature of human existence. Scientific inquiry is often carried out in teams. Even if it is not, the research undertaken presupposes a body of other knowledge and practices that defines the status of that branch of science. Results of inquiry are accepted only as they are processed through a social system of review. What counts as interesting and even valid scientific pursuits at any given time is largely a function of values shared by the scientific community. Even scientific education partakes of this social nature, as the student is led, apprenticelike, through the procedures and practices and modes of question-posing that initiate one into the scientific community. In these respects, initiation into the scientific community affords us an analogy with initiation into the human community. We become persons in the way in which one becomes a scientist. Becoming a scientist is a matter of learning to think and practice in certain ways and of learning to see some things as more important than other things. This learning is an intensely interpersonal process. So it is with becoming a person. Our entry into the social order is an entry into the realm of persons and we do so by means of interpersonal interactions. In this way, learning, communication, and knowledge are all aspects of the same process of becoming persons. Their social nature points toward the essentially relational nature of the human person.

In the domain of distinctively human behavior we are justified in speaking of final causation (teleology) in the form of purposive behavior. In the inorganic and organic worlds, the present moment is largely a repetition of the past as causal forces thrust themselves forward. Whatever novelty occurs is due almost completely to contingency. Human beings, however, employ intelligence to solve problems, with the result that planning is a prominent phenomenon in human behavior. Planning is possible only because for us the future represents an ideal that may be actualized. On the basis of this projected future, we act in ways intended to bring about this actualization. For humankind, then, causation is not merely from the past into the future but also from the future into the present. The future, functioning as an ideal, brings about and explains activity in the present. Because of the role of the future in human behavior, the causal influences on us include psychological motivation and rationality. Although the role of physical causation in explaining human actions and beliefs can never be denied, given the physical substratum that makes human being possible, it would also be a mistake to deny the special role that motivation and reasoning have in human action. Human beings undertake certain courses of action not only because of physical causes (such as hormonal or perceptual stimuli) but also because of conceptions that we form and to which we are attracted. Naturally conceptions alone will not yield a full explanation of behavior. But they also are not a negligible aspect of behavior and they underline the relational character of human behavior, for conceptions (such as ideas and values) are inescapably social.

Motivation and rationality figure into human behavior. Their relational character is seen in the phenomenon of persuasion. It is true that humans can exercise physical causation on one another through bumps and pushes. Rational persuasion, however, is the form of causation that is distinctively human. Persuasion does not cause action in the physical sense of cause but may be said to induce action, at least when the object of persuasion feels the force of the reasons given. We must immediately acknowledge that persuasion is sometimes practically and psychologically coercive, as when kidnappers demand ransom money. At other times, persuasion takes the form of material or emotional inducements to action that fail to take seriously the status of human beings as moral persons. Nonetheless, we customarily give at least lip service to the ideal of rational persuasion as the preferred mode of causal interaction between persons. In fact, rational persuasion is operative in many areas of life, even if it is not uniformly applied. Modern judicial systems, for example, seek to arrive at decisions far more by argumentation than by brute force. The same is true, perhaps to a less extent, of governmental deliberations.

Rational persuasion is an expression of human relatedness because, through our participation in rational discourse, we enter into a mutually conditioning network of learning, communication, and knowledge and allow the possibility of our thinking and behavior being changed. In such a network we are affected by each other. What I think and how I act are in part conditioned by the ideas of others. Certainly we must not pretend that by rational persuasion we mean only the force of logic. Many things go into making an idea persuasive. We are motivated by the rhetorical form in which the idea's logic is presented, the demeanor of the proponent, and what we know about the life of the proponent. These other considerations signify that persuasion is broader than the canons of logic.

Rational persuasion shows forth our essential relatedness by revealing that all human thought and action take place in a context. Our thinking and acting are always in response to some prior thought or action that has been presented to us. Our response may be highly creative and even original. Nonetheless, it always presupposes a context of interpersonal relations. Proof of this is that we can almost always find an explanation for the origin of an idea or action in the surrounding circumstances that helped call it forth. The fact that we are induced to action through persuasion points to the additional fact that our thinking and acting are never fully original with us but are called forth by the personal contexts in which we find ourselves. This observation in turn provides further exposition of the thesis that human being is essentially relational in character.

This discussion of motivation and rationality brings into consideration another aspect of human behavior. This is the aspect of morality. Like rational persuasion, morality is a thoroughly relational aspect of human behavior, for we are not born moral persons. We become so only through the acquisition of a moral character and moral conceptions, a process that is every bit as social as is language acquisition. As a result, the moral community in which we find ourselves is of capital importance in any understanding of human moral development. There is no particular form that the moral community must take. It may be small, as in the case of the family, or large, as in the case of the nation. It may be formally structured, as are voluntary associations and institutions, or loosely structured, as are friendships. The main thing is that we are formed into moral persons by our interactions with other persons.

The character of morality is determined by the future, which has an ideal character and is experienced by us as the field of possibility and as a project. To say that human beings have a future that functions as an ideal is to say that our conception of reality is not completely restricted to what is and has been actual. We are able to contemplate possibilities of various sorts. Morality, therefore, is not merely a matter of conventional behavior. It involves as well a conception of what ought to be the case and the ability to discern the difference between what is and what should be. For this reason, the most comprehensive claims of sociobiology with respect to morality can be accepted only with reservations. We must certainly admit that morality finds its context in human society and that society has evolutionary roots. We may also agree that, due to evolutionary pressures, certain types of human behavior generally associated with morality have been selected over the millennia. Nothing in these admissions, however, negates the importance of the sense of "ought" for human moral activity. It may well be true that this sense of ought has evolved in human history. Nonetheless, the validity of moral ideals and of this sense of ought neither depends on nor is compromised by their evolutionary history. If humans act today in ways that have been selected by evolutionary pressure, then, to the extent that we are acting consciously and with knowledge of our motives, we have chosen to act in these ways. Hence we should grant the validity of the moral sense on its own terms while not denying the important role that the evolutionary history of humankind must have played in the development of that moral sense.

There is one more aspect of human relatedness—our relation to God. Human beings are more than social beings. Our constitutive relations extend beyond our relations to other persons in our social environment. We are also called to live in the presence of God. To do so is to live mindful of the transcendent ground of all finite reality. It is to acknowledge and affirm our finitude and to take our place with the rest of the created world before the creator. It is to cultivate the virtues of wisdom and humility and to give praise to the creator. To the extent to which we stand in God's presence with praise, wisdom, and humility, our lives are given a distinctive character. We are then drawn into the trinitarian life of God, not only in the natural way in which all finite creatures participate, but with conscious intentionality and with the recognition that such a life is the necessary condition of humankind's highest good.

Humankind, however, persistently falls into a state of forgetfulness of the world's transcendent ground. We live unmindful of our highest calling. Because our participation in and relation to God falls far short of its full possibility, the other aspects of our relatedness suffer not only from the limitations of finitude but also from the distortions of sin. I will return to this subject in the last part of this chapter.

The Relations between Humankind's Communities

Relatedness occurs not only between persons but also between human communities. As with other aspects of human being, this mode of relatedness too is grounded in our participation in the physical universe and especially in the biological world. There it is not just individual organisms but also systems of cells and societies of individual beings that relate to one another in terms of behavior and space. In human society, whether we consider the relations between families, voluntary associations, communities, or nations, we find that no group is fully autonomous. Each group exercises an effect on others and in turn is affected by others just as in interpersonal relations. Further, the thoughts and actions of any given group are always situated in a particular context that is determined by the net effect of the thoughts and actions of the groups to which it is related. As with individual persons, one group's relations to other groups is an essential component of its being, insofar as it is partially determined by those relations. In this way, human community also exhibits the trinitarian dialectics of identity and difference that issues forth in essential relatedness.

With regards to relatedness in the form of behavior, there are significant differences between interpersonal relations and relations between groups, at least at global scales. One nation may not share the language of another nation or a common store of knowledge. Nonetheless, as with individual persons, there can be a process in which a nation, or at least a portion of a nation, enters into the thinking and ethos of another nation and thus shares (or at least becomes familiar with and favorably disposed to) its beliefs, values, knowledge, and customs. In this case, the relation between nations would be more profound than the oft-witnessed relation marked by misunderstanding, distrust, and power politics. There is also an analogy between interpersonal relations and relations between groups with respect to morality. Here, between nations, relationality has assumed a moral dimension in the form of international law, treaties, and institutions. Of course, the actual morality of current international relations is far from perfect; however, there is at present a genuine if rudimentary basis for moral relations between nations. Perhaps even more significant is the growing acceptance of the idea of human rights. With this idea nations have come to acknowledge the reality and importance of a moral standard that transcends the laws of particular nations.

With regards to relatedness in the form of space, we can speak of a shared space between human communities analogous to interpersonal space. In its most physical and international sense, intergroup space appears in the form of borders that separate one nation from another. Here, space demarcates but also unites, at least in the narrow region of the border. In order to overcome the separation of the border and to allow communication between nations, it is necessary to insert a bit of one nation into another—the embassy. Less formally there is shared space in the form of international forums and agencies that create a communicative space in which nations may cooperate. The space of groups appears also in the sacred spaces of communities. The most notable of these are the places associated with religions. In these cases, particular places have a holy character about them and become foci of religious practices. But overtly religious places are only the obvious example of a more general phenomenon. Every community and nation has sacred spaces that embody the beliefs, values, and commitments of its members. Cemeteries, national shrines, and even sport stadiums are also sacred places in which rituals of communal importance are enacted and social myths are recited.

Humankind's Relation to the Natural Environment

A final consideration in this discussion of human relationality is our relation to the natural environment (this subject will be taken up again in chapter ten in its specifically moral dimension).

As with the relation of one person to others and of one community to others, understanding our relation to the natural environment is essential to any adequate understanding of humankind. Our biological relation to the environment is largely a matter of adaptation through genetic modification and selection; however, the issue in this section is cultural adaptation, the use of knowledge and technology in the process of adapting to our environment and of finding our place in it. All species have the capacity to adapt to the environment. In most species, this adaptation is completely a function of fortuitous genetic composition. Some animals, however, are able to adapt in other ways as well, for example, by relocating if their original environment changes. The capacity of human beings, however, to adapt to their environment far surpasses that of other animals. Through artificial means such as clothing and agriculture we are able to survive and flourish in a variety of environments that would otherwise be closed off to us. The same is true of manipulating the environment through the use of tools. Human toolmaking, while a development of behavior exhibited by certain animals, has progressed dramatically beyond that of other animals and shows no sign of coming to an end. If anything, the rate of toolmaking is increasing. The relational significance of tookmaking lies in the fact that through it we define ourselves as the sort of being that relates to our surroundings in this way and find our identity in it. We understand ourselves in terms of the environment, even if often in negative or exclusionary ways. In so doing we testify to our essential relatedness to the environment. We declare that a full understanding of human being requires that we think of ourselves together with the natural environment.

However, our relation to the natural environment goes beyond our cultural adaptation to it. Consider our relation to other species. Physically and biologically, we are essentially related to them in the sense that we are physically dependent on them. They have places in the food chain whose top we occupy. We need bees to pollinate our fruit trees. We need ants and other insects to decompose organic materials and help create soil. But our relatedness to other species goes far beyond physical dependency. We define ourselves in relation to other species. We understand ourselves to be the being that is different from the rest of the living world, important similarities notwithstanding. Just as the individual person is constituted, at least partially, by relations with other persons, so the human species is constituted, at least in part, by its relations with other species. As I noted previously, the basic structure of human existence is to be in relation to something, whether other persons or other species. This is true even when, as is generally the case with urban and suburban dwellers, we have little direct contact with other species. Even here the world of thought, values, and institutions that we build for ourselves and the role that we assign to ourselves in that world cannot be divorced from our conceptions of the biological world and its members. Our relation with other species is, it is true, often negative, as when we see ourselves as something completely different from them. Additionally, other species are perceived as (and sometimes are) a threat to us and are experienced as something to be feared, exterminated, or domesticated in some way. If we can control them through taming or killing or otherwise restricting them, our sense of assurance in the world is reinforced. But more positive conceptions of our relation to other species are possible as well, conceptions in which we understand our relation to them in terms other than competitive and adversarial. The same is true, on a larger scale, of our relation to the physical environment in general. We define ourselves as a species by our relation to the surrounding world. Naturally our self-definition varies with the ways in which we represent the surrounding world to ourselves. In some conceptions, as with the ancient Stoic philosophy, humankind is an integral part of the physical universe and we feel an essential kinship with it. In other, more dualistic conceptions, the universe is something alien, something important mainly as the arena of human activities and something available for exploitation.

The character of our relatedness to other species and to the surrounding physical world appears in the space that we share with those species and that world. This space is often marked by a sharp distinction between urban and rural. As with the relation of nation to nation, there is a concern to provide a clear boundary between human space and natural space. Human encroachment on the natural domain is then often described as development. The remaining portions of the natural domain are then often designated as wildernesses and preserves, depending on whether we conceive of them as original and untouched or as something that humankind has set aside and protected. In the space between humankind and other species and the surrounding world, zoos play a special role. They are like embassies in the sense that they represent the artificial creation of one space in the midst of another. An embassy is the territory of one nation located in another. A zoo is the space of nature in the midst of human space. In this sense, it is a kind of shared space but it is so on strictly human terms. A zoo is, in fact, a strange sort of space because it is something deliberately created by us for us, as a way of representing to ourselves certain ideal images of other species and the world that surrounds us.

The character of our relation to other species and the world is also indicated by our behavior in that relation. As is the case with the other relations that define us, our relation to other species and the world signifies an important limitation of our autonomy. We exercise causal efficacy toward these other species and the environment and in turn are causally affected. Our relation here is marked by reciprocity.

Further, even as moral beings who in a way transcend the natural domain and differ significantly from other species, our acting and thinking always take place in a worldly context that comprises other species and the natural world. This is not to say that our thinking and action are concretely determined by these external factors but that they presuppose conditions over which we do not exercise full control and which partially determine the outcomes of our actions and the pathways of our thoughts.

In connection with our behavior in relation to the natural environment, we may ask about the moral dimension of our relation to other species and the world at large. If we conceive of the world and our place in the world in such a way that we utterly transcend the natural world and its members, then the moral quality of our relation to this world will be void. We will think of the world as a thing to be used at our discretion. But if we conceive of the world differently, then our relation to it may well take on a moral quality. We will then regard ourselves as having duties in relation to the world and will cultivate the sort of character that relates to the natural world in a consciously moral fashion (in chapter ten I present a fuller account of this subject).

Under the Conditions of Finitude

The relatedness that characterizes creatures implies the finitude of the universe and everything within it, for each thing is an element in the web of relations in which it stands. Because all things in the universe are essentially relational, nothing in the universe may be thought of as absolute, i.e., as ultimately real apart from its connections with the totality of other realities. This is the meaning of creatures' finitude.[5]

Perhaps the easiest way of seeing the finitude resulting from relatedness is to consider causal relations. The universe as a whole may be considered a single, enormous nexus in which every entity and field is bound to others by causal relations.[6] This means that any given entity or other physical reality exerts a conditioning effect on other entities and realities and in turn is affected by others. Nothing in the physical universe is fully self-determining. Each thing or process is what it is because of its causal relations to other things or processes. This observation leads us to the conclusion that every single thing within the universe is finite, for to be finite means to be limited or restricted by something else. The causal relations within the universe, then, which help make the universe to be a complex whole, also bring it about that the entities and processes within the universe exhibit the finitude of mutual determination. As a result, created entities in the physical universe and biological world do not possess complete self-determination and most lack any measure of self-determination. Their relatedness is such that they are utterly determined by networks of causal relations. Each contributes to the causal network and in turn receives its effects. Each receives passively the net effect of the causal chains in which it is embedded and just as passively exerts an influence on its neighbors.

The finitude resulting from relatedness appears in additional forms in the biological world. As noted previously, organisms are essential to and dependent on their environmental spaces. But the environment may suffer degradation to the extent that it cannot support life. There is also the possibility of an organism's niche being encroached upon by competitors. Besides these sorts of event, the natural environment's finitude is grounded in its own relatedness to external factors. The biological world is not all-encompassing, as is the physical universe. This means that it is subject to the contingencies of external factors. It is, for example, totally dependent on energy, ultimately derived from the sun. This energy is not inexhaustible. Someday, life on earth will come to an end when our star has come to the end of its natural cycle. A different sort of threat is posed by collisions with comets and asteroids. It appears likely that several times in the past such collisions have brought about massive extinctions. The prospects of avoiding future collisions does not seem promising, unless some technological means of destroying approaching objects is developed. Climatic and other environmental changes are yet another source of contingency that can have a considerable effect on the possibility and development of life. In these and other ways, then, biological space exists contingently and, at times, highly precariously. Its finitude is a function of the role that contingency plays in it.

The finite character of the biological world can be seen as well in the behavior of living things. The behavior of particles, atoms, and larger physical realities is determined by physical forces. In the biological world, however, we find, in addition to this sort of physical causation, manipulation of the environment and other forms of purposive behavior. Nonetheless, behavior in the biological world is still a largely deterministic phenomenon. Novelty is not self-generated but is instead due to such contingent events as random genetic mutation and environmental change. Purposeful behavior in relation to the environment is, except for the few animals in which authentic learning occurs, completely determined by genetic composition and chemical reaction. Even when learning is associated with purposive behavior, it occurs without significant degrees of conscious intentionality. Apart from learning, purposive behavior is, so to speak, programmed into the organism's genetic constitution. The activities of cells and organisms are effective but essentially limited to one admittedly important purpose, the survival and reproduction of the population to which the cells and organisms belong. The capacity for adaptation and complex behaviors such as learning, manipulation of the environment, and communication are extraordinarily limited and almost exclusively serve the purpose of survival and reproduction. As a result, the individual being is subordinated entirely to the well-being of the population and its genetic legacy.

The same is true of organs and societies in the biological world. Judged from a human perspective, they suffer from at least one serious limitation. Unlike human societies, they have a very limited capacity to act. The function of an organ, such as the heart, or of a system, such as the nerve system, seems to be a conglomeration of the functioning of the individual cells composing the organ or system. Although the cells composing an organ or system exercise a reciprocal effect on each other, organs such as the heart do not have the ability to act as a unit by directing the functioning of their members. That is, the organ or system lacks the identity and unity characteristic of the cell or organism. Whatever coordination there is among the constituent members seems to arise from the action of one member on the others, not from the action of the organ or system on its members. In this sense, biological composites are quite like physical composites such as stars and galaxies, whose activity is simply the net effect of the activities of their constituent parts. Only in animal societies does there appear to be unity of action on the part of the whole. This phenomenon receives its most developed form in human societies, which have the ability to act corporately on their members, as when an organization or society is regulated by laws that are binding on members. Here the community acts on its members directly; its action is not merely the sum of the acts of members on one another.

Like everything else in the universe, human existence is subject to the limitations of finitude. This is a consequence of our essential relatedness. Because of this relatedness, every one of us affects others and in turn is affected by them. We are for this reason radically dependent on each other and our experience is constituted by these relations. This is true of all things in the universe, but in human being this fact becomes a matter of conscious knowledge. Human beings are distinguished by the fact that we know of our radical dependence and take steps to regulate it, improve and manipulate it. Government, education, and many other human endeavors are attempts at shaping our mutual dependency. But under the conditions of human sin, these attempts often take the form of trying to avoid this sense of dependence, either through ideologies that emphasize human freedom and autonomy or through totalitarian government that restricts the semblance of autonomy to unelected leaders. But the death of loved ones brings back to us in ways that cannot be contradicted the fact of our mutual dependency. The experience of another's death brings home with undeniable certainty the truth that who and what we are is a matter of the relations into which we have entered. A similar feeling arises within when we experience the destruction of an institution to which we have devoted ourselves. In its demise we experience not only its death but, in a measure, our own, for we are it and it is we. Its death, like the death of a loved one, is our own participation in death, a tearing away of our selves, a tearing that leaves ragged edges that can never be fully mended.

Characteristic human activities such as learning and knowledge likewise participate in finitude. Even in those of high intelligence learning is associated with effort. The very fact that we must acquire knowledge by a process (especially one prone to error) in itself shows the finite character of human being. On the scale of human communities, we can see that the process of learning implies the possibility of loss. The tedious accumulation of knowledge by civilizations can be lost forever in the destruction of history. Cognition likewise does not escape the limitations of human life. At least since the philosophy of Immanuel Kant the essential finitude of human thought has been recognized. Whereas Aristotle could assert that intellect is humankind's attaining to a divine mode of existence, it has since become clear that intellect is a human, all-too-human phenomenon. Indeed, it is in the study of the natural sciences, one of the outstanding examples of human cognition, that the finitude of cognition becomes most evident. It is in the sciences that any human pretension to completeness of knowledge is stripped away by the slow, laborious and sometimes errant path of patient inquiry.

Human learning and knowledge serve social and other purposes. It is a measure of the finite character of our participation in God that human learning and knowledge are incomplete and incompletely serve their ends. However, under the conditions of sin, learning and knowledge go beyond incompleteness and become instruments employed for evil ends and for unworthy social purposes. When this happens learning is no longer a liberating experience but instead becomes a constriction on the human project. This occurs, for example, when learning is framed in narrowly utilitarian terms. In this case, learning is reduced to just those aspects needed to accomplish some narrowly conceived purpose. The value of learning becomes limited to immediate productivity. It becomes an investment that must pay quick dividends. It is even further degraded when it is forced to serve the perverse goals of the nation or other educating entity. Whereas the utilitarian approach impoverishes learning by pruning it of subjects deemed irrelevant for the immediate need, the political perversion of learning results in the adulteration of the subject of learning. The results of history, literature, the sciences, and other subjects are subtly or not so subtly manipulated in order to support the approved version of truth. No institution concerned with learning is exempt from this temptation, least of all the church, which understands itself to be charged with propagating God's truth.

Communication is another expression of human relatedness. It too will always be attended by finitude, at least if the analysis proposed by the deconstructionist program in philosophy is at all viable. According to this analysis, every use of language is inherently implicated in polyvalence and interpretation. Naturally, this is a problem only on the assumption that language ought to be able to convey thoughts with ideal clarity and without distortion. But even without this assumption we can see that language and communication are not transcendental objects but are instead embedded in the finitude of human life and are subject to all manner of conditions.

Under the condition of sin, social communication becomes perverted in ways that resemble the perversion of learning and knowledge. The most egregious form of this in the last century has been propaganda. George Orwell's *1984* is a classic presentation of the thesis that opinion in the industrial world is a product to be made, packaged, and sold. This is true not only of totalitarian regimes, in which the government has a monopoly on the news media. It is true also of the democratic nations in which news is manufactured and truth has become a commodity. Truth and speech are no less controlled by a plurality of commercial entities than they are by a single despotic government. They are no less distorted by capitalization than by politicization. Speech, which should be one of the means by which free subjects participate in the public life of the community, often becomes the means by which the community is closed off and its members become subjects of manipulation. No less dangerous is the role that advertising plays in the commodification of speech and communication.

What is true of learning, knowledge, and communication is true all the more of morality. It would seem that morality, having an ideal character, would be exempt from the claims of finitude. But we must also keep in mind that the ideals of morality cannot be divorced from fallible human judgments. Even the ideals of morality are relative to our moral vision, a vision that is always to some extent impaired. Evidence for this is the fact that yesterday's moral ideals often embarrass us, a fact that suggests how our own ideals today will be received by future generations. For example, ideals of humane treatment of prisoners and of human rights have changed substantially within the last century in, we trust, a progressive direction. Our understanding of these ideals, however, to say nothing of our capacity or willingness to actualize them, is as limited as any other aspect of human being. This is the limited truth possessed by the theory of ethical relativism. It is not that there are no moral norms but that the norms we adopt are only in a limited sense transhistorical and transcultural. The idea of freedom, for instance, traverses history, but not without change as it is conceived variously in this and that cultural epoch. If moral ideals did not depend on our conception of them, then perhaps we could speak of an utterly unconditioned realm of moral values. As it is, our perception of any such unconditioned realm is itself conditioned by many factors.

Under the conditions of sin, morality is not only limited but is also perverted. It is perverted, for instance, in the public's cynical and often well-deserved attitude toward government. In this case government is generally acknowledged to be not subject to the commonly accepted norms of behavior. It is not just that the agents of government do not subject themselves to moral norms; it is also and mostly that the public acknowledges and even accepts the discrepancy between governmental action and what most people hold to be morally upright behavior. The same cynicism is evident when any institution, including the church, is generally regarded as existing in a separate moral category, one that flatly contradicts basic notions of right and wrong. Another form of morality being perverted under the conditions of sin is the wholesale abandoning of moral norms by a society even while those norms are publicly extolled as ideals. Morality is also distorted by sin whenever the letter of the law is elevated above the spirit of the law and turned into an immutable rule admitting of no exceptions. When this happens, the goal of law—human well-being—has been ignored and a concern for abstract and punctilious legalism substituted in its place.

Finally, humankind's relation to the natural environment is subject to finitude. Although humans, through the use of intelligence and technology, are highly adaptive to our environment, neither we nor our technology have an unlimited capacity for adaptation. Even though we have made tentative steps in genetic engineering, we are far from being able to successfully meet all the challenges that the environment brings to us. The frustrating history of treating the AIDS virus is an example. Although there is little doubt that eventually a vaccine will be developed to control this particular virus, there is also every reason to suspect that human adaptation to other environmental challenges will be accompanied by laborious effort. Our use of technology to manipulate the environment is similarly constrained by the inherent limitations of the materials used in the technology and by the strength of our imagination in devising technology. Although technological development in the last three centuries has sometimes painted a Promethean picture of human activity, both the occasional technological disaster and the everyday frustrations with modern gadgets reminds us of their essentially finite character.

Under the condition of sin, the limitations of finitude are exacerbated. Our refined capacity for adaptation to the environment is no longer enough for us. We now wish to become masters of our destiny by controlling our genetic composition and by manipulating the environment through technology. At the present moment it is not possible to be specific about the moral dimension of attempting to control our genetic composition because the technology is new, because public discussion about it has just begun, and because laws and ethical norms are still in the formative stage. Certainly there are no theological grounds for hindering the attempt to remedy genetic defects by altering the genes in germ cells. The history of humanity and its use of new and powerful technology, however, warn us to be cautious of proceeding with genetic engineering without the concomitant work of ethical reflection. As these words are being written, it is being reported that at least one team of scientists is attempting to clone a human being and also that cloning animals is fraught with grave difficulties and perils due to the fact that in cloning the process by which cells come to have differentiated functions proceeds in a much smaller time frame than it does in the natural process of development. There can be little doubt that this technical problem will one day be resolved and that in the future human beings will be cloned and subject to other sorts of genetic manipulation. However, humankind's moral history does not fill us with unalloyed optimism about this project.

The other way in which we seek to master our own destiny is through manipulation of the environment through the use of tools. Perhaps once in history such manipulation was the simple expression of human need. Now, however, it takes the form of an overweening lust for dominance. The natural world has become for us, to a great extent, merely a resource, a great treasury of economically exploitable goods. But doesn't the Genesis account of creation sanction such a rapacious stance toward the natural world? After all, it represents God as commanding humanity to have dominion over every other creature and to subdue the earth (Gen 1:28). Although a fuller response to this question will be offered in the next two chapters, it can at least be noted here that this command must be understood in its ancient context, with its (by our standards) extraordinarily primitive agricultural technology and its realistic danger of famine and starvation. God's command to humankind today, with our vastly more powerful technology and with our material abundance, is quite different. In ancient times, with a small population, the primary task was physical survival and the maintenance of civilization. Today it is not civilization that is in desperate straits, but the natural world.

The Kingdom of God

The kingdom of God stands for the redemption of creatures' relatedness insofar as they suffer from the distortion of sin. In the fullness of the kingdom of God, trinitarian relatedness reigns, although its actualization in any given individual or community will be subject to the limitations of finitude.

In the kingdom of God, human forms of relationality come to mirror the relatedness that characterizes the Trinity. Practically speaking, this means the end of self-asserting moral autonomy, whether of individuals toward each other, or of communities toward each other, or of humankind toward the natural environment, or of humankind toward God. In every case, human life is lived out in the conscious knowledge that each of us depends upon others and that our identity is constituted by our relations with other individuals and communities and with the natural environment and, ultimately, with God.

The historical anticipation of the Kingdom is the church, which exists under the condition of finitude and which has not been able to escape the distortions of sin. Nonetheless, in the church there should be special attention to the quality of human relations, since it is these relations that constitute those who are in the kingdom. These relations should be characterized by the same sort of mutual love and giving that the persons of the Trinity show to each other. If, as the Christian tradition has taught, the life of the Trinity is a life of self-giving love, then our participation in the trinitarian life in the kingdom of God (and in its historical anticipation in the church) should reflect that self-giving love. As God allows the divine being to be drawn into the world in the incarnation and the giving of the Spirit, so those in the kingdom are called to allow their lives to be drawn into the lives of others and into the existence of communities and into the natural environment. Although at one level we are naturally related to each other and to communities and to the natural environment, the kingdom of God means the actualization of this relatedness in conscious and intentional moral action and in a spirit of grateful response and obedience. Further, although in one sense every human being is naturally related to God, since human existence in all its dimensions is a participation in God, in another sense we are called to actualize that relation with conscious intentionality and thus bring the totality of our lives under God's lordship. It is the church's task in the world to call humankind to realize, as much as is humanly possible, trinitarian relatedness and to model that relatedness as a testimony of God's grace.

The future that God wills for creation is a future in which we realize the essential interconnectedness of all things and act on the basis of this realization. It is a future in which harm and exploitation are no longer moral options because we each see the folly of harming and exploiting that to which we are essentially related and of which we are an integral part. It is a future in which there is a convergence of individual good and corporate good, due to our knowing that each of us is a part of an integral whole, that our relation to that whole constitutes our being, and that the good of that integral whole is our own good.

PART THREE

A TRINITARIAN ETHICS

9

The Ethical Dimension of the Doctrine of Creation in Christian History

The considerations offered at the end of chapter eight about the convergence of individual and corporate good lead us to the topic of this chapter. The Christian faith has not only cognitive and hermeneutical dimensions but also an ethical aspect. This must be the case if, as the Bible claims, God is love and those who do not love do not know God. The Christian faith, especially the doctrine of creation, is associated with a way of being in the world, and belief in such a doctrine includes commitment to this way of being. One who persistently lives without this commitment does not really believe the doctrine, in the Christian sense of "believe." While one may affirm a doctrine intellectually, such affirmation falls far short of Christian faith. The ethical dimension of the Christian faith is grounded in this fact.

Broadly speaking, there are two impulses in the ethical dimension of the doctrine of creation. Both are grounded in the trinitarian life of God, which, as noted in previous chapters, is a life of identity and difference. Human existence in the kingdom of God is marked by a more profound participation in this life of identity and difference than is found outside life in the kingdom. In relation to our existence in the world, the dialectics of identity and difference appears in two impulses. One is the tendency toward world transcendence. This impulse is the necessity of differentiating the Christian community from the created world. The other is the tendency toward participation in the world. This impulse is the necessity of identifying with the created world. We are called on to be distinguished from the world while participating in the world. This means that "world" has a twofold significance. On one hand, it is alienated from God and hence must be overcome through ethical transcendence. On the other hand, the world remains the good creation of God and the context of our human existence. These two tendencies are contrasts but are not contradictory. They are dialectically related. Their inseparability is grounded in the fact that they arise from our participation in the trinitarian life of God, the life of identity and difference.

The Tendency toward World Transcendence

The phrase "world transcendence" suggests that, in some respect, the world is regarded as problematic for the Christian life. In the New Testament, for example, the world is often regarded as an evil system that arrays itself defiantly against God. There are also passages suggesting that this world, together with the heavens, is destined to be destroyed and replaced by another. Hence there is a need to maintain an ethical distinction between the Christian community and the world. This problematic character, however, should not be taken to imply that Christianity is a religion of world rejection. Although individuals and movements within Christian history have denounced the world as utterly evil, they do not represent the mainstream. The world is fallen, but it is not evil. It remains the good creation of God and the site of the new creation.

In the Bible, the world receives a negative connotation when it is identified with the political and demonic structures that oppress the people of God. When, in John's Gospel, Jesus says to the disciples, "If the world hates you, be aware that it hated me before it hated you" (15:18), it is clear that "world" means the totality of sinful humanity that steadfastly disobeys God and rejects those whom God sends. Likewise, when Ephesians counsels that "our struggle is not against enemies of blood and flesh . . . but . . . against the cosmic powers of this present darkness" (6:12), it is evident that the cosmic powers are the fallen and demonic structures of the universe that struggle against God and God's people. Finding themselves a small and beleaguered community in a politically and culturally hostile environment, it is not surprising that early Christians urgently felt the need to overcome the world in an act of ethical transcendence. The Christian doctrine of creation, then, is not solely about the universe in its physicality or as a spatial-temporal manifold. On the contrary, it is a doctrine about the universe in all its aspects, including its ethical aspects.

The impulse toward world transcendence rests on seeing the world as something over which the believer must win a victory and that is or contains an obstacle to salvation, even as it remains the good creation of God. The way the problematic character of the world is conceived, however, varies in history and across cultures. As a result, world transcendence takes various forms in Christian history. These forms are highly dependent on the cultural situation in which the church finds itself. The following pages will illustrate some of the forms that this impulse has taken. The next chapter will indicate one direction that this impulse may take today.

World Transcendence in New Testament Apocalypticism

The form taken by early Christianity's tendency toward world transcendence was drawn from the apocalyptic worldview of first-century Judaism. The feature of apocalypticism most pertinent to the doctrine of creation is its dualistic thinking with respect to humankind and history. It divided humankind into two camps, a minority faithful to God and the unfaithful majority. Additionally, there is a sharp distinction between the present evil age and the age that is soon to come. The present time of oppression requires of God's people patience and faithfulness. The entire universe seems to be arrayed against the people of God. Within a short time, however, the end of this age will come. The nations will be judged, the wicked will be condemned, and the righteous will be rewarded. Then God will reign on earth. The earth will be restored to the paradisiacal condition it enjoyed before human sin.

This dualistic mind-set is the intellectual framework that underlies the form of world transcendence advocated in the New Testament. For instance, Paul's theology is built on an ensemble of contrasts. In our current state we bear the image of *Adam*, the man of dust; however, in the new age we will bear the image of *Jesus*, the man of heaven (1 Cor 15:49). The powers of *darkness*, from which we have been rescued, are opposed to the kingdom of *Christ* (Col 1:13). We must forsake life according to the *flesh* and live instead in the *Spirit* (Gal 5:16-17). As a result, there is an ethical life stipulated for the people of God. Because we have been transferred from the evil system of the world into the kingdom of Christ, we are no longer to live as though still a part of the evil world-system. Instead we are to seek those things that transcend the world (Col 2:20; 3:1-2). By living according to the Spirit of God, we will be enabled to resist the desires of the flesh (Gal 5:16-17) and to be unconcerned about mundane affairs. Paul and the rest of the New Testament urged an attitude of detachment in light of the dawning new age that renders everything worldly insignificant.[1] The New Testament writers, convinced that the moral and political fabric of society is fallen and in a state of rebellion against God, urged the people of God to drop out of that society to the extent feasible. Practically speaking, this meant that practices clearly at odds with the kingdom of God must be avoided and that one must hope only in the coming kingdom of God. This is the meaning of world transcendence in its first-century form.

It is both possible and valid to distinguish the New Testament's world-transcending impulse from the apocalyptic worldview in which it is embedded and which furnished its form. This is because, according to the New Testament, the kingdom of God is not only a future reality that will replace this world but has in fact already made its presence known as a redemptive reality in this world. We are called to transcend the world while living in it and while being a part of it. As a result, the redemptive nature of world transcendence becomes evident without implicating us in a theology that regards the world as evil in itself. This message—the powerful and redemptive presence of the future in the present and the resulting possibility of liberation—is the enduring message of New Testament apocalypticism.

World Transcendence in Early Christian Asceticism

After the first century the vivacity of apocalyptic fervor began to subside,[2] but the world-transcending impetus remained, although in new forms. It remained mainly because it was firmly embedded in the New Testament and because the New Testament was increasingly being read apart from its original apocalyptic context. In the early centuries of Christianity, the main form of world transcendence was asceticism, often in the context of monastic life.[3]

Asceticism is a form of world transcendence because, as in apocalypticism, the world or some aspect of the world is seen as in some sense problematic. Whereas in apocalypticism the problematic aspect is the oppressive and demonic structures that threaten to destroy the people of God, in asceticism the problem is worldly and often bodily desires that deter the believer from the path of perfection, such as desire for physical pleasure and for wealth. Augustine illustrates well the ascetic tendencies of early Christianity, especially with regard to marriage and sexuality. Fundamental to his theology is the conviction that the world in its created state was characterized by order. Above all, this meant the obedience of the body to the commands of the soul. Sin, however, virtually destroyed this order, so that now, in our sinful condition, the body does not spontaneously obey the soul but must be forced to do so by discipline. This sinful condition was brought about, he argued, by humankind seeking pleasure, beauty, and truth in worldly things instead of in God.[4] The practical manifestation of disorder is temptation and concupiscence, the overwhelming desire for pleasures of all sorts. Since our sin consists in seeking pleasure in things other than God, Augustine was convinced that the only antidote to concupiscence is rigorous self-control. Only by rigidly controlling our desires could we hope to regain the wholeness of soul and body that characterized our original state.[5] For example, eating represented grave dangers to the soul. The pleasure associated with eating threatened, he wrote, to make him its captive. His only recourse was continuous fasting, attempting to force his body to obey.[6] The pleasures of sound had likewise formerly enthralled him, so that he required God to deliver him from bondage to this pleasure, knowing that the pleasures of the senses will, if unchecked, come between him and God. Even singing could be an occasion for sin if he found himself attending more to the act itself than to the words conveyed by the song.[7] Worse than these pleasures of the senses is the mind's curiosity, which has a pleasure of its own as the mind seeks satisfaction through vain and valueless learning.[8]

Augustine's view of marriage and sexuality is consistent with the rest of his theology. Not unexpectedly, he followed Paul in holding that celibacy is preferable to marriage.[9] But he went beyond Paul in the variety of rationales he offered for this view. On the premise that modesty in marriage is a virtue, he argued for the superiority of celibacy, for in celibacy the flesh is consecrated to and kept for the creator alone and not shared with a spouse.[10] He also regarded celibacy as an angelic life because it represents the practice of incorruption within the corruptible flesh. The celibates, he argued, were already now in this world living the heavenly life in advance of their heavenly glorification.[11] Further, they could look forward to a greater heavenly reward than could the married. Although, he allowed, marriage is no hindrance to receiving eternal life, the celibates were to receive a greater share of heavenly glory and honor.[12] Finally, he urged celibacy on the grounds that it represents a significant way in which we may imitate Jesus, whom he called the pattern of celibate purity.[13]

With the lessening of the apocalyptic spirit, the impetus toward world transcendence found an outlet in asceticism. The New Testament texts that enjoined renunciation in light of the approaching kingdom of God served also to buttress the ascetic tendency of Christianity, a tendency that has never died out as an ideal. Even Protestants critical of monasticism nonetheless incorporated the monastic ideal of the ascetic and disciplined life into their theology. John Calvin's *Institutes of the Christian Religion* describes the Christian life in terms of self-denial.[14] Across the spectrum of the Christian tradition, the ascetic impulse in its many forms has been one of the enduring and strongest expressions of the tendency toward world transcendence. To be sure, few Christians today would approve of Augustine's view of sexuality and marriage, rightly judging that he had emphasized certain aspects of the Bible's ethics at the expense of others. It is nonetheless incumbent on us to maintain continuity with the world-transcending impulse, even if for us it will take a somewhat different form.

World Transcendence in Christian Mysticism

It may seem odd to classify mysticism under the ethical dimension of the doctrine of creation. For many people, mysticism connotes a quietistic and contemplative state of mind—the opposite of an ethical posture. But it would be a mistake to regard Christian mysticism as merely a state of mind or a type of experience. It involves certain practices and beliefs, as did apocalypticism and asceticism. Further, at least in the Roman Catholic and Orthodox churches, mysticism has sustained an institutional role through its influence on theology. Moreover, ethics is not simply reducible to practice. It includes also our conception of the world and our practical orientation to it.

Just as Christian asceticism presupposed New Testament texts arising out of the apocalyptic matrix, so Christian mysticism presupposes the ascetic tradition and may be regarded as an outgrowth of that tradition. This helps explain the world-transcending character of mysticism. In it, as in asceticism, we must go beyond the world if we are to attain spiritual perfection. Because the things of the world are sources of temptation, the mystical path must begin with ascetic practices. In comparison with apocalypticism and asceticism, however, mysticism has tended to have a somewhat more positive view of the world. This is because, in mysticism, ascetic practices were joined with the medieval sense that the world is a mirror of God's nature, so that the soul can use worldly entities as stepping-stones in its journey to God. Christian mysticism, then, points the way toward a helpful use of the world-transcending impulse in expounding the doctrine of creation.

The medieval mystic and theologian Bonaventure (1221–1274) will serve as an illustration. For Bonaventure, transcending the world means directly experiencing a reality that exceeds this natural world and doing so by being lifted out of one's own natural abilities by the power of grace. The eternal is, as it were, above the earth, and the soul must go up to it.[15] Accordingly, the things of the world can be compared to rungs on a ladder by which the soul climbs to God.[16] Alternatively, worldly things can be seen as mirrors dimly reflecting God's nature and as vestiges of God's creative activity.[17] The soul, since it is embodied, begins with material things around it, which it knows by means of the senses. By meditating first on the physical properties of sensible objects, the soul can come to a knowledge of the power, wisdom, and goodness of God the creator.[18] Also, by distinguishing the more transitory from the more permanent, the soul is led to meditate on the unchangeable and incorruptible divine reality.[19] At a higher level of ascent, consciousness of the *act* of knowledge points us toward God. In the act of knowledge the physical thing makes an impression, an image, on the mind. Meditation on the mental image, Bonaventure asserted, ultimately can lead the soul to a knowledge of the trinitarian relation between Father and Son, for the Son is the eternal image of the Father. Similarly, the laws by which the mind judges between one thing and another (as in, "x is more beautiful than y"), are, Bonaventure averred, immutable. This immutability likewise points us to God, who is alone truly immutable.[20] In short, everything in the created world is a sign that denotes God as first cause, final end, and exemplar of perfection.[21] Each thing retains traces of its divine origin. The discerning soul can recognize these traces and use them as stepping-stones to regain the direct knowledge of the triune God. In this way, although material things are not denigrated, their value is grounded in their role as signs of a spiritual and transcendent reality.

The full extent of mysticism's world-transcending character is seen in what Bonaventure regarded as its ultimate earthly goal, the direct experience of the Trinity. Short of this step, the human intellect exercises itself in finding traces of God among creatures. But the ascent of knowledge terminates in a state in which intellect is set aside and the Trinity is experienced directly. The mystic has here transcended human nature.[22] This state is characterized by grace, not doctrine; by desire, not understanding; by praying, not reading.[23] Here, in the ultimate state of world transcendence, both the world and human nature itself have been left behind and perfection attained, if only temporarily. In mysticism, then, it is not the world alone that is transcended but particularly the human mind in its finite limitations. The mystical ascent consists in drawing the mind's attention away from mundane entities and toward the triune God.

World Transcendence in the Age of Modern Science

The modern scientific view of the universe has generated its own intellectual context in which the impulse toward world transcendence has taken shape. This is particularly the case when, for example, this scientific view has been associated with a materialistic and mechanistic philosophy. In this association, the world appears to be a hostile place, not only to the people of God but to a meaningful human existence in any sense.

As an illustration of theology's response to a philosophically charged scientific worldview, consider Albrecht Ritschl (1822–1889), the leading German theologian of the late nineteenth century. Writing in a period when materialistic philosophy was dominant, Ritschl regarded the natural world as a threat to human being—not a physical threat, but an existential one. As Ritschl conceived it, humankind's chief problem in relation to nature is the possibility of the natural world hindering our freedom. Ideally, the natural world would be incorporated by us into our life as a resource. In this way we would achieve a harmony between human life and the natural order.[24] This ideal state is not something won easily; it is a task that we must work at. Consequently, we feel the physical world to be something that we must surmount. Yet, with God's help we can attain lordship over the world by actualizing those spiritual and personal qualities that we share with God.[25]

What accounts for Ritschl's conception of the world and of humanity's place in the world? One source is surely the scientific milieu. While scientific materialism was not unknown earlier in previous generations, it was a minority voice amid idealistic philosophical alternatives. These idealistic systems inclined thinkers of previous generations to view the world and humanity's relation to the world in organic and dialectical terms. Humans were thought to be both a part of but also in a sense distinct from the world. In this way, theologians could take up a positive attitude toward the natural world without fear of thereby reducing humankind to the status of mere parts in a great mechanical world-system. Ritschl, however, found himself in quite a different intellectual setting. With the collapse of the idealistic philosophies in the 1840s and the following decades, a strident form of materialistic philosophy became ascendant. Ritschl perceived a great danger that human persons would in fact be seen as pieces of the cosmic natural and deterministic machine. Accordingly, he was concerned to represent salvation as freedom from mechanistic determinism and as transcendence over the world.

According to Ritschl, humanity's relation to nature is one of the fundamental problems that gives rise to religion. We have, he argued, a need to resolve two contrary facts: first, that we are a part of the natural world and, second, that we are spiritual persons who transcend nature. As a part of nature, humankind is dependent on and subjected to the world of finite realities. As a result we feel ourselves constrained. As beings that transcend nature,[26] we feel ourselves distinct from and independent of nature. The resolution of this conflict consists in our attaining freedom from the world while always continuing to exist in some dependence on a material environment.[27] This freedom is to be understood teleologically as a purpose that God has established for the human race and in which God invites humankind to participate by ethical activity. In turn, the character of this freedom gives content to the conception of God, who is for us the power that enables human beings to realize the attainment of the highest good, i.e., transcendence.[28] In Christianity, this highest good is understood to be the kingdom of God, which is both a reality that God accomplishes and also a task that humans work at by rendering obedience to God.[29] Jesus was for Ritschl the model of the human person who had transcended the world for the sake of the kingdom of God and been able to live ethically in the world. This is what, according to Ritschl, made Jesus the founder of the kingdom. He is thus the enduring pattern for us. It is no exaggeration to say, then, that the purpose of transcending the world, according to Ritschl, is that we may participate in the highest good, which he understood to be a this-worldly task. The freedom resulting from world transcendence establishes the possibility of humankind's ethical activity in the world.

A few concluding comments: (1) The impetus toward ethical world transcendence is a permanent aspect of the Christian faith. It is grounded in our participation in the trinitarian life of God, a life in which difference is an essential aspect. With regard to our ethical posture toward the world, this means that it is always necessary to maintain a distinction between the Christian community and the world, at least insofar as the world is conceived as fallen. Hence we are called to transcend the world. (2) Although the dialectics of participation and transcendence is permanent, the forms that it takes differ from epoch to epoch. In the first century, it was lodged in an apocalyptic mind-set. Later, it emerged in ascetic practices. Still later it took form as mysticism and then Ritschl's conception of freedom. History presents us with different forms in which the impulse toward world transcendence occurs. (3) We must exercise critical judgment over these historical forms. None of them should be identified with the Christian faith, for each is historically contingent. The apocalyptic way of thinking in its first-century form was a response to first-century political conditions. Asceticism and mysticism may be and have been taken in extreme directions. Ritschl's proposal unnecessarily devalues the natural world. (4) In spite of these limitations and distortions, the history of Christianity provides us with powerful testimonies to the need to recognize the impulse toward world transcendence.

The task today is, by means of a dialogue with this tradition, to fashion an understanding of world transcendence that is faithful to the regulative dimension of the Christian faith while also sensitive to our contemporary moral situation (this is the subject of chapter ten). Ritschl's conviction that the purpose of transcending the world is to make possible our ethical life in the world is particularly worthy of attention in this respect, for it connects world transcendence in a powerful way to participation in the world.

The Tendency toward World Participation

Whereas the impulse toward world transcendence expresses the problematic nature of the world and the individual's need to go beyond it
in the quest for salvation, the impulse toward world participation
expresses the importance of the world as the context of ethical action.
World transcendence rests on the affirmation that the world is fallen.
World participation rests on the affirmation that, in spite of its fallenness, the world remains the good creation of God and the site of the
new creation. The twofold character of the ethical dimension thus
reflects the ambivalent attitude toward the world found in the doctrine
of creation. But this twofold character is not a simple opposition. The
world cannot be divided into good and evil parts or epochs. Instead,
world transcendence and world participation are related dialectically.
Neither in itself is the full truth of the ethical aspect of the doctrine of
creation. Taken separately, each is false and leads to distortions. It is
only the two together that give us the truth. This can be seen from
Ritschl's presentation of world transcendence, the purpose of which is
to enable us to live ethically *in* the world. Here world transcendence is
the ground of world participation.

World Participation in the Bible

One of the ways the Bible signals humankind's participation in the
world is its emphasis on humility and praise. Both arise from our sense
of being part of the created world that God has created. Both remind
us of our essential solidarity with other creatures and our difference
from the creator.

The importance of humility, mixed with fear and awe, comes to
poetic expression in the final chapters of Job. Throughout most of the
book, Job longs to locate God. God, he charges, has unjustifiably
harassed Job and has unaccountably refused Job's requests for an inter-
view so that Job could discover the reason for his torment. With
increasing frustration Job demands an audience with God so that
God's actions can be explained. Finally, in chapter 38 God appears—
enigmatically, in a whirlwind—and turns the tables on Job. Job
receives the encounter with God he had sought, but it is God who now

makes demands. In the space of four chapters, Job is reduced to a state of fear and trembling, for God's recitation of the mysteries of the world puts Job in his human but very humble place. In chapter 42 Job is forced to confess not only his ignorance but also his insignificant place in a universe he can scarcely begin to comprehend. Paradoxically, in spite of the threatening questions of God, who seemed ready to condemn Job for his insolence, God pronounces Job righteous (vv. 7-8). The lesson to draw from these chapters is that our encounter with the creator, which is at the same time an encounter with the incomprehensibility of creation, does not bring an answer to the sorts of questions we wish to pose to the creator. Instead, this encounter leads us to consider our finitude and our place in the created world.

The New Testament's version of this motif is found in the first chapter of Romans. According to verses 18-32, in spite of the fact that God's power and nature are knowable through created things, humankind (especially the Gentile world) has refused to honor God, to render thanks to God, and even to acknowledge God. From this basal sin has resulted the full range of human faults—envy, murder, strife, and so on. In other words, Romans represents sin principally as humankind's refusal to acknowledge God and its tendency to worship creatures in place of the creator. What the text here condemns is the tendency to subvert the relation between creator and creature, between infinite and finite, between the creatureliness of the creature and the deity of the creator. Accordingly, righteousness is represented as submitting to and trusting in the creator, the one "who gives life to the dead and calls into existence the things that do not exist" (4:17).

Related to humility is praise. Humankind is called on to praise God the creator for, as the book of Revelation shows, the reality and lordship of the creator are disputed in the human community. For human beings, therefore, praise is one of the forms that humility takes. To praise the creator is to acknowledge our place among the created things. Praise of the creator is essential to being human, for by participating in the same act of praise as does the rest of creation, we affirm our essential creatureliness. Praise, consequently, is the opposite of idolatry. As Ps 96:1, 4-5 explains, God is to be praised above all other gods, for whereas they are mere idols, God is the creator of the heavens in which these gods purportedly dwell. In the Bible, praise is due to God the creator precisely because God is the creator. The act of creation establishes a divide between the creator and the created world that forbids the worship of created things. Not surprisingly, the Gospels represent Jesus as exemplary with respect to the praise of God. The best illustration of this is the Lord's Prayer, in which Jesus begins with the wish that God's name be sanctified. John's Gospel makes this point by portraying Jesus as glorifying the Father by his ministry (e.g., John 17:4).

In summary, praise is an act of world participation, because we thereby take our place alongside other creatures and give testimony to the power and wisdom of God. Refusal to praise God is idolatry, because it means ignoring the distinction between creator and created world and, by implication, attempting to escape our finite humanity.

Another aspect of world participation disclosed in the Bible is wisdom. As noted in chapter three, above, Proverbs 8 and other biblical passages portray the creator as the wise architect and builder of the universe. But wisdom is not possessed only by the creator. Humankind is invited to share in God's wisdom by learning from the created order and becoming wise. Since the created world manifests God's wisdom, meditation on that world reveals wisdom and enables us to partake of it.

The wisdom of which the Bible speaks is closely linked with practical ethical activity.[30] For example, Proverbs 2 promises that those who receive God's wisdom will understand righteousness, justice, equity, and every other good thing (v. 8). This feature is grounded in God's own justice, which Ps 146:5-7 connects closely to God's act of creation: "Happy are those whose help is the God of Jacob . . . who made heaven and earth, the sea, and all that is in them; who keeps faith forever; who executes justice for the oppressed; who gives food to the hungry." Humankind, accordingly, is to emulate God by practicing acts of justice. To fail to do so is serious business, as Prov 14:31 indicates: "Those who oppress the poor insult their Maker, but those who are kind to the needy honor him." Furthermore, the practical activity of the wise is to be characterized by prudent and generous behavior in other ways as well. For instance, Prov 11:1 calls for the use of fair balances, and 12:10 urges considerate care for work animals. Other examples abound in Proverbs. Wisdom themes are not limited to the Old Testament, for the New Testament depicts Jesus as the embodiment of wisdom. The most overt such depiction is in 1 Cor 1:24, in which Paul flatly declares Christ to be the wisdom of God. But there are other indications in the New Testament.[31] Perhaps the clearest occurs in Matt 11:19, which seems to identify the Son of Man with divine wisdom. Certainly Jesus' ethical concern, for example, his call for right judgment (Matt 23:23 points to wisdom themes in his ministry).

In the Bible, to be wise is not an otherworldly attitude. It is to be actively involved in the things of this life and to be involved in ways that reflect God's own nature. To be wise is to live according to the wisdom with which God has created the universe. It is to fit our lives into a larger reality of which the whole created world partakes. Above all it is a matter of acting justly and seeking to bring about justice. It is in this way that wisdom, as the Bible understands it, is a mode of participating in the world.

A third aspect of world participation in the Bible is the belief that humankind has been created in the image of God. At first consideration, this belief might be thought to counteract any tendency toward world participation, at least if it is thought to imply our essential similarity with God. After all, no other creature in Genesis 1 is said to be created in God's image. In truth, however, the meaning of the image of God points directly to world participation, because humankind is to be God's image *in the world*. Genesis alludes to this when it associates the image with dominion over the rest of the created world.[32] Being God's image is therefore an exercise in world participation. Humans are here to cultivate the earth and to care for it. Although we have been given dominion over the earth, we must also render an account to the creator for its use. The Bible consistently represents humanity's task as a matter of participation in the world, not as flight from the world. To be sure, the New Testament, with its more pronounced apocalyptic view of things, has a diminished sense of worldly work as stewardship. Accordingly, it is important to preserve the canonical authority of the Old Testament, so that a misplaced emphasis on the New Testament does not result in an unbalanced theology.

In sum: the life of those who live by the doctrine of creation is one of humility, praise, wisdom, justice, and lived according to the image of God, Jesus Christ. Naturally, the way in which we understand these characteristics depends in part on our understanding of the doctrine of creation. That, in turn, depends on our intellectual context and on the present state of human knowledge. Nonetheless, these characteristics help to define the fundamental aspects of ethical world participation.

World Participation in the Christian Tradition:
Thomas Aquinas and Natural Law

Like the impulse toward world transcendence, the impulse toward world participation has developed in the history of Christian thought. One example of such development is Thomas Aquinas's understanding of natural law, which is an extension of the biblical conception of wisdom.

For Thomas, things in the created world are ruled by God's eternal law. This means that God has directed all things toward their proper ends, for example by instilling instincts into animals, so that they naturally but unthinkingly act in purposeful ways. God's directive activity, which results in the natural law, reflects God's creative wisdom. God stands in relation to the created world as the artisan stands in relation to the product. And just as the artisan's conception is the model for the product, so God's wisdom is the archetype of the natures of all things. Everything, in its own way, reflects the perfection of the creator. As the one who moves all things to their ordained ends, God is portrayed as a wise governor, with the result that the natural law is itself God's eternal wisdom in its role of directing all things to their ends.[33]

Even though every created thing is ruled by natural law, humans have a special relation to it. Humans, he argued, have a share of God's eternal reason. We participate in God's reason and so are able to employ our own rationality to distinguish between good and evil.[34] This has implications for human laws. If they are based on a right use of reason, then they are in conformity with natural law and reflect God's eternal law. To the extent that human laws deviate from right reason, then they are neither laws nor natural but simply cases of injustice.[35] As a result, human ethical activity is in accordance with God's eternal reason and wisdom to the extent that it conforms to natural law. But, as with all creatures, the natural law for humans pertains to the teleological ends that are endemic to human nature.

The world-participatory character of the ethics of natural law is seen when we consider these teleological ends. Relying on Aristotle's definition of goodness as an end that is sought,[36] Thomas argued that our reason recognizes as good and desirable all that to which we are naturally inclined. But there is a hierarchy of inclinations based on human nature. First, because we are living beings, we have inclinations that we share with all other living beings. For example, all entities pursue self-preservation. Accordingly, he asserted, natural law includes all means of preserving life. Then, because we participate also in animal life, we share some natural inclinations (for example, toward sexual intercourse and the rearing of offspring) with other animals. Third, because we are rational beings, we have distinctive inclinations, such as the desire to know God and to live socially with other humans.[37]

The theory of right reason and of natural law is an expression of human participation in the world. Each sort of inclination that is natural to humans is legitimate and, assuming that we abide by the dictates of right reason, none conflicts with the others. Each is capable of being satisfied in harmony with the law of the creator. With this theory, a way is opened to regard natural human life in positive terms. Thus created order, although subordinated to the supernatural, does not essentially contradict it.

World Participation in the Christian Tradition:

The Protestant Doctrine of Vocation

The Protestant version of world-participating ethics is associated with the term *vocation*. In the medieval Roman Catholic context, vocation referred to the religious life of the monk or the priest. In the view of such reformers as Martin Luther and John Calvin, the restriction of vocation to the religious life had the undesirable consequence of devaluing worldly occupations and daily human pursuits. They responded by enlarging the notion of vocation to include all sorts of occupations, both overtly religious and worldly.

For Luther all vocations are ordained by God.[38] Worldly vocations include being a parent, a servant or maid, a lord or subject, or, in general, any other office or duty of human life.[39] Rather than regarding these as merely human contrivances for purposes of convenience or utility, Luther saw them as divinely ordained for human well-being and therefore as intrinsically honorable and praiseworthy. Nor did Luther arrange these vocations hierarchically. Since each is ordained by God, those who fulfill these tasks are doing a holy work and are living as saints. Indeed, those who labor in legitimate vocations should feel great joy, knowing that they are glorious in the sight of God.[40] Luther went so far as to say that those who work in vocations are thereby holy. Whether lord or servant, a life of faithfulness in a vocation is a life of holiness before God. Mundane work is not only, as for Thomas, natural and legitimate; it is also a means of serving God and fulfilling the command of God.[41] Luther's conception, then, is a development of the Bible's conviction about the praise of God. All things as they perform their ordained functions are praise to God. For Luther, working faithfully in our vocations constitutes our holiness.

Apart from their benefits for the individual's standing before God, worldly vocations are the means that God has ordained for the preservation and functioning of society. When the vocations are well served, the result is stability, order, and social peace. Unfortunately, what Luther meant by order and stability is largely a matter of maintaining the social hierarchy. That is, the doctrine of vocations discouraged people from disrupting social boundaries by seeking to inhabit a higher class than is due. The doctrine ensures that people find solace in performing their tasks in life, no matter how humble, without scheming to usurp another's position. In this way, social peace is maintained.[42] Calvin, although equally committed to the need for peace and just as anxious about social disturbance, was somewhat more liberal in allowing for social mobility.[43] Because of the importance to society of maintaining peace, Calvin considered worldly government to be not only holy but actually the most holy and honorable of all the vocations.[44]

In spite of the socially conservative tenor of this doctrine, it is a legitimate expression of the world-participating aspect of the doctrine of creation. It legitimates and sanctifies daily work. According to Calvin, in performing our vocation, we can know that our lives are in conformity with God's will and only thus will they be "properly framed." We will be free of rash impulses because we will know ourselves to be in the station of life to which God has appointed us. The daily burdens of life will be endurable with the knowledge that whatever comes our way has been ordained by God. Finally, every aspect of work, even the most lowly, is adorned with value in the sight of God.[45]

Although we today rightly censure certain aspects of the doctrine of vocation, especially its static view of society and its unnecessary restrictions on individuals, it is not difficult to see that it, like Thomas's theory of natural law and right reason, is essentially an affirmative view of humanity's worldly life. In both Thomas's and the reformers' views there is an affirmation of this life even with the recognition that those who participate in it may not be a part of the redeemed people of God. For both, the natural order of life has its own integrity, is grounded in God's act of creation, and does not depend on the order of salvation, although its full development requires a positive relation with the economy of salvation.

Conclusion

It is important to retain the ethical dimension in any discussion of the doctrine of creation, because we face a constant temptation to interpret the doctrine as a theory about the natural world and especially about its origins. The practical aspect of the doctrine can be retained only if we continually advert to the ethical dimension, which unequivocally reminds us that the doctrine of creation is not principally a theory but necessarily includes, as do all theological doctrines, a definite way of being in the world. Although the doctrine has a cognitive aspect, it is not solely an intellectual account of the universe but also practice and life in the world. The ethical dimension reminds us of the connection in the Christian faith between verbal formulations of doctrine and the practice of doctrine.

There are also problems if the ethical dimension becomes the *only* emphasis in the doctrine of creation. It is important to remember the dialectical character of the doctrine of creation. Any loosening of the dialectics by emphasizing one function at the expense of the others results in serious distortion and imbalance. If the regulative dimension of the doctrine is lost, then the ethical loses its Christian character, as sometimes happens in the liberal theological tendency to reduce doctrine to its ethical dimension. It is then no longer a dialogue carried on with a particular tradition. If the hermeneutical dimension is lost, then the ethical can easily ossify into a rigid form of life that quickly becomes outdated because of its failure to engage in a dialogue with the various branches of human knowledge. Recent interest in ecological theology provides an illustration of the dependence of the ethical dimension on the hermeneutical. Until scientists became concerned about the environment, theologians showed little interest. But by listening to the emerging concerns of scientists, theologians have been able to open a new horizon in the ethical aspect of the doctrine of creation. It seems obvious that this horizon would not have been opened without the contribution of the hermeneutical dimension of the doctrine. Without input from scientific disciplines, even ethically sensitive theologians would likely have been oblivious to the issue of ecology.

The theological task today with regard to the ethical function is to maintain the dialectical balance of the doctrine. On one level, this means maintaining faithfulness to the doctrine of creation in its regulative dimension and also attending to the hermeneutical task by incorporating the results of scientific learning into the ethical function. On another level, it means maintaining the dialectical balance of the world-transcending and the world-participating tendencies. The theologian today must ask what it means to transcend the world and also how we are to participate in the world. This is the subject of chapter ten.

10

The Ethical Dimension
of the Doctrine of Creation Today

In the preceding chapter I suggested that there are two distinct impulses in the ethical dimension of the doctrine of creation, world transcendence and world participation. World transcendence denotes the necessity of overcoming the world and maintaining an ethical difference from the world. Participation in the world denotes not only the fact that we are a part of the world but also that we acknowledge our identity with and membership in the finite world. These two impulses are grounded in the trinitarian dialectics of identity and difference. I also suggested that the distinction between transcendence and participation expresses the ambivalence of the conception of *world*. Insofar as it is conceived of as fallen and as something morally or spiritually problematic, it is something we must transcend. Insofar as it is conceived of as God's good creation and the arena of the new creation, it is something of which we are a part. Finally, I argued that the historical forms that these impulses take depend on each culture's understanding of the world. This helps us see why Christian theology showed no more interest in environmental problems than did adherents of other religions and philosophies until the scientific community began to express concern. It was not the result of a moral obtuseness peculiar to Christianity but the fact that Christian ethical sensitivity in this matter depends in part on the state of scientific knowledge—on an understanding of the world in which environmental issues are recognized as urgent problems. It is the understanding of the world in terms of ecosystems and the effects of consumption and waste that has made it possible for Christians to recognize this additional component of their ethical responsibility. As a result, Christian theologians have understood the implications of the ethical dimension in various ways. The task in our current cultural situation with its distinctive problems is to think anew the implications and forms of world transcendence and participation.

What do world participation and world transcendence entail in our situation, especially as we meditate on the doctrine of creation? First, given the contextual nature of theology, it is important to specify that "our situation" means relatively affluent Christians in the industrial-technological societies, which are marked by high levels of production and consumption, modified free market economies, and democratic forms of government. In our situation perhaps the most urgent ethical issue relating to world participation is the state of the natural environment and the attitude and actions that we should take toward it. Concern for the environment is a matter of participation in the world, because we are tempted to misuse and degrade the natural environment mainly because we refuse to think of ourselves as a part of it. Identifying with the world by acknowledging both its goodness as God's creation and our own participation in it provides the theological (and utilitarian) grounds for a sound and sensitive ecological ethics. But there is more to the world than simply its character as the good creation of God. There is also the world that we, under the condition of sin, make for ourselves. In our cultural situation, one form that this world takes is designated by the term *consumerism*. It is a world marked by manic consumption that is required for national economies to sustain themselves. Such manic consumption, although lacking the dramatic quality of the demonized Roman Empire represented in the biblical book of Revelation, is nonetheless as great a threat to our well-being as the Roman Empire was to the early church. Accordingly, we are called on to resist it through ethical transcendence, just as Christians of earlier centuries were called on to transcend the human-made worlds in which they found themselves. Taking a cue from the theology of Albrecht Ritschl, however, the act of transcending the world is not an end in itself. It serves our participation in the world in two ways. On one hand, it frees us from the consumer mentality and thus reduces our expenditure of natural resources. On the other hand, transcending the consumer culture delivers us from our egocentric obsession with individual well-being and allows us to consider the good of the natural environment and other transindividual realities.

The Ethical Transcendence of the World

An Analysis of the World to Be Transcended

Before discussing what world transcendence means in our contemporary context, it may be helpful to indicate from a theological perspective why we are prey to the consumer-culture. As noted above in chapter five, human being is a project that always aims at some ideal form. As a result, our nature is not fully determined. Theologically expressed, we are created from nothing. Human being, in its distinctive features, has nothing substantial on which it rests. Although it presupposes our participation in the physical universe and the biological world, it is something beyond them and is not simply the result of their forces. It comes about as a project under construction in history. Our nature must be fashioned from usable materials of the past and from projected ideals. This means that we make decisions about the past and about how we will employ the past in the project of becoming human. It also means that we make decisions about the projected ideal that will guide our becoming human. But we have a tendency to engage in the task of becoming human in disregard of the knowledge of God and of God's command. We refuse to accept the ideal of human existence that God has set before us—the New Testament portrait of Jesus Christ—and the new past and new future that God gives to us. In short, we refuse to participate in the new creation. But, since human being is a project under construction, it is something to be created. If we refuse participation in God's new creation, then we must necessarily create ourselves out of our own resources. We must create our own past and project our own future. We then establish our own ideal of human being. Along with that ideal is a self-made world of meaning in which we dwell. Ultimately, however, the attempt to create ourselves and our world from our own self-made resources is destructive, for it makes human being the origin, center, and goal of all. It inevitably becomes narcissistic instead of theocentric. So, it is easy to see why the consumer-culture appeals to us, for it is a modern form of narcissism. It is the world that we are making for ourselves in our cultural situation.

One of the noteworthy aspects of this culture is the tendency to define the human person as a consumer of commodities.[1] Of course, humans *are* consumers of commodities, but it is characteristic of our world to narrow the conception of the human person until it is identical with "consumer." The person is seen as an abyss of needs and desires, the counterpart of which is the endless variety of commodities. We learn from advertising of urgent needs of which we were previously ignorant and are enticed into desires of which we formerly had no inkling. We learn, for instance, that we deserve vacations, which the airlines and tourism industry are ready to supply. We discover that problems hitherto insoluble can be fixed through technological advances. For example, loose skin around the eyes can be tightened with creams, which as a bonus provide a luminous finish for the skin. People from a technologically less sophisticated era may be shocked to discover the impossibility of living without such cutting-edge gadgets as mobile phones and the latest software. Financial freedom turns out to be around the corner if we subscribe to a bargain-basement wireless phone service. Filial guilt can be assuaged by buying Dad a Rolex watch.[2] The centrality of consumption and of the human being as consumer is illustrated by the fact that television advertising is not so much about the products being touted as it is about the consumers of those products. Advertisements do not reveal the defining characteristics of the product but instead disclose (and perhaps even induce) the anxieties and hopes of potential buyers. What is crucial for the advertising technician is not the virtues of the product but the problems of the consumer.[3] It could hardly be otherwise when the consumer is faced with so many more or less identical brands of consumer goods. Advertising the merits of a product would hardly differentiate one brand of toothpaste from another. Instead, the commercial focuses on consumers, informing them of needs and problems.[4] In summary, the world of consumers and consumption promises a new physical and psychological image that can be either purchased through the consumption of commodities or obtained through technology.

Not only are persons defined as consumers, but their relations are likewise defined in terms of consumption. For example, the relation of patient to physician is frequently turned into an instance of a consumer using a product, a tendency abetted but not completely caused by the trend toward health maintenance organizations being run strictly as businesses. Education likewise has become consumption, with students being no longer learners but consumers. Not surprisingly, the benefits of university education are usually explained in financial terms, with statistics showing the typical salary advantage of those with higher education over those without. In these cases, what has traditionally been an intimate relation between persons is now commonly represented as an economic relation between a consumer and the provider of a commodity. The fact that education and health care do not naturally lend themselves to being thought of as commodities seems increasingly to be beside the point. Even familial relations have not escaped. Mother's Day and Father's Day, which might be thought of as celebrations of natural ties, have become major opportunities for consumption, as we have become convinced that the surest sign of love and affection is the giving of consumer items.

Just as the human person is reduced to the single activity of consumption, so all things tend to be turned into commodities. Although *commodity* still has the technical meaning of goods (such as pork bellies and soybeans) bought and sold in enormous quantities, in fact we today tend to think of all manner of things and relations as commodities (even if we do not use the term itself): health care, education, and even religion. Even though we may cringe at the crass appeals for money on televised religious programs, such appeals are only the symptom of a culture-wide attitude. This attitude holds that we are consumers with spiritual needs that can be satisfied by the appropriate religious product. Entering the religious marketplace, the consumer of religion is faced with a bewildering variety of products and hence has no choice except either to sample or to make arbitrary choices. Churches, like physicians and educators, become providers of a product and religion becomes a commodity about which people make economic decisions as consumers based on their needs and desires. In a different way, news and information have become commodities, as the valiant struggle of network journalists to maintain autonomy from their corporate overlords demonstrates.

It is not only human relations that are commodified. Happiness, beauty, and a host of other ethereal qualities have become things subject to buying and selling. Much of this is indirect. Few would consciously acknowledge trying to buy happiness, but happiness is indirectly promised and sought by means of the purchase of consumer goods. In the case of beauty the aspect of commodity is more direct as the booming industry of plastic surgery offers a variety of medical procedures that promise to bring beauty for a price. In each case, our world promises an unending series of new experiences or some new technology that will fulfill some need. Of course, not everyone in our culture plays the role of consumer with fanatical devotion. Moreover, few are completely taken in by the power of advertising. In a culture dominated by images and advertising, however, the image may have a greater claim to reality than do concrete individuals.[5] With the power of the image this world does not need coercive political and military means to extend its sway. We willingly embrace it along with its materialistic ideology in spite of our knowledge of its techniques of persuasion and of the vacuity of its philosophy. We know that happiness cannot be bought and that spiritual and moral realities cannot be commodified. We know that the version of truth and reality proposed by this culture is false, and yet we find ourselves unable to resist entering into its world and living by its values. We see here the nature of sin. Sin is not something into which we are tricked or coerced but something we know to be false and destructive but to which we find ourselves yielding.

A preliminary and thoughtful theological response to the world of consumption has been provided by the Roman Catholic Church. In *Centesimus Annus*, it draws attention to the limitations of the consumer market by arguing that there are important human needs that cannot be supplied by commodities and that some good things cannot be treated like commodities. It also calls attention to the danger of an idolatry of the market, whereby all things are considered important only insofar as they conform to the logic of the consumer market.[6] The language of idolatry suggests that the world we have made for ourselves possesses a truly if distorted religious character. Its religious nature is more evident if we think of religion not only as certain types of ceremonies, customs, and beliefs but as an interpretation of reality in which issues of truth and value are decided. The consumer world is, in fact, an interpretation of reality or, more accurately, the creation of a world of meaning. In it human beings learn what they are—consumers—and what is real—commodities. They are also taught what is true, namely, the image, for in this culture it is the image above all that constitutes reality. Besides all this, this world does in fact have many of the overt trappings of religion. It has ceremonies (such as beauty pageants and the Super Bowl), in which cultural ideals are set forth in powerful images and linked to advertised commodities. It has official representatives (celebrities) who embody its ideals. It is associated with a distinctive set of practices (buying and consumption) by which one participates sacramentally in this world and is validated in it.

Centesimus Annus goes on to argue for the necessity of transcending a merely economic understanding of human nature. In an economic view, there is no way of distinguishing genuine human needs from those that have been artificially induced and that may be obstacles to human development.[7] If human beings are considered mainly or totally as consumers and everything else is a commodity, the result is a leveling of all things and values. In this process the only thing that counts is the satisfaction of needs and desires through the consumption of commodities. The intrinsic importance of those needs and the relative value of commodities do not enter into consideration, for every commodity by definition satisfies some need or desire, and needs and desires are considered solely in themselves, not in relation to some other aspect of human well-being. The origin of these needs and desires, their validity, and their place in human life and society likewise fall outside of notice.

It is therefore ironic that this world of ours, especially in its union with the free-market economy, is regarded as a great triumph over the planned-market economies of the cold war communist regimes. In fact, the proliferation of consumer goods and our extraordinarily high level of consumption are often held up as proof of the superiority of our world to others. Of course, there is no denying that an economy in which people's basic needs are satisfied is superior to one in which they are not. A free market may also be an important buttress for political democracy. But the issue at hand is not the merits or liabilities of the free market in itself but instead the character of the world of meaning that we have created for ourselves. *Centesimus Annus* argues that the distinction between our world and that of Marxist regimes of the twentieth century is insignificant in light of their more profound philosophical similarity. Although our world of consumption has indeed generated a higher material standard of living, it has brought with it a reductionistic philosophical materialism every bit as insidious as that characterizing communist regimes. By reducing human beings to the status of consumer and all other things to the status of commodity, it shows itself to be, like Marxism, a variety of materialism.[8]

As a result of our acquiescence to the world of consumption, we have suffered what can be described from a theological perspective only as a trivialization of human life. Whereas human life might be about the questions of human existence and God, we find ourselves obsessed with pleasure and comfort and with gadgets promised to deliver pleasure and comfort.[9] Television is both a symptom and cause of this trivialization, for in it everything is consistently represented as entertainment. Even profound philosophical issues and wrenching moral dilemmas are put to work in the service of show business.[10] Nor is televised news exempt from the process of trivialization. Television would seem to be an ideal medium for the communication of information. It can present news within seconds of its occurring, and it specializes in vivid images. But it delivers material to us that can have the mere and deceiving appearance of information, for news of important events comes to us in small, disconnected bits that lack a context that would make it meaningful to us.[11]

As human being comes to be defined in terms of consumption and things become commodities for consumption, consumption comes to have a life (or logic) of its own and to become an end in itself. Hence the "shop till you drop" mentality. This is not just a catchy phrase; it illustrates one of the most dominant behaviors of our culture, one with its own religious and symbolic functions and one of our most popular forms of therapy. Given the vast range of commodities to purchase and our large amount of disposable income, it is no wonder that shopping has become one of our most characteristic activities. In earlier times, shopping afforded people an opportunity to get out of the house for a purpose other than work. Now, however, with the various shopping channels on television and with the growth of shopping and banking on the Internet, even the home is a commercial location. In preindustrial Europe the home was a place of production where small crafts were manufactured. Now the home is a place where commercial transactions occur in an antiseptic electronic setting. Not surprisingly, shopping has become a kind of competitive sport, with magazines such as *Consumer Reports* devoted to helping us hone our skills.

The logic of consumption is ordered by the concepts of novelty and quantity. Since the well-being of the national economy demands that consumers spend their disposable income, it is necessary for commodities to be packaged as "new" so that consumers have a reason to continue spending and accumulating without the sense that they are buying the same goods again and again as when the new item on fast-food menus is unveiled with a media ceremony. Although there are only so many ways to prepare a hamburger and even though it would seem that all those ways have already been discovered, the word *new* consecrates the item for the consumer as something that is needed because of its sheer novelty, not because it satisfies certain nutritional requirements. Whereas novelty encourages accumulation of commodities over time, the concept of quantity aims at inducing an instantaneous increase in consumption. This is the strategy behind the practice of fast-food restaurants that offer to double the portion of food for only a marginal increase in cost. Although few of us need that extra helping of food for nutrition, the consumer mentality forbids us from passing up a bargain. Just as sellers can make money by selling in volume, so we have been persuaded to be good consumers by purchasing in volume.

The problem with the logic of novelty and quantity is that there seems to be no end. No matter what we buy, there will always be something newer and, presumably, better. With consumption an end in itself, there are no norms that tell us when to stop. Without a more adequate view of human being, there is no way of discerning when the sequence of novel commodities has exhausted true novelty and when the quantity of consumable items exceeds our true need for consumption. In other words, the consumer culture, which seems predicated on the satisfaction of needs and desires, is in truth founded on dissatisfaction. If consumers were suddenly to decide to be content with their current supply of consumer goods and to forgo further purchases until those goods were fully used up, the shock to the national economy would be incalculable. The economy works only if our level of dissatisfaction is great enough to induce us to buy what is new and to do so in large quantities. We must be convinced that what we have is not good enough. We must be dissatisfied. Although humankind has been acquisitive from the beginning, it is characteristic of our world that it has found a way to create dissatisfaction consistently and then provide means of addressing that dissatisfaction, means that in turn create more dissatisfaction.[12]

The consuming self has two distinctive features that deserve further exposition. First, we understand ourselves to be autonomous persons who exercise free choice. Second, we understand ourselves to be individuals.

The consuming self is the latest in a series of self-conceptions characteristic of the modern era, in which the subject, its fulfillment, and its power of choice have become first principles. The consuming self represents a maximum of subjectivity, for its own needs and desires are the basis not only of its own life but also of the national economy and of the entire world of meaning. Self-satisfaction and self-fulfillment are the highest values, to be achieved by choosing. Whether those choices are for material goods or moral and spiritual paths, the self's choice is the primary thing. Choice is understood as the power to select autonomously among alternatives. And this conception of freedom, which has a long history, takes on new meaning in an age when the range of alternative goods is unprecedented and institutional guidance in making choices is discounted.

But this notion of choice is in truth a false freedom. Although it is true that we may choose from a nearly unbounded range of alternatives, this capacity to choose is from a theological perspective an emaciated and even dangerous conception of freedom. It is in fact an abstract sort of freedom, because it has been torn from the wholeness of human life and isolated from the rest of our existence. The results, in the words of *Centesimus Annus,* are alienation and oppression.[13] Additionally, the conception of freedom as the power of alternative choice falls far short of the Christian view that true freedom consists in a life of obedience to God. Only such a life corresponds to our true being. Our self-made world's conception of freedom alienates the power of choice from the totality of our being and unleashes destructive power, just as any aspect of our lives, when cut off from the rest, can in isolation turn against us.[14] This conception of freedom proves to be self-alienating and a symptom of our alienation from God.

What is paradoxical about this conception of freedom is not only that it is inadequate but also that it hides our essential lack of freedom. While convincing ourselves that we have this unlimited and uncoerced power of choice, we make ourselves vulnerable to the subtle pressure of advertising and other cultural images. The accomplishment of modern advertising has been to convey and reinforce our conviction that we are free while simultaneously using all manner of stratagems to manipulate our needs and to create new and thoroughly unnecessary desires. So, while we are free in the restricted sense that we can choose from any number of types of fast food, the conditioning we have undergone that makes us desire fast food has constrained those choices in impressive ways.

The consuming self is represented not only as free but also as an individual. This means that consumption is more than just an economic phenomenon; it is one of the dominant factors in the formation of social relations.[15] In contrast to collective forms of social organization, in which the basic unit is the family or clan and one's identity arises in connection with family and other social relations, our world is populated with individual consumers who are united not by social and familial bonds but by economic bonds and by their capacity to participate actively in the world of consumption.

The excessive individualizing of the person in a consumer culture is illustrated by the fate of some of the ideals of the women's movement. Notions such as liberation and equality, which originally had distinctly political meanings, have been pressed into service by the advertising and commodity industry. Their strategy, according to Susan J. Douglas, has been to take these social-political ideals and turn them into personal-individual ideals. Instead of being elements of a political agenda, they are now presented as components of the self-fulfillment of individual women. Freedom has became permission to indulge oneself narcissistically and to seek fulfillment of private desires.[16]

The individualism of the consumer culture is, in the analysis offered by *Centesimus Annus,* a falsehood, for such a person is alienated from genuine human community and from fellowship with God. The society composed of such individuals is inadequate, because the prevailing conception of the person inhibits the sort of community in which genuine human life is possible.[17] Although we are promised that authentic existence is to be obtained by the fulfillment of individually felt needs and desires, this is in fact the path that leads to destruction, for we do not realize that this ideal is an artificial production of our own making.

The world of consumers and commodities is a world created and projected by us. At the heart of this creative and projecting activity lies the advertising image. Our world presents its ideals, its vision of human life, and its picture of reality through the images of advertising and the various media. To be sure, images have always been important in culture. Ancient Greek and Roman societies set forth their ideals in statues of the gods; the Christian church has used icons to represent its convictions. Today, the image has been connected to a different conception of human being—the consumer—and to the consumer's typical activities. It is by means of the image that desires and needs are stimulated and in some cases produced. Images coordinate and regulate the production of consumer desire and the production of commodities.

It could be otherwise. Advertising could be primarily informative, relying on propositional forms of communication. But in the television era the proposition has been largely replaced by the image.

Instead of providing information, advertising images create for us an ideal world, centered on the consumer's need and the product's capacity for satisfying that need. It associates the product with ideal images of human life.[18] To this end, the people and physical settings of these images are uniformly attractive, far more so than is typical in our daily experience of people and physical surroundings. It is by the power of these attractive images portraying an ideal life that we are convinced that we need everything from liposuction to the latest, most technologically sophisticated brand of dish soap.

The image is not only instrumental in fashioning consumers but also determines how we experience the world. Television, again, is instructive, for it has become our chief source of information, in spite of its being primarily a medium for entertainment. Yet we depend on it for information in a way in which we depend on no other entertainment medium. No one would think, for example, of learning of governmental policies from the movie or recording industry. Television has become a (perhaps the) dominant form of contact with the world.[19] The result is that we come to expect reality to have the sort of characteristics that it has on television. Local television news, for example, typically does not report the day's happenings by means of verbal discourse but consists of a series of on-the-scene video shots of events or people describing events. Presidential debates likewise do not consist in an exchange of ideas but are structured by the sort of reality that television specializes in—images. Today we expect experience to have a strongly visual, imagelike character. This might explain the growing use of videotapes and other visual media in education and the common complaint that academic lectures are both boring and passé.

Ultimately, the images of this world coalesce to constitute a systematic symbolic order in which values, truth, and reality are determined. It provides a vision of the human life well-lived and even proposes to supply the institutions and mechanisms by which the components of that life can be obtained.[20] What is most striking about this symbolic order is the combination of its ideal character and its visual orientation. It is an ideal world in the sense that it presents problems and then immediately offers solutions to them in the form of consumer products. In this ideal world there are no problems that a commodity cannot solve. At the same time, this order is mediated to us by means of images, frequently images of stunning beauty and desirability. But even here the ideal quality of this order is evident, for both the beautiful people of the images and the images themselves are the result of considerable technological effort and expense devoted to erasing any imperfection of nature.

As a result, just as we are alienated from our bodies, from God, and human community, so we are alienated from the natural world. Consumption on the scale encouraged by our culture signals our separation from nature. We simply don't know where the material for all of our commodities comes from. If we did know the source and its limitations and the environmental cost of procuring the materials, then we might have a different perspective on the value of unrestricted consumption. As it is, however, we live in a world of images, not of natural processes and things. Nature itself is mediated to us by images in magazines and television. This separation from nature was necessary for a consumer culture to come about, for it is doubtful that a people who were conscious of being dependent on nature would find value in a continuous quest for novelty and the consumption of ever-increasing quantities of goods. In turn, the emphasis on novelty and quantity gives rise to the phenomenon of built-in obsolescence. A wide range of consumer goods these days resists repair and demands instead to be thrown away and replaced. In this phenomenon we see perhaps the clearest link between the consumer culture and our environmental problems.[21]

A Trinitarian Ethics of World Transcendence

If we can describe the world that we are to transcend, how can we shape an ethics of world transcendence based on the trinitarian God of the new creation?

In 1 Cor 8:6 God, the Father, is said to be the one *from* whom all things come to be and for whom we exist. This verse affirms that God is the creator and that our lives should be directed toward God. Although God is the creator of the finite universe in its totality, it is good for us if God is also the creator of the world of meaning in which we live. As it is, humankind manifests a persistent tendency to make worlds of its own that prove to be destructive and even demonic. This verse calls us to transcend our self-created worlds and to accept the new world that God is creating. It is only as we orient ourselves to God and transcend the world that we avoid the temptation to create worlds of our own making.

The model that guides us in transcending the world is Jesus Christ, the Son. The doctrine of creation asserts that humankind is the image of God; however, we are a distortion of that image, since we exist under the condition of sin. The New Testament presents Jesus Christ as the true image of God. He is the true humanity, for his being was to know and obey God. Because his life stands in contrast to the images of the good life that we have created for ourselves and that we try to achieve by acquisition and affluence, it is he who should be our model and not the cultural images that we have created. Jesus Christ is the new creation and the eruption into history of the true and restored image of God. Our participation in the new creation means being renewed in the image that is Christ.

Concretely, participation in the new creation and being renewed in the image of Christ means living in the kingdom of God by the power of God's Spirit. The kingdom that Jesus preached and introduced was in his day the reversal of the world's values. In this kingdom the first would be last and the last would be first. Those who would lead must become servants. The poor are blessed, the rich are judged. Life in the kingdom through the power of the Spirit today must be equally committed to the reversal of values to the extent that the world's values inculcate not knowledge of God but ignorance of God. Life in the kingdom through the power of the Spirit means accepting Jesus as the authentic image of God. It means striving to be renewed according to this image and to accept his life as the authentic vision of the good life. This life takes social form in the community of the church, a community that seeks to transcend the world by becoming aware of its destructive and idolatrous nature, by devising strategies for transcending it and by cultivating a life based on Jesus as the authentic image of God in contrast to the self-made images of our culture. The church is to offer the world an alternative world of meaning, one reflecting God's kingdom instead of distorted human ideals. Above all, the kingdom of God calls us to a life of love, which is oriented to the good of others and to our participation in something that transcends narrowly conceived human desires.

With this in mind, we are in a position to see the truth of previous attempts at transcending the world in the Christian tradition. As noted in chapter nine, in early Christianity world transcendence took the form of apocalypticism. Although the apocalyptic worldview is not an option for most of us today, it has a valuable contribution to make to the ethics of world transcendence. It indicates in a powerful way that the fallen world has transindividual aspects, that the fallen world is not simply a collection of individuals with problems. On the contrary the truly problematic aspect of the fallen world is the fact that its fallenness is transparent to us. Because it so envelops us and shapes us, it distorts our capacity to see its destructive effects. The fallenness of the world is thus different from the oppression of a despotic regime in which it is possible to identify those at the top who make obviously harmful decisions. The fallen world is something that we have all contributed to and in which we all live. Apocalypticism reminds us that the world's fallenness forms a system of which we are all a part and which is so pervasive that we do not notice its effects.

The ascetic tradition in Christianity likewise contributes to our attempt to transcend the world today. Although asceticism has been popularly associated with the belief that the body and all material things are evil or at least dangerous to the soul, we may regard this belief as a distortion of the legitimate insight that danger lies in the inordinate desire for finite realities of all sorts. It is not the body that is evil but the desire for bodily pleasures that threatens the soul's well-being. It is not youth, beauty, wealth, and power that are evil, but rather our fixation on obtaining them and making them the highest or even sole good in life. The ascetic tradition, then, has much to teach us about the vital importance of freeing ourselves from desires, especially when these desires have been artificially induced by commercial interests. This tradition can also remind us of the importance of practical disciplines that are effective in overcoming inordinate desire.

The contribution of mysticism to the task of world transcendence today is twofold. First, the mystical tradition reminds us that human good cannot be reduced to our physical and emotional well-being and that the source of our good lies beyond the finite world. It warns us against seeking our ultimate good in creatures and it continually directs our attention to the true source of that good. Second, at the same time this tradition refuses to denigrate the finite and the physical but regards the finite as that which mediates God to us. For the mystic, the finite is a transparent medium that conveys to us the God who cannot be seen. The mystical tradition testifies to the fact that overcoming the world does not mean leaving the world behind but consists in seeing the world rightly in its relation to God.

Finally, the theology of Albrecht Ritschl has the enduring value of pointing out that our transcendence of the world is not a flight from the world or a quietistic detachment from the world. God calls us to be agents with God in the new creation, a role that can be ours only as we are free of the world's spiritual hold on us. We are called to transcend the world so that we may authentically participate in the world without the distorting effects of sin.

Ethical Participation in the World

Introduction

I have described the principal theological objection to the world of consumption. But we should not overlook the secondary objection that this world engenders unfortunate consequences because of its false orientation to the natural environment. In its own way it perpetuates the dualistic separation of humankind from the natural world that has characterized both modern and premodern Western civilization. This orientation declares that the natural world exists primarily as an object of use and that its value consists totally in its capacity to generate raw materials for commodities. As a result, the consumer mentality is complicit in our environmental problems. Although the extraordinary levels of consumption characteristic of technological and consumer-oriented societies are not the sole or perhaps even the main cause of our environmental difficulties, they do contribute to it. More significant than consumption itself are the underlying beliefs of the world of consumption about the natural world and humankind's relation to the natural world. Because these underlying beliefs are pervasive, it is necessary to reframe the issue of environmental problems. It is not sufficient to employ prudential or utilitarian considerations as a premise for environmental policy. Although these may be effective rhetorical and political strategies, they can fall within and perpetuate the narcissistic and consumer mentality that contributes to our environmental problems. A prudential or utilitarian approach, if it portrays ethical decisions only in terms of what is good for humankind or the individual, may perpetuate a view of the natural world that is both theologically objectionable and environmentally perilous. We need a better rationale for environment ethics, one that helps us overcome the narcissism inherent in our condition.

To transcend the world presented by the consumer-oriented culture does not mean abandoning or negating the world that remains God's creation. On the contrary, we are called to participate in this world. My purpose in this section is to describe the general implications of world participation for environmental ethics. Certain matters of critical importance to environmental ethics cannot be considered in this context, for example, an enumeration and description of current ecological problems, a complete diagnosis of the causes of these problems, and proposals for policies and political agendas. In lieu of a fuller treatment, I refer the reader to authors who have developed these topics in greater detail.[22]

The first step in offering a theological view of environmental ethics is an apologetic one. It is necessary to state forthrightly that neither the Bible nor Christianity is the cause or at least the only cause of our ecological problems. This is not to deny the role that Christians individually and corporately have played in such problems. Sins of omission and commission abound and have been found in every era. But there is no sound historical basis for claiming that the biblical-Christian tradition is inherently antagonistic toward the natural environment and that it induces in its adherents an unusually destructive attitude toward the world. Many have undertaken to establish this point, and I will not repeat their arguments or their refutations. But I do want to underline the contextual nature of this tradition. The Bible and most Christian literature were written before there was an ecological problem or before it became known. As a result, such writings—up to a few decades ago—may not offer much direct support for ecology. Further, some teachings of the Bible and traditional theology may, when interpreted in a certain way, easily be taken to support a rapacious attitude toward nature. For these reasons, it is vital that we keep in mind the contextual and occasional nature of biblical and theological writings. Not surprisingly, ecological concern lay beyond their hermeneutical horizon. This is not to say that Christian theology has no resources for addressing ecology but only that such resources do not consist of explicit statements. Instead of scouring the Bible in support of sound environmental ethics, an alternative strategy is to approach our ecological responsibility from the perspective of world participation as discussed in chapter nine.

The Elements of World Participation

One aspect of world participation is humility and the praise of God. Although it is evident that we do in fact participate in the world, it is an act of humble obedience to acknowledge and affirm this factual participation by means of ethical and spiritual activity. By doing so we recognize both our essential finitude and God's status as creator.

It is a lesson in humility to learn that we are rooted in the physical universe and biological world and consequently are a part of the world. Human beings are not exceptions to the cosmic rules but instead exemplifications of those rules in particular circumstances and at an advanced level of structural organization. Even life in the kingdom of God is not a contradiction of our participation in the universe. It presupposes that participation. As a result, it is difficult to sustain the view (which recurs often in the history of human thought) that humankind is metaphysically and utterly distinct from the rest of the world. Nothing in Christian theology supports the view that humankind is essentially different from the rest of creation. Although the Christian tradition does insist on the special status of humankind before God, such status does not nullify our status as creatures and our solidarity with and connection to the rest of the world. In short, we are the world in one form of organization.

Hence we must reject an anthropocentric interpretation of the universe. But immediately we must confront the apparently anthropocentric character of the Bible. By this I mean the tendency of the Bible to focus on human affairs and to portray God's relation to the world almost exclusively in terms of its impact on human well-being. Without question, social, political, and economic—that is, human—matters far outweigh cosmic and other concerns in the Bible. Further, scholarly interpretations of the Bible have over the years augmented this sense of the Bible's anthropocentric character. Interest in the Bible's view of nature was, until recently, far from the attention of biblical scholars, whose main preoccupation was with God's intervention in *human* history. Another factor here was the concern of scholars to distinguish Israel from its neighbors by portraying the latter as pagans, whose religion was based on nature, in contrast to Israel, whose God utterly transcended nature.[23] Today, however, a more balanced view has emerged, with many biblical scholars concerned to show that the Bible does not have an anthropocentric viewpoint. For example, Bernard Anderson states that Genesis in no way teaches that the world exists merely for the sake of human beings but presents us with a world in which each sort of entity, including humankind, has a place and function assigned to it by God. The effect of this is to locate humankind relative to other beings and not in absolute distinction from them. He also calls attention to the cadence of the first chapter of Genesis, with its preliminary climax on the third day (the furnishing of the earth with vegetation) and with a second climax on the sixth day (the creation of land animals, including humankind). The emphasis, he argues, is not on the status of humankind but instead on the earth as a habitat and home for all living things. He also finds it significant that terrestrial animals and humans are both created on the sixth day, a literary device that also tends to undercut any conception of humankind as utterly distinct from the rest of nature.[24]

If we abandon an anthropocentric metaphysics, then we must admit that the universe had a history with God before humankind's appearance and will presumably have a history with God if humankind ever disappears. Although we cannot imagine what the history between God and the universe is apart from our relation to God and to the universe, the doctrine of creation affirms that God's relation to the universe does not depend on us and in certain ways does not involve us. Consequently, the universe does not exist for us. The drama of this conclusion should not be overlooked. From ancient times until recently, humankind's intellectual horizon was centered on our own existence. Even the Copernican revolution did not substantially change this viewpoint. Although as a result of astronomical studies we acknowledged that we are not the center of the physical universe, we preserved our metaphysical status by locating ourselves at the pinnacle of value. In this way we were able to maintain a fundamental distinction between human being and other sorts of being. For theological as well as scientific reasons, however, we must see ourselves as a part of the universe, not the center.

Acknowledging this is more than an act of intellectual humility, it is also an act of piety. To enter into the new creation means to acknowledge our own creaturely status and to recognize that God alone is uncreated. Such acknowledgment means that we must leave behind the domain of sin in which we create a world for ourselves. It is to acknowledge our solidarity with the rest of the created world. It is to relinquish a false sense of lordship or ownership and instead to stand in the presence of God with the rest of the created world in the act of praise. This does not rule out the Bible's keen sense of humankind's distinctive importance in relation to God, nor does it imply that all things stand on the same level of value. It is sound Christian judgment to assert that exploitation of minerals is far less a moral and spiritual concern than is the destruction of organic life. Likewise, extinction of a species has greater consequences than does the death of an individual animal. Moreover, affirming our participation in the world does not rule out acting in our own self-interest. Like all living beings, we inevitably use other entities as instruments for our own well-being. Some parts of the world are more directly pertinent to our well-being. Nonetheless, because we are part of a system and because our good depends on the well-being of that system (or at least of that portion most directly pertinent to us), there is no justification for an attitude that treats the rest of the created world as though it exists for our benefit alone. We do not have sovereign rights of ownership over the universe, except as we selfishly take them to our own destruction. A helpful recent suggestion has been offered. Building on Martin Buber's distinction between I-thou and I-it relations, H. Paul Santmire has proposed the category of I-ens relations to describe our relation to nonhuman beings. Unlike the I-thou relation, our relation with the ens may not be reciprocal. At the same time, the ens is more than just an instrument available for human use, as in the I-it relation. Santmire wishes the concept of the I-ens relation to denote an attitude whereby we contemplate the world of nature as something created by God with its own integrity and value. Included in this attitude would be a sense of gratitude for this natural world, a sense that would exclude our usual greed.[25] Thoughts such as these can help us attain reverence for the God who made all and who makes all things new. Such reverence demands that we care for the world of which we are a part and on which we depend and also that we abnegate our false claims to ownership.

The obverse of humility is praise. Praise is directed to God because God is the creator—the one from whom are all things and for whom are all things. We should understand this praise to be more than vocal proclamation of God's greatness, more than a subjectively intended act. We should, with the Bible, think of praise as the greatness of God reflected in finite beings when they fill their place in the created world. On this understanding, praise is an act of all creatures. Although we tend to think of praise as a cognitive and volitional act and therefore as a human act, the Bible persistently portrays the whole of the created world offering praise to God. Psalm 148 calls on all creation to praise God. Sun, Moon, stars, the heavens, the waters above the heavens, sea monsters and the deeps, fire, hail, snow, frost, wind, mountains, hills, fruit trees, cedars, wild animals, cattle, creeping things, and birds are successively commanded to praise the creator. The New Testament ends with this same motif, with Rev 5:13-14 recounting the offering of praise to God and to the lamb of God by every creature in heaven, on the earth, under the earth, and in the sea. We must regard these passages as more than mere anthropomorphism. The regular course of the created universe is in itself a testimony to God's power and wisdom. For this reason, Ps 19:1-4 can announce that "the heavens are telling the glory of God; and the firmament proclaims his handiwork. Day to day pours forth speech, and night to night declares knowledge." Accordingly, Psalm 104 links together praise and God's wisdom as it enumerates the works of God in their mystery and their harmony. As creatures behave according to their natures, they exhibit the wisdom of God and thereby offer praise to God. Praise, therefore, is not simply a verbal act. It is identical with the being of creatures that shows forth the greatness of God. Each entity, in its distinctive role and in its part in the whole, is a mode of praise to God as it participates in the Trinity. For humans (in the distinctly human aspect of our existence), praise takes the form of verbal utterance and faithful observance of our duties.

The universe of finite beings, then, in whole and in part, is a praise to the greatness of God. Terence Fretheim has argued that this understanding of praise can inform a Christian environmental ethics insofar as it makes us sensitive to the role that each entity plays in God's world and to humankind's capacity to compromise and even destroy components of the universe's silent choir of praise.[26] Each being has a distinctive part to play in the universal symphony. Diminishing one part of the cosmic symphony (by environmental destruction and species extinction) reduces the unity and richness of the whole.[27] Consequently, all created things possess an intrinsic value that transcends the instrumental value they may have for human use.

Humility and praise, accordingly, are important antidotes to the concept of ownership prevalent in the consumer culture. In this conception, anything that is owned, such as land or forest, is at the complete disposal of the owner. The biblical view, on the contrary, is that the universe is God's. God has given us use of the world but not ownership. This conviction introduces a note of responsibility about our use of the world.

Another aspect of world participation is associated with the concept of being created in the image of God (Gen 1:28). This verse asserts that humankind is created in God's image and that God has given us dominion over all other creatures. In spite of the long history of discussion concerning the image of God, the immediate context encourages us to connect being created in the image with being granted dominion. The problem is that dominion appears to offer a biblical warrant for the exploitation of nature. As a resource for the contemporary religious life, it remains problematic insofar as it seems to grant to humankind license to exploit the natural environment. Accordingly, care must be taken lest we misunderstand the nature of this dominion. The human tendency toward self-aggrandizement can easily find in this notion a justification for rapacious behavior toward the earth and its inhabitants.

Contemporary biblical scholars, however, have shown that this conclusion is unwarranted. It is true that the Hebrew word for dominion has violent connotations in some of the contexts in which it appears. For example, it can describe a king trampling down foreigners. What is decisive, however, is not its lexical meaning but its meaning in context. In fact there is a notable absence of violence in the first chapter of Genesis, humans not being given permission by God to eat animals until after the flood in the ninth chapter. It is also significant that the same word is used in Gen 1:16, where the sun and moon are placed in the sky in order to rule (i.e., have dominion) over the day and the night. Here the word is clearly not associated with violence.[28]

How has this passage affected Christian thought about nature?[29] In the opinion of James Barr, it is unlikely that it had much effect on the idea of nature, for most Christian exegesis of Gen 1:28 understood the image of God to be our possession of a rational soul and not our exercise of dominion. Or it was understood as an allegory about the need to conquer the animalistic elements of the human character.[30] Dominion, he avers, became a point of discussion only when scholars stopped interpreting the image of God in terms of a rational soul.[31] Even when dominion was a matter of interest, it was not taken to imply humankind's mastery over nature or the right to radically reshape nature but was understood to sanction the sort of limited use of nature that had been prevalent for centuries.[32] To whatever extent nature was modified in the Middle Ages, for example, such use was motivated more by fundamental human needs than by religious considerations.[33]

Scholars are agreed that dominion did not receive the meaning of mastery over nature until the rise of modern science in the seventeenth century, when dominion came to be linked to the notion of scientific progress and to the power of technology.[34] Another contributing factor may have been Protestant theology, which favored the plain sense of Scripture over the allegorical. In the medieval allegorical view, physical things (and not just words) possessed meaning, for they were thought, like words, to refer to objectives realities. In a Protestant setting, however, things were not like words and so had no intrinsic meaning; stripped of their allegorical meaning, things could have only an instrumental purpose in the service of human well-being.[35]

One modern way of interpreting dominion favorably is to identify it with stewardship. Psalm 24:1 reminds us that the earth is God's, suggesting that, even though God is said in Psalm 115 to have given the earth to humankind, this grant has more the character of a loan than a gift. At any rate, Genesis understands humankind to have been placed on earth as in a garden in order to cultivate it (2:15). Although the Bible does not elaborate on this theme, it is no injustice to the Bible for us to think of this cultivation as a matter of caring for the well-being of the earth and its inhabitants. Even the New Testament is aware of our responsibility to God for this care. Revelation 11:18 asserts that with God's eschatological wrath comes the time when God will destroy those who destroy the earth. Although it is unlikely that John the seer had today's ecological sensitivity, it is not inconsistent with this statement and the Bible's teaching about stewardship to interpret them in ecological terms.

With the concept of stewardship, the emphasis is placed on humankind's responsibility to care for the natural world. In this view, humans are to manage the earth in the place of God. As such, our management must testify to God's lordship and must be of the same benevolent character as God's rule. Such an interpretation has the added bonus of illuminating the notion of being created in God's image. If humankind, as steward, exercises dominion in the place of God, then we are God's representatives, an idea not far from the ancient concept of image.[36] It makes much more sense (in the Bible's frame of reference) to interpret the image of God in this way than to see it as our possessing a rational soul. But even the notion of steward-ship contains plenty of interpretive latitude. It does not in itself fully determine our ethical responsibilities. Up until the last couple of decades, the common view was that stewardship was a matter of man-aging nature wisely and benevolently in order to sustain human life.[37] Dominion, in this view, is not a matter of letting nature take its course, for such a tactic would mean accepting starvation as an apparently natural solution to food shortages.[38] Technology, accordingly, would not be our main problem but rather the solution, for the goal would not be to return the earth to a state of nature but to use technology carefully in the service of human well-being.[39]

Contemporary theologians are much less impressed with this idea of stewardship. Richard Bauckham, for one, conjectures that the con-cept of stewardship cannot be successfully divorced from our modern obsession with technology and from the assumption that humans are fundamentally different from the rest of the natural world.[40] As a result of this sort of thinking, Christian thought in the last two decades has shifted the emphasis from management of and intervention into the environment to its preservation and protection. The concept of stew-ardship, at least in its modern development, connotes that nature exists in two states, either a humanly maintained garden or a wasteland wrought by human misuse. Contemporary theologians are eager to find an alternative to this choice.

A way forward in understanding the concepts of the image of God and dominion appears if we advert to the principle that Jesus Christ is the image of God in the primary sense (2 Cor 4:4 and Col 1:15). This christological interpretation of the conception of the image of God points the way toward an adequate appropriation of the notion of dominion today. If Jesus Christ is the image of God, then it is he who determines the meaning of dominion over nature and of power more generally. Gospel statements indicating that power is not to be abused but used in humble servitude suggest how the notion of dominion can be put to use today in a way that does not imply a rapacious attitude toward nature. Once we attend to the Bible's portrait of Christ, we learn that true dominion, in God's kingdom, is a matter of humble ser-vanthood (Mark 10:42-45). The purpose of rule is not financial gain (1 Pet 5:3). The lordship of Jesus is the lordship of love, which wills the good of the other. Furthermore, love is to be shown unconditionally to all, as God's love is shown to all (Matt 5:43-48). To be sure, there may be practical difficulty in seeing how this sort of love is to be shown to all things. It is not clear, for instance, what the good of mineral deposits is and how we are to promote that good. However, this practical difficulty is ameliorated when we recall that life occurs in ecosystems, which include both living beings and also the inorganic materials and structures that make life possible. It is these systems that should be the object of our love as we actively seek to do what is good for them. In this way it is possible to love all created things, even those that are not living.

Another aspect of world participation is wisdom and its ethical expression in justice. The twofold conviction about our relation to the nonhuman world (arising from the practice of humility and praise) and our responsibility for the use of the world (arising from a reformed sense of stewardship) leads us to a consideration of wisdom. In the Bible, it is the wisdom literature that calls our attention to the order of the universe, an order of which humankind is a part and which elicits our praise of God. It is the mark of the wise person to discern the way in which each being fits into God's created world and to appreciate the distinctive role of each. It is also the mark of a wise person to take our role in the universe as a matter of ethical seriousness and accept the responsibility that has been given to us.

One dimension of wisdom is prudence. It is the ability to understand and navigate effectively through politics and other human affairs and to bring ethical convictions to bear on those affairs. This aspect of wisdom is required for a Christian environmental ethics in order to discern the precise forms that ethical activity should take. It is not sufficient to repeat such true but extraordinarily general propositions as that the created world is good and that we should act responsibly in our use of the world. An ethical posture must eventually issue forth in particular policies. It is here that prudence is required, for the recommendation of policies inevitably uncovers the problem that in human affairs there are competing goods that must be balanced. In the absence of dramatic advances in technology, our society will continue to require large quantities of fossil fuels and other sources of energy that harm the environment. While it is good to protect the environment, it is also good to promote human well-being, something that requires the expending of energy. These two goods are in conflict; both cannot be simultaneously pursued without some sort of adjudication.

It is the task of prudence to guide us as we attempt to find the best solution to this conflict, all things considered. Wisdom in the form of prudence, therefore, mediates between our theological convictions and the demands of political practice. It is concerned with finding workable solutions that represent the best possible options under the circumstances but without losing sight of the ideals present in our convictions. An example of the application of prudence can be found in a document prepared by the Roman Catholic bishops of the Pacific Northwest region of the U.S. and Canada with regard to the Columbia River watershed. The proposals build on theological convictions about the created world and our responsibility for it. At the same time, they recognize the political and social obstacles to a simplistic demand for environmental protection. For example, bishops urge action to preserve the salmon population, but they also recognize that specific proposals, such as breaching dams, will have an impact on a wide variety of people. They indicate the importance of taking into consideration the well-being of local native people and other affected groups such as commercial fishermen. Other proposals include fostering owner-operated, economically viable family and cooperative farms, conserving energy, and establish environmentally integrated alternative energy sources.[41] These proposals, drawing on prudential wisdom, point the way forward for a Christian environmental ethics.

The proposals of the bishops' letter point to the question of justice, for they are concerned with what is truly good for all concerned—property owners, those who lives depend on the forests and rivers, native people, and nature itself. This concern reflects the development, within the last two or so decades, of the concept of ecojustice.[42] Ecojustice is an attempt to move beyond the view that protection of the environment and providing economically for the poor are in conflict. A previous generation, anxious about the material poverty of a large percentage of the world's human population, tended to subordinate environmental ethics to social justice. Ecojustice rests on the premise that the needs of the poor cannot be met without considering also the health of the natural environment.[43] Additionally, justice calls us to consider our responsibility to future generations. Even if depleting our natural resources did no harm to the environment, it would still violate the demands of justice to the extent that it would deprive future generations of the resources necessary to live well. This is not to say that the assumed needs of future generations override the pressing needs of today, but they must be considered in any use of resources.[44]

It may seem incongruous to speak of justice with respect to the natural world, for justice in our modern context is usually associated with civil rights or with the distribution of goods. The ideas that the natural world enjoys civil rights or that we can distribute society's goods to nature make little sense unless we advert to biblical perspectives. Justice in the biblical sense is an active concern for the well-being of those who lack the power necessary to assert their rights or achieve their own good. In the Bible itself, the recipients of justice are always those whose social status puts them at a gross disadvantage and who are virtually helpless. They include foreigners, widows, orphans, and the desperately poor. A recent development in Christian environmental thought has been to think of nature as among those who need the protection that biblical justice demands, on the grounds that nature is unable to protect itself against human exploitation. Just as the relation between the poor and the rich is marked by a substantial imbalance of power, so is the relation between nature and humankind.[45] The result is that it becomes a Christian duty to care for nature together with the poor and other oppressed people.

Besides humility and praise, justice, and dominion and stewardship, we might find grounds for an environmental ethics from an unexpected source, biblical eschatology. To see how this might be, it is necessary to grasp the connection between eschatology and the new creation. The Christian life is grounded in the new creation—in eschatology—for the Christian life is eschatological existence. "Eschatological existence" expresses the Christian belief that the kingdom of God and the gift of the Spirit are not merely promised for the future but are also present realities. To be sure, the kingdom of God and the world's complete reception of the Holy Spirit are for us a matter of promise, and we look to the future for their full arrival. At the same time, the kingdom and the Spirit were already present in the ministry of Jesus. As a result, Christian existence is life that participates simultaneously in the present and the future. The Christian ethical life is carried out in the dialectics between the present sinful world that is, according to the New Testament, passing away and God's future that is present but not fully manifest. It is our response to God's command that we live on the basis of a future whose reality we experience but which is still a matter of faith and hope, in the midst of a present fallen world that persists and resists God's kingdom.

It remains to be shown that an ethics of world participation is grounded in the new creation and eschatological existence. What is needed is to show that the new creation implies not only an ethical life but a world-participatory ethical life—that it both encourages and demands our active participation in and affirmation of the world. The problem is that such a view seems to contradict biblical eschatology and its view of the future. In places the Bible states that the future of the cosmos has been determined by the will of God and that, in view of the fallenness of the world (1 John 2:17), all we can do is wait—hence counsels of patience in apocalyptic literature (Rev 2:3; 6:11). In short, the ethics that arises from biblical eschatology does not readily suggest world participation. On the contrary, it presents the eschatological future as an alternative to this present, sinful world and thus seems to encourage the world transcendence pole of the Christian life exclusively. Perhaps the clearest statement of this conviction is 2 Pet 3:10-13, which declares that the present cosmos is to be destroyed and from this fact delivers an exhortation to personal holiness and patient waiting for the new heavens and earth. On the basis of this and other like passages, the picture of apocalyptic groups as utterly other-worldly and world-denying has become popular. The issue may be put simply: Does the new creation, which includes a new heaven and earth (Rev 21:1), negate the old creation and encourage world-denying ethics?

The key to understanding the world-participatory nature of Christian ethics is to see that God's new creation is still a *creation*. The newness of the new creation does not eliminate continuity with the original creation but must be understood as transformation, not as destruction and replacement. It is not as though God destroys this heaven and earth in order to make room for the new heavens and earth, as though this world is utterly unredeemable. The paradigm for us is the resurrection of Christ.[46] "Just as Christ was raised from the dead by the glory of the Father, so we too might walk in newness of life" (Rom 6:4). Resurrection is associated with newness of life. But Christ's new resurrection life does not contradict his mortal life—it is the same Jesus who is resurrected. So newness does not rule out continuity with the old. Instead newness means transformation of the old: "We will all be changed. . . . The dead will be raised imperishable and we will be changed. For this perishable body must put on imperishability, and this mortal body must put on immortality" (1 Cor 15:51-53). Likewise, "Be transformed by the renewing of your minds" (Rom

12:2). So the world to come, the new creation, does not mean the destruction of the present world but its transformation. The new creation is still God's good *created* world. There is only one world. The world that is to be redeemed through new creation is this world.

We may state the connection between the new creation and world participation succinctly by noting that those who participate in the new creation are still *creatures* and are still a part of this world. The new creation does not make us into spirits who leave the world, in either a literal or a figurative sense. Although this eschatological life is life in the Spirit, we are still located in the world. We have not and will not transcend our finitude. Even if it is necessary to transcend the fallen world ethically, we are still a part of the world. This factual participation calls for ethical participation.

This sort of general affirmation still leaves open the question of how we may interpret the eschatological passages of the Bible in a way that is consonant with a world-participatory ethics. The following points are relevant.

First, just as we distinguish the enduring biblical doctrine of creation from the ancient cosmologies that accompany it (chapter 3), so we are justified in distinguishing biblical eschatology from the apocalyptic worldview that often accompanies it. There are important biblical eschatological affirmations that can be separated from and do not depend on the apocalyptic worldview, just as there are affirmations about creation that can be separated from and do not depend on the ancient Near Eastern cosmologies.[47] The premise of this distinction is that, regardless of the extent to which the Bible is the word of God, it is also a thoroughly human work, using the modes of thought typical of ancient people. Since this premise is commonly accepted in the case of creation, there is no reason to decline its application to eschatological passages. But if we separate biblical eschatology from the apocalyptic worldview, what is left? What is left is the message that the God of eschatological life is the God who makes all things new: "If anyone is in Christ, there is a new creation: everything old has passed away; see, everything has become new!" (2 Cor 5:17). Above all, it is the God "who gives life to the dead and calls into existence the things that do not exist" (Rom 4:17). To live eschatologically is to have been given a future that has already begun in the present and to be commanded to live in that future, forsaking the past (insofar as the past is constituted by sin). This future is the kingdom of God and the gift of the Spirit, which are matters of promise but also present realities. The first point, then, consists in the claim that biblical eschatology is more about the new creation and about eschatological existence in the Holy Spirit than it is about apocalyptic predictions concerning the end of the world. In this view, the future is not a set of events already determined by God (as is often implied in apocalyptic literature) but the power that transforms the present.

Second, apocalyptically oriented religious groups are not invariably composed of disaffected people who have been deprived of power and whose apocalyptic worldview functions as a form of consolation or compensation. They are not inherently world-denying groups. Recent research on apocalyptic groups, ancient and modern, does not support the thesis that apocalypticism is rooted in social and economic deprivation.[48] Although the origins of apocalyptic literature in many cases are and will remain shrouded in mystery, there is no good reason to assume that the apocalyptic literature of the Bible represents any particular tendency toward a world-denying ethics.

Finally, it is important to note that the eschatological and apocalyptic passages of the Bible have not been interpreted monolithically in Christian history. These texts have been and can today be interpreted in more than one way. There is historical justification for not thinking of them as coded messages about future events, even though that is their ostensible meaning and even though they have often been understood that way. Stephen D. O'Leary has offered an illuminating key to the history of interpreting these passages. He argues that there are two fundamental understandings of human history and destiny that he (borrowing from Kenneth Burke) calls the tragic and the comic. The tragic view regards the human problem as guilt that must be assuaged by redemption through a sacrificial victim, a sacrifice that restores the moral order of the universe. It conceives of destiny in terms of fate and predetermination. It sees history as progressive and as moving to a final resolution. The comic regards the problem not as guilt but as human error. As a result, redemption occurs as human fallibility is disclosed and recognized. History is under the control of fortune, not fate, which gives greater emphasis to historical change and human activity. History is also conceived as episodic, not progressive. It is clear that the usual interpretation of apocalyptic passages as predictions of the future represents the tragic mode of interpretation. But this interpretation overlooks the ways in which these passages and books have functioned in and for the communities for which they were written. They were intended to speak to the concerns of their contemporary readers. For example, the book of Revelation encourages its readers to stand firm in the faith and counsels repentance, an attitude that incorporates the comic emphasis on change and human activity. Further, the history of interpretation shows a tendency, as expectations of the imminent end of the world fade, for Revelation to be interpreted not as a predictive book but instead as an allegory of the church's ongoing struggle against its enemies.[49] Along the same lines, contemporary research into the book of Revelation emphasizes that the political conflict portrayed in the book is in fact a literary screen on which has been drawn the ideological conflict between the Christian and the Roman views of the universe.[50] If this claim is correct, then the purpose of Revelation must be reassessed and its ostensibly predictive character must be questioned. Instead we must regard Revelation and other apocalyptic books as creating, in the words of Elisabeth Schüssler Fiorenza, a "'symbolic universe' that invites imaginative participation." They use symbols not to predict but to evoke response, to instill convictions and to compel decision.[51] The future that apocalyptic books describe is not a predetermined future subject to prediction but a possible future about which the seers warn.[52]

In the words of John T. Carroll, "Human fidelity to covenant, persevering commitment to the ways of God, active resistance to powerful systems that oppress the needy—these are part and parcel of the moral vision commended by John [in Revelation] and kindred visionaries."[53] Although the problem that the church faces today differs from the problem it faced in John's day, the same concern for obedience to God evidenced in Revelation will induce us to care for the earth. This means that we must regard the future that the new creation opens up to us as something in which we are to cooperate with God. Of course, nothing must diminish our conviction that ultimately salvation is not self-made. Without God's new creation, human activity will perpetuate the conditions of sin under which we labor. Nonetheless, although the promised kingdom of God comes as an act of God, it does not come without us and our active participation.

If the future lies before us as a task in which we cooperate with God, then what are we to make of the eschatological promises of a complete renewal of the universe in such books as Revelation? As argued above in chapters five through eight, we should not think of the universe as a whole or even the earth as participating in or suffering from the consequences of sin, except insofar as human misdeeds have resulted in harm. The universe as a whole, in its inorganic and organic aspects, does not need redemption. Further, the biblical texts that seem to announce an eschatological return to paradise probably should not be interpreted as statements about the entire cosmos.[54] In short, eschatological texts do not necessarily envision a complete abrogation of the facts of nature.

What, then, may we hope for? We cannot, on the basis of the Bible or the Christian faith, assert that there is a predetermined future in which God will dramatically and definitively alter the course of nature, so as, for example, to eliminate predation or transform carnivores into herbivores. We also cannot assume that God will step in before it is too late and fix whatever problems humankind has created. Instead, we must understand the promised future in light of the new creation. The God who calls us into the kingdom is not the God who determines the future in the way in which a novelist prepares an ending. Instead we have to do with the God who makes all things new by opening up a future where none was previously imagined. This is the God who provides a child for Abraham and Sarah, who returns Israel from exile, who raises Jesus from the dead, and who brings us into newness of life. Eschatological life in the kingdom is not receiving a future that has been fixed from eternity but is instead a summons to enter into a future that is newly created and to cooperate in the creation of that future. The God of Christian hope is the God who sustains the present course of the world insofar as it retains its created goodness and who creates a new future into which we may enter when we stray from the appointed path. This is the Father of Jesus Christ, who brings us into the kingdom by the power of the Spirit.

Postscript

The purpose of these concluding thoughts is to indicate further paths along which these trinitarian considerations may proceed.

In the preceding chapters I have used the results of the natural sciences to understand the doctrine of creation. I have presented them in a highly selective way with many generalizations. I have necessarily taken a synoptic view of the scientific picture of the world. Any comprehensive account of the doctrine of creation must probe more deeply into the details of each branch of the natural sciences and present the results of those branches in a more thorough and rigorous way. At the same time, such an account would necessarily remain an interpretation, i.e., a theological understanding of the created world. Breadth of scientific detail must be combined with unity of theological vision. In particular, it will be important for any such account to consider the results of the sciences synoptically, so that the universal participation of creatures in God is not overlooked in the wealth of detail, theory, and conception peculiar to each branch and sub-branch of the sciences.

A more comprehensive doctrine of the Trinity must also include an account of the nature of the language that it employs. In discussing the participation of creatures in the trinitarian life of God, it may easily appear that what is being offered is a theory, analogous to scientific or philosophical theories, about a being, God, and the relation between that being and the universe. In fact, however, God is not the sort of being that we can talk *about*. God is not the object of theoretical inquiry and study. Whenever we begin to talk *about* God, as we may talk about the weather or other physical systems, then we have stepped away from an authentic engagement with the subject matter of theology. The reason for this is that human knowledge of God is participatory, not theoretical. God is not an object available for study. As a result, no theological *theory* of God is possible. If it is true that God is love and that this love is the trinitarian love between the Father and the Son, then human knowledge of God that is theologically authentic must consist in our entering into and participating in this love. In short, love and not a objectively theoretical disposition is the proper form of knowing God. (None of this precludes the possibility and validity of a *philosophical* account of God that would constitute a theory or at least have elements of a theoretical disposition. The theologian is obligated to take notice of these philosophical accounts, to assess their compatibility with the Christian faith, and to interpret their significance for the Christian community. At the same time, it is always important to maintain the distinction between a philosophical or other sort of theory about God and a genuinely theological account.)

As a result, the language that we use in the doctrine of creation must not be regarded as descriptive of God in the sense in which scientific statements are descriptive of material events and processes. Although understanding the doctrine of creation is an intellectual exercise, its purpose is not ultimately informative but anagogic. By anagogic I mean that its purpose is to draw the human mind upward to the knowledge of God, which is love, and not to inform us about God. The way forward in this matter was laid out by St. Augustine in his work on the Trinity. There he argued that in such phenomena as human love and knowledge we can discern vestiges of the triune creator, for in these phenomena we find the dialectics of the trinitarian life. Created phenomena thus provide us with analogies for the Trinity. By meditating on these finite phenomena, we can discern something about the triune God, even though our knowledge remains analogical and not direct. But he argued that the highest analogy to the Trinity is found not in the structure of love and knowledge as such but in the mind that knows and loves *God*. Here the true image of the Trinity is discovered. But, at this point, analogy passes over into anagogy. In other words, at this point we leave behind indirect knowledge about God and arrive at the proper knowledge of God, which is equivalent to our love of God. Here we leave behind the theory-like words of investigation and take up the language of prayer and glorification. Our thoughts may not seem like prayers (they may lack the formal characteristics of prayers), but they should be offered up to God as prayers and acts of adoration. We should not, however, think that the prayer-like nature of this investigation prevents rigor of thought. On the contrary, since the goal of this investigation is knowledge of the triune creator, thinking in the mode of prayer is the form in which rigorous thought appears. Offering up our thoughts as a prayer and entering into the love of God is the form of thought ultimately appropriate to theology.

Finally, in offering a theological interpretation of the world, I have concentrated on assimilating the scientific picture of the world into the doctrine of creation. I have necessarily emphasized the importance of adjusting our understanding of creation in light of this scientific picture. Any comprehensive theology of creation, however, would also take account of scientific knowledge and indicate the ways in which the Christian faith may contribute to scientific practices and inquiry. Such a theology would build on the considerable body of historical studies that show that a given scientist always works within some philosophical frame of reference, whether consciously articulated or not, and that, in the case of many scientists, the Christian faith has functioned as that philosophical frame of reference. The further task is to show the implications of the Christian faith for the sciences today.

The goal of this task is not to create a distinctively Christian form of science. The natural sciences, like most intellectual disciplines, have a technical or practical aspect that allows them to be practiced by people of widely diverse philosophical and religious commitments. Laboratory and field work as well as the devising and testing of theories cannot be segmented into particular religious communities without loss of the scientific community and of the sciences. This is not to say that the Christian faith has nothing to contribute to the sciences. As historical study has shown, it has contributed in the past (just as the philosophical and religious convictions of other traditions have contributed), and there is every reason to believe that such contribution is possible today.

Two types of contribution may be briefly mentioned here. On one hand, theology has the responsibility of calling attention to every attempt to associate natural science exclusively with one philosophical stance. In our day, it is common to portray natural science as though it were simply identical with a reductively naturalistic philosophy. While it is true that many scientists today work within such a philosophical frame of reference, such a philosophy is not implied by the practices and theories of the natural sciences and need not be presupposed by the sciences. Numerous competent scientists do not adhere to such a philosophy. Theology can perform a service by calling attention to this fact.

Second, the Christian faith can have a more positive role in scientific inquiry, to the extent that individual scientists are informed by that faith. In combination with other considerations one's faith could, for example, guide one in choosing research topics and agenda. Being a Christian may affect the sorts of questions that one finds interesting and worth investigating scientifically. This does not mean that one's faith will determine in advance the results obtained by inquiry. Such determination would mean that one had stepped outside the bounds of science. It does mean that the initial choice of research agenda and its direction will be affected by one's larger philosophical frame of reference, at least part of which could include one's religious faith. Additionally, it is conceivable that one's faith could bring ethical considerations to bear on the course of research, particularly in those areas of research that are intimately connected to emerging technologies. Research that will result in technology destructive to human well-being or to the natural environment may understandably be avoided by those with religious faith, not because that research lacks scientific merit but because of ethical considerations.

In no case does the Christian faith dictate what scientists as scientists should do or what they should find interesting and worthy of scientific inquiry. But it does stand against any pretensions to the effect that the scientific picture of reality is alone true or comprehensive. While granting full validity to the natural sciences in their domains of knowledge, and granting also the potential contribution that the sciences can make to the understanding of the Christian faith, theology cannot allow to go unanswered unwarranted intellectual claims made by representatives of the scientific community. At the same time, Christians who are scientists may, as they meditate on the convictions and significance of the Christian faith, find resources for the direction that their research should or should not take.

Christian theology is true to its calling when it helps the church faithfully maintain the rule of faith, when it helps the church understand the faith by assimilating human knowledge, and when it helps the church live out its doctrines faithfully and in an intellectually responsible way. In seeking to fulfill this calling, its constant hope is that its words may become a prayer of praise and thanksgiving to the God who made the world and who continues to make all things new.

Notes

1. The Historical Development of the Doctrine of Creation

1. These words of warning are apropos of any attempt to extract doctrine from the Bible: "When the content of the narratives and poems is taken out of these forms and shaped into a systematic presentation, a different rendering of faith and its meaning occurs. . . . To give an account of Old Testament faith we need to begin by paying careful attention to the language of the narratives and poems themselves." "Form, rhetoric, and content belong together, for they are the constituent parts of language. To separate them is to alter the meaning of the text" (Leo G. Perdue, *Wisdom and Creation: The Theology of Wisdom Literature* [Nashville: Abingdon, 1994], 325 and 326).

2. For an orientation to the place of the doctrine of creation in the biblical narrative, see Bernhard W. Anderson, *Creation versus Chaos: The Reinterpretation of Mythical Symbolism in the Bible* (Philadelphia: Fortress Press, 1987), 35–38, and idem, *From Creation to New Creation: Old Testament Perspectives* (Overtures to Biblical Theology; Minneapolis: Fortress Press, 1994), 1–4.

3. This view of metaphysics is common to both Alfred North Whitehead and Martin Heidegger. See Whitehead, *Process and Reality: An Essay in Cosmology* (corrected ed., ed. David Ray Griffin and Donald W. Sherburne; New York: The Free Press, 1978), 90, 116, 219, and Heidegger, "The Way Back into the Ground of Metaphysics," in *Existentialism from Dostoevsky to Sartre,* ed. and trans. Walter Kaufmann (New York: Meridian, 1956), 217.

4. This threefold distinction is not equivalent to the core-peripheral distinction, for core-peripheral distinguishes between two sorts of doctrine, one essential, the other not. My point is that it is the one doctrine (e.g., creation) that exhibits all three dimensions. However, we can regard the hermeneutical dimension as a matter of adiaphora in contrast to the authoritative regulative dimension.

5. What I am calling the regulative dimension corresponds to what the early church called the rule of faith. It is not simply identical with the Bible but with what the church has regarded as the central teachings of the Bible.

6. Origen, *On First Principles*, preface, trans. G. W. Butterworth (New York: Harper and Row, 1966).

7. "The church teaches what has been believed everywhere, always, and by all."

Vincent of Lérins, *A Commonitory*, in Nicene and Post-Nicene Fathers of the Christian Church, series two (Grand Rapids: Eerdmans, 1955), 11:132.

8. An exception occurs when, as in the case of Thomas Aquinas, a hermeneutical project attains exemplary status and becomes a classic. As the work of an individual, it can never become truly authoritative unless the community is willing to sanctify a particular and culturally conditioned understanding and declare it to be true.

2. The Regulative Dimension of the Doctrine of Creation

1. When discussing the Bible, I refer to "writers" because, first, in most cases the number and identities of the authors are unknown to us and, second, the ancient world had no concept of authorship similar to ours.

2. On the polemical character of the opening chapters of Genesis, see Gerhard F. Hasel, "The Polemical Nature of the Genesis Cosmology," *Evangelical Quarterly* 46 (1974): 81–102, and Gordon J. Wenham, *Genesis 1–15,* Word Biblical Commentary (Waco, Tx.: Word, 1987), 9.

3. Bernhard W. Anderson, *Creation versus Chaos: The Reinterpretation of Mythical Symbolism in the Bible* (Philadelphia: Fortress Press, 1987), 21.

4. Claus Westermann, *Genesis 1–11: A Commentary,* trans. John J. Scullion (Minneapolis: Augsburg, 1984), 127.

5. Ibid., 159.

6. Hasel, "Polemical Nature," 88, and Wenham, *Genesis 1–15*, xlix.

7. See, for example, Michael Allen Williams, *Rethinking "Gnosticism": An Argument for Dismantling a Dubious Category* (Princeton: Princeton Univ. Press, 1996), 97, 108 and 117, for caution against allowing traditional pictures of Gnosticism to determine the way they are regarded today.

8. Irenaeus, "Against Heresies," in *The Writings of Irenaeus,* trans. Alexander Roberts and W. H. Rambaut; Ante-Nicene Christian Library 1 (New York: Christian Literature Co., 1885), 1.22.1 and 2.2.5.

9. Ibid., 2.9.2.

10. Ibid., 1.22.1.

11. Ibid., 2.1.1.

12. Ibid., 4.20.1.

13. Ibid., 2.10.2–4.

14. Ibid., 3.22.1 and 5.14.1–2.

15. *Creeds of the Churches: A Reader in Christian Doctrine from the Bible to the Present,* ed. John H. Leith, 3d ed. (Atlanta: John Knox, 1982), 33.

16. Athanasius, "Against the Heathen," in *St. Athanasius: Select Works and Letters,* trans. Archibald Robertson; A Select Library of Nicene and Post-Nicene Fathers of the Christian Church, vol. 4 (New York: Christian Literature Co., 1892), 40.1–2 and 42.1–2.

17. Ibid., 41.2–3.

18. Ibid., 6.1.

19. Ibid., 4.4 and 7.3.

20. Ibid., 28.1.

21. Ibid., 27.4–5.

22. Ibid., 28.3.

23. Ibid., 29.1.

24. Athanasius, "On the Incarnation," in *St. Athanasius: Select Works and Letters*, 2.4.

25. Basil, "The Hexaemeron," in *St. Basil: Letters and Select Works*, trans. Blomfield Jackson; A Select Library of Nicene and Post-Nicene Fathers of the Christian Church 8 (New York: Christian Literature Co., 1895), 1.8.

26. Ibid., 1.10.

27. Ibid., 1.9.

28. Ibid., 1.9, 1.11 and 9.1.

29. Ibid., 1.8.

30. Ibid., 1.6.

31. Ibid., 1.3.

32. Ibid., 2.2.

33. The Dordrecht Confession (1632), section 1, and the Westminster Confession (1646), chapter 4, section 1, expressly affirm that God created the world in six days. For the texts see *Creeds of the Churches*, 293 and 199.

3. The Hermeneutical Dimension of the Doctrine of Creation

1. For an overview of the relevant Babylonian myth, see Bernhard W. Anderson, *Creation versus Chaos: The Reinterpretation of Mythical Symbolism in the Bible* (Philadelphia: Fortress Press, 1987), 17–22. A more detailed discussion can be found in Ronald A. Simkins, *Creator and Creation: Nature in the Worldview of Ancient Israel* (Peabody, Mass.: Hendrickson, 1994). See also Gordon J. Wenham, *Genesis 1–15*, Word Biblical Commentary (Waco, Tex.: Word Books, 1987), 163, for an orientation to the scholarly discussion about the extent to which the Old Testament used the mythologies of the surrounding nations.

2. For an overview of medieval science and its relation to Christian thought, see David C. Lindberg, *The Beginnings of Western Science: The European Scientific Tradition in Philosophical, Religious, and Institutional Context, 600 B.C. to A.D. 1450* (Chicago: Univ. of Chicago Press, 1992); 245–80 and Christopher B. Kaiser, *Creation and the History of Science* (Grand Rapids: Eerdmans, 1991), 53–95.

3. Thomas Aquinas, *Summa Theologiae*, Blackfriars English translation, ed. Thomas Gilby (Garden City, N.Y.: Image, 1969), 1.44.2.

4. Ibid., 1.46.2.

5. Ibid., 1.65.3.

6. Ibid., 1.47.3.

7. Ibid., 1.103.1.

8. Kaiser, *Creation*, 236, also mentions Basil and Thomas as earlier representatives of this tradition.

9. Ibid., 191–93.

10. Ibid., 218.

11. John Hedley Brooke, *Science and Religion: Some Historical Perspectives* (Cambridge: Cambridge Univ. Press, 1991), 125.

12. For an illustration, see the remarks on Boyle in Brooke, *Science and Religion*, 132.

13. Ibid., 127.

14. Ibid., 127, and Kaiser, *Creation*, 203.

15. Kaiser, *Creation*, 226.

16. Jon H. Roberts, *Darwinism and the Divine in America: Protestant Intellectuals and Organic Development 1859–1900* (Madison: Univ. of Wisconsin Press, 1988), 117. The Roman Catholic response to evolution was much slower to accommodate itself to evolutionary biology.

17. Frederick Gregory, "The Impact of Darwinian Evolution on Protestant Theology in the Nineteenth Century," in *God and Nature: Historical Essays on the Encounter between Christianity and Science,* ed. David C. Lindberg and Ronald L. Numbers (Berkeley: Univ. of California Press, 1986), 379.

18. Roberts, *Darwinism*, 192.

19. Ibid., 118 and 120.

20. Gregory, "Impact," 379.

21. Roberts, *Darwinism*, 120–24.

22. A. Hunter Dupree, "Christianity and the Scientific Community in the Age of Darwin," in *God and Nature*, 360–61.

23. Roberts, *Darwinism*, 131.

24. Gregory, "Impact," 381.

25. Ibid., 380.

26. Roberts, *Darwinism*, 156.

4. Creatures' Participation in the Trinitarian Life of God

1. My exposition of wisdom in the Old Testament has been guided by the following: Joseph Blenkinsopp, *Wisdom and Law in the Old Testament: The Ordering of Life in Israel and Early Judaism,* Oxford Bible Series (Oxford: Oxford Univ. Press, 1995); Ronald E. Clements, *Wisdom in Theology* (Carlisle: Paternoster/Grand Rapids: Eerdmans, 1992); John J. Collins, *Jewish Wisdom in the Hellenistic Age,* The Old Testament Library (Louisville: Westminster John Knox, 1997); and Leo G. Perdue, *Wisdom and Creation: The Theology of Wisdom Literature* (Nashville: Abingdon, 1994). The discussion of spirit has been guided by the following: Marie E. Isaacs, *The Concept of Spirit: A Study of Pneuma in Hellenistic Judaism and Its Bearing on the New Testament,* Heythrop Monographs; London: Heythrop College, 1976), and Friedrich Baumgärtel et al., *"Pneuma, ktl.," Theological Dictionary of the New Testament* (Grand Rapids: Eerdmans, 1968), 6:359–68.

2. The Old Testament also knows that this moral order has exceptions. The book of Job is concerned with the individual who is blameless (Job 31) and yet suffers the fate of the wicked. The author of Psalm 37 and others take up the converse question of why the wicked prosper. So the moral order of the universe, although an expression of God's will, is from a human perspective not fully comprehensible. Nonetheless, even these exceptional cases are regarded as being under the supervision of God in a mysterious way. After all, Job's tormentor is not an abstract natural law but is the inscrutable God. It is God who authorizes Job's sufferings and sets limits to them (Job 1:12). At the same time, all human activity is under the supervision of God (Prov 15:3), who will eventually dispense justice (Prov 16:5). In fact, the wicked have their own role to play

in the moral order of the world: "The Lord has made everything for its purpose, even the wicked for the day of trouble" (Prov 16:4). Wickedness, then, although ostensibly contrary to the divinely imposed moral order, fits into a larger and mysterious order that nonetheless displays God's wisdom (Clements, *Wisdom*, 159).

3. This understanding of the spirit as the ability to perform superhuman feats is not limited to the Old Testament. For example, 1 Corinthians 12 is an exposition of the gifts of the Holy Spirit. It is clear that Paul regarded them as transhuman phenomena. Similarly, Luke 1:35 notes that it is by the Holy Spirit that Mary conceived Jesus, an event clearly regarded as miraculous.

4. Acts 2 regards this prophecy as fulfilled, or at least as beginning to be fulfilled, in the early church. In other words, it is the teaching of Acts and of the New Testament generally that the eschatological day has already begun.

5. A fuller biblical account of God's relation to the world would need to discuss, in addition to wisdom and spirit, such notions as God's word, glory, and the angel of presence. Nonetheless, in the sifting out of the biblical tradition, particularly in its New Testament form, increasing emphasis was laid on wisdom and spirit, with other aspects of God being assimilated to these.

6. Athanasius, "Against the Heathen," in *St. Athanasius: Select Works and Letters,* trans. Archibald Robertson; Select Library of Nicene and Post-Nicene Fathers of the Christian Church, vol. 4 (New York: Christian Literature Co., 1892), 40:1–2.

7. Ibid., 37.3.

8. Ibid., 38.2.

9. Ibid., 41.2.

10. Ibid., 41.3.

11. Ibid., 42.1.

12. Ibid., 42.2.

13. Athanasius, "On the Incarnation," ibid., 54.3.

14. Athanasius, "Against the Arians, Discourse I," trans. John Henry Cardinal Newman, rev. Archibald. Robertson, in *St. Athanasius: Select Works and Letters* (A Select Library of Nicene and Post-Nicene Fathers of the Christian Church, vol. 4; New York: Christian Literature Co., 1892), section 9.

15. Athanasius, "Defense of the Nicene Definition," trans. John Henry Cardinal Newman, in ibid., section 14.

16. According to the creed of Constantinople (381), the Spirit is the one who gives life.

17. Athanasius, "On the Incarnation," 2.3.

18. Ibid., 5.1.

19. Thomas Aquinas, *Summa Theologiae*, 1.4.2.

20. Ibid., 1.44.1.

21. Thomas went on to argue that God is not contained in any genus. Ibid., 1.3.5.

22. Ibid., 1.4.3.

23. Ibid., 1.104.1.

24. Ibid., 1.15.2.

25. Ibid., 1.44.3.

26. Ibid.

27. Ibid., 1.12.1.

28. Ibid., 1.12.4.

29. Ibid., 1.12.2.

30. Ibid., 1.34.3.

31. In one place Thomas establishes a threefold distinction: insofar as creatures represent their cause they reveal the Father; insofar as they have form they represent the Word; and insofar as they are ordered one to another they represent the Spirit. The rationale is that the Spirit corresponds roughly to will in the divine nature and the act of ordering is the result of the exercise of will (ibid., 1.45.7).

32. Paul Tillich, *Systematic Theology: Three Volumes in One* (Chicago: Univ. of Chicago Press, 1951–1963), 1:164. There are two other pairs of ontological elements: freedom and destiny, and form and dynamics. In order to simplify the exposition I am concentrating on individualization and participation.

33. Ibid., 1:245.

34. Ibid., 1:238.

35. Ibid., 1:235.

36. Ibid., 1:189.

37. Ibid., 3:32.

38. Ibid., 1:235. For the same reason, God is not *a* person, although God is personal (1:244–245).

39. Ibid., 1:237.

40. For Tillich, Jesus Christ is the new being. Our participation in the new being is our participation in the being of Jesus Christ.

41. Ibid., 2:174–75.

42. Ibid., 2:176.

43. For the same reason that God is not *a* being, God is not *a* spirit.

44. Ibid., 1:249–51.

45. The trinitarian principles do not constitute the doctrine of the Trinity. The doctrine of the Trinity, i.e., the doctrine of the Father, Son, and Holy Spirit, depends on and could not have been formulated before the historical revelation of Jesus Christ. The trinitarian principles are a preparation for the doctrine in the sense that they expound, somewhat philosophically, what it means to say that God is the living God (ibid., 1:251).

46. Ibid., 3:20.

47. Ibid., 3:21–24.

48. This understanding of the Spirit's role within the eternal Trinity goes back at least as far as Augustine.

49. Tillich, *Systematic Theology*, 3:19.

50. It is not possible here to give a full justification for every point in the following interpretation. Many parts of the interpretation must be presented as theses, with references to theological and scientific literature taking the place of full discussion. Further, since it is the aim of this chapter to present a *theological* interpretation of the created world, many important philosophical questions are omitted.

5. Persistence and Change in Time

1. A complete account would have to take note of atoms losing electrons but remaining substantially identical in spite of this change.

2. Catalytic molecules represent an interesting variation on this pattern. As agents of catalysis, they undergo chemical change but then return to their original composition. Both their processes of change and their resumption of persistence are cyclical.

3. One might suggest certain exceptions to this general rule. For example, internal regulation of temperature, in which the organism seeks to return itself to a prior state. But these processes are not so much time-indifferent as they are cyclical or repetitive.

4. This tendency toward static repetition is not something negative. It is this physical and biological stability that makes life possible.

5. The appropriation of the past as tradition is not always a conscious act. Especially in societies that are not pluralistic, appropriation of one's tradition may not be a matter of reflection but even in these societies appropriation is ultimately a matter of decision. Religious conversion affords us an example of dropping allegiance to one's original tradition and adopting another tradition.

6 . This is not to say that there are no progressive movements within human history. Although progress is neither inevitable nor irreversible, it is possible. The abolition of slavery affords an example. It took a long time for its evil character to be generally accepted and even more time for it to be eliminated. Yet the fact that it is practiced far less today and is almost universally condemned is surely a moral advance.

7. This does not necessarily mean that the envisioned future differs radically from the past. The future could well be regarded as the fulfillment of the past.

8. The question of the universe's finitude in a larger sense is raised by the possibility of a pretemporal state of the universe. On one hand, the universe's infinity is practically axiomatic, since in that state it would not be bound by time and would comprise whatever space there was. On the other hand, and theologically considered, the universe even in this pretemporal state is finite in relation to God, unless we wish, as a philosophical decision, to posit the existence of such a state as a metaphysical first principle. Otherwise, the universe even in this state will depend for its being on God, even if we are thereby forced to concede that the creation of the universe lies not only before time but outside all time.

9. It is, of course, possible that some animals, perhaps among the primates, experience death in ways that approximate the human experience of death. This is not surprising if cognition and other human functions have an organic basis that we share in certain ways with other animals.

7. Part-Whole Relations

1. Protons may represent an exception. Although proton decay has been predicted by theory, it has not been experimentally confirmed.

2. Notably in Psalm 22 and Job.

3. Again we note a modern and liberal form of religion, such as we find in Judaism and Protestantism, that eschews overt claims to totality. Whether such claims can be consistently carried through is debatable.

8. The Relatedness of All Things

1. Thomas Aquinas, *Summa Theologica* 1.29.4.

2. By "without cause" I mean that no reason can be assigned for the radioactive decay of *this* atom in contrast to some other atom in the sample. The mechanism of decay is well known; however there seems to be no reason for any particular atom decaying *now* instead of at some other time.

3. Naturally, we should not simply conflate the conceptual results of quantum field theory and relativity theory, as though they were saying the same thing. In describing particles in terms of fields, quantum field theory is stipulating the appropriate conceptual schemes for discussing physical reality under varied experimental conditions. In relating energy and matter, relativity theory is not proposing a conceptual scheme for defining matter and energy, but instead is offering an explanation of the conversion of one into the other. The philosophical consequence of these theories is that we can comprehend a physical thing only as we conceptualize its material thingness in relation to other physical realities—fields and energy.

4. As might be expected, the concept of dominion presents theology with another kind of problem. This will be considered in chapter ten.

5. A question arises here: Since, as previously discussed, the trinitarian persons are defined by their relations, are the persons finite? The answer is no, because each person is the entire divine nature (and not a part of it). The persons are the relations within the divine being and hence are not finite. Another question may also be asked: Is God essentially related to the universe? If so, this implies that God is finite. Since it is not the purpose of this book to give a complete account of God's relation to the universe, I can offer here only a brief answer. It is my belief that God's relation to the universe is asymmetrical. In this way, although the world bears a necessary relation to God, God bears no necessary relation to the world. As a result, the world is inherently finite while God is infinite.

6. This view of the universe as a causal nexus must be qualified for the realities of the quantum world, in which causation is of only limited usefulness as an explanatory tool. Such qualification, however, does not alter any judgment about the universe's essential finitude.

9. The Ethical Dimension of the Doctrine of Creation in Christian History

1. On the Christian attitude toward wealth in Paul's letters, see Martin Hengel, *Poverty and Riches in the Early Church: Aspects of a Social History of Early Christianity,* trans. John Bowden (Philadelphia: Fortress Press, 1974), 35–41.

2. Christine Trevett, *Montanism: Gender, Authority, and the New Prophecy* (Cambridge: Cambridge Univ. Press, 1996), 103, argues that expectation of Christ's second coming was still common in the second century.

3. See Peter Brown, *The Body and Society: Men, Women, and Sexual Renunciation in Early Christianity,* Lectures on the History of Religions; New York: Columbia Univ.

Press, 1988), 17–22, for the ideological context of Christian asceticism in pagan society. Although not identical with Christian views, Hellenistic philosophical opinions about sexual mores bore a resemblance to Christian asceticism.

4. Augustine, *Confessions,* trans. R. S. Pine-Coffin (Baltimore: Penguin, 1976), 1.20.

5. Ibid., 10.29.

6. Ibid., 10.31.

7. Ibid., 10.33.

8. Ibid., §35.

9. Ibid., §30.

10. Augustine, "Of Holy Virginity," in *St. Augustin: On the Holy Trinity, Doctrinal Treatises, Moral Treatises,* trans. C. I. Cornish; Select Library of Nicene and Post-Nicene Fathers of the Christian Church, vol. 3 (Grand Rapids: Eerdmans, 1978), §8.

11. Ibid., §12.

12. Ibid., §§19, 21, and 24.

13. Ibid., §35.

14. John Calvin, *Institutes of the Christian Religion,* trans. Ford Lewis Battles; ed. John T. McNeill; Library of Christian Classics 20 (Philadelphia: Westminster, 1960), 1.3.7.

15. Bonaventure, *Saint Bonaventure's Itinerarium Mentis in Deum,* trans. by Philotheus Boehner; Works 2 (St. Bonaventure, N.Y.: Franciscan Institute, Saint Bonaventure University, 1956), chap. 1, §§1–2.

16. Ibid., §9.

17. Ibid. chap. 1, §9 and chap. 2, §1.

18. Ibid., chap. 1, §11.

19. Ibid., chap. 1, §13.

20. Ibid., chap. 2, §§7 and 9.

21. Ibid., chap. 2, §12.

22. Ibid., chap. 7, §§1 and 4.

23. Ibid., chap. 7, §6.

24. Albrecht Ritschl, *The Christian Doctrine of Justification and Reconciliation: The Positive Development of the Doctrine,* trans. H. R. Mackintosh and A. B. Macaulay (New York: Scribners, 1900), 234.

25. Ibid., 202.

26. Ibid., 199.

27. Ibid., 609.

28. Ibid., 201.

29. Ibid., 30.

30. See Leo G. Perdue, *Wisdom and Creation: The Theology of Wisdom Literature* (Nashville: Abingdon Press, 1994), 101–4, for further exposition of this theme.

31. See Elisabeth Schüssler Fiorenza, "Wisdom Mythology and the Christological Hymns of the New Testament," in *Aspects of Wisdom in Judaism and Early Christianity,* ed. Robert L. Wilken (Notre Dame, Ind.: Univ. of Notre Dame Press, 1975); and James M. Robinson, "Jesus as Sophos and Sophia: Wisdom Tradition and the Gospels," in idem. M. Jack Suggs, *Wisdom, Christology and Law in Matthew's Gospel* (Cambridge: Harvard Univ. Press, 1970), and Silvia Schroer, *Wisdom Has Built Her House: Studies on the Figure of Sophia in the Bible,* trans. Linda M. Maloney and William McDonough (Collegeville, Minn.: Liturgical, 2000).

32. This interpretation of the image of God is supported by Ps 8:5-8, which notes

that humankind has been created just a bit lower than the members of the divine assembly, has been crowned with glory and honor, and been given dominion over earth's animals. Psalm 115:16 likewise asserts that "The heavens are the Lord's heavens, but the earth he has given to human beings."

33. Thomas Aquinas, *Summa Theologiae*, 1/2.93.1.

34. Ibid., 1/2.91.2.

35. Ibid., 1/2.93.3, reply to objection 2.

36. Aristotle, *The Ethics of Aristotle: The Nicomachean Ethics,* trans. J. A. K. Thomson; rev. ed. (London: Penguin, 1976), 1:1.

37. Thomas Aquinas, *Summa Theologiae*, 1/2.94.2.

38. Martin Luther, "Psalm 111," in *Selected Psalms II,* Luther's Works, vol. 13, ed. Jaroslav Pelikan, trans. Daniel E. Poellot (St. Louis: Concordia, 1956), 368.

39. Ibid., 358 and 368.

40. Martin Luther, "Confession concerning Christ's Supper (1528)," in *Word and Sacrament III,* Luther's Works, vol. 37, trans. and ed. Robert H. Fischer (Philadelphia: Fortress Press, 1961), 364.

41. Ibid., 365.

42. Luther, "Psalm 111," 369.

43. John Calvin, *Commentary on the Epistles of Paul the Apostle to the Corinthians,* trans. John Pringle (Grand Rapids, Mich.: Eerdmans, 1948), 1: 248–49. But see also Calvin, *Institutes,* 3.10.6, for a conservative view closer to Luther's.

44. Calvin, *Institutes,* 4.20.4.

45. Ibid., 3.10.6.

10. The Ethical Dimension of the Doctrine of Creation Today

1. In the discussion of this topic, I have drawn on the thoughts of Rodney Clapp, "The Theology of Consumption and the Consumption of Theology: Toward a Christian Response to Consumerism," in *The Consuming Passion: Christianity and the Consumer Culture,* ed. Rodney Clapp (Downers Grove, Ill.: InterVarsity, 1998), 169–204.

2. See Stuart Ewen and Elizabeth Ewen, *Channels of Desire: Mass Images and the Shaping of American Consciousness* (New York: McGraw-Hill, 1982), 74.

3. Neil Postman, *Amusing Ourselves to Death: Public Discourse in the Age of Show Business* (New York: Penguin, 1986), 128.

4. It should not be concluded from this analysis that consumption is a bad thing or that legitimate human needs and desires are to be ascetically denied. For much of the world's population, a chief obstacle to well-being is not enough consumption. The problem is not consumption and needs in the context of a human life well lived. The problem is consumption considered as the defining characteristic of a human life well lived and with the proliferation of needs in the consumer-culture. In short, the problem lies in consumption becoming an end in itself instead of being a means to higher ends.

5. Stuart Ewen and Elizabeth Ewen, *Channels of Desire,* 76.

6. John Paul II, *Centesimus Annus,* §40. Papal Encyclical, 1991. See the following website: http://www.vatican.va/holy_father/john_paul_ii/encyclicals/documents/hf_jp-ii_enc_01051991_centesimus-annus_en.html.

7. Ibid., §36.

8. Ibid., §19.

9. This rather harsh critique of contemporary culture should not be taken as an endorsement of some other historical culture, on the supposition that there was some culture in the past that was devoted to profound matters in an unalloyed way. The present critique aims only at showing the form that human sin takes in our current situation.

10. Postman, *Amusing Ourselves to Death*, 80.

11. Ibid., 107.

12. See Craig M. Gay, "Sensualists without Heart: Contemporary Consumerism in Light of the Modern Project," in *The Consuming Passion*, 19–39, esp. 36; Clapp, "The Theology of Consumption," esp. 189; and Stuart Ewen and Elizabeth Ewen., *Channels of Desire*, 75.

13. John Paul II, *Centesimus Annus*, §§39 and 55.

14. The problem of intellect, in the form of scientific knowledge, cut off from humane values, is another example of this problem.

15. Stuart Ewen and Elizabeth Ewen, *Channels of Desire*, 262–63.

16. Susan J. Douglas, *Where the Girls Are: Growing Up Female with the Mass Media* (New York: Random House, 1994), 246.

17. John Paul II, *Centesimus Annus*, §41.

18. Postman, *Amusing Ourselves to Death*, 128.

19. Ibid., 92.

20. Stuart Ewen and Elizabeth Ewen, *Channels of Desire*, 42 and 256–57.

21. Ibid., 52, 58, and 76.

22. The following are good surveys of contemporary thought: *The Care of Creation: Focusing Concern and Action*, ed. R. J. Berry (Leicester, England: InterVarsity, 2000); the articles in *Christian Scholar's Review* 28, no. 2 (1998), give a good picture of evangelical thought; H. Paul Santmire, "Healing the Protestant Mind: Beyond the Theology of Human Dominion," in *After Nature's Revolt: Eco-Justice and Theology*, ed. Dieter T. Hessel (Minneapolis: Fortress Press, 1992) presents leading authors who emphasize ecojustice. For a historical presentation of recent Protestant thought on the subject, see Robert Booth Fowler, *The Greening of Protestant Thought* (Chapel Hill, N.C.: Univ. of North Carolina Press, 1995).

23. See Ronald A. Simkins, *Creator and Creation: Nature in the Worldview of Ancient Israel* (Peabody, Mass.: Hendrickson, 1994), 256, for a critique of the previous generation of biblical scholarship.

24. Bernhard W. Anderson, "Creation and the Noachic Covenant," in *From Creation to New Creation: Old Testament Perspectives*, Overtures to Biblical Theology (Minneapolis: Fortress Press, 1994), 155; idem, "Human Dominion over Nature," in *From Creation to New Creation*, 131; and idem, "Relation between the Human and Nonhuman Creation in the Biblical Primeval History," in *From Creation to New Creation*, 139. See also Simkins, *Creator*, 261.

25. Santmire, "Healing the Protestant Mind," 75–76.

26. Terence E. Fretheim, "Nature's Praise of God in the Psalms," *Creation* 3 (1987): 29, speaks forcefully on this point.

27. Ibid., 22–23.

28. Anderson, "Human Dominion over Nature," 130; James Barr, "Man and Nature: The Ecological Controversy and the Old Testament," in *Ecology and Religion in History*, ed. David Spring and Eileen Spring (New York: Harper & Row, 1974), 61–63; and

Claus Westermann, *Genesis 1–11: A Commentary,* trans. John J. Scullion, S. J. (Minneapolis: Augsburg, 1984), 159.

29. Peter Harrison, "Subduing the Earth: Genesis 1, Early Modern Science, and the Exploitation of Nature," *Journal of Religion* 79/1 (1999): 89.

30. Ibid., 91.

31. Barr, "Man and Nature," 65.

32. Richard Bauckham, "Stewardship and Relationship," in *The Care of Creation: Focusing Concern and Action,* ed. R. J. Berry (Leicester, England: InterVarsity, 2000), 100.

33. Harrison, "Subduing the Earth," 95.

34. Bauckham, "Stewardship and Relationship," 100–101.

35. Harrison, "Subduing the Earth," 97–98. Harrison believes that dominion, as envisaged in the seventeenth century, was seen as an attempt at restoring the earth to the condition it had before sin. Infertility, weeds, and other deleterious features were regarded not as natural but instead as the result of God's curse in response to human sin. As a result, dominion was to be exercised not in order to shape nature in conformity with human purposes but instead in order to restore nature. See pp.103–4.

36. Anderson, "Human Dominion over Nature," 128 and 130.

37. See, for example, Thomas Sieger Derr, *Ecology and Human Liberation: A Theological Critique of the Use and Abuse of Our Birthright* (Geneva: World Council of Churches, 1973), 54.

38. Ibid., 50–51.

39. Ibid., 54.

40. Bauckham, "Stewardship and Relationship," 102–3. H. Paul Santmire, "Healing the Protestant Mind," 75, concurs.

41. Columbia River Pastoral Letter Project, "The Columbia River Watershed: Caring for Creation and the Common Good, an International Pastoral Letter by the Catholic Bishops of the region," (2001). See the following website for more details: http://www.columbiariver.org/main_pages/Watershed/watershed.html.

42. See Dieter T. Hessel, "Introduction: Eco-Justice Theology after Nature's Revolt," in *After Nature's Revolt,* 9, for a concise discussion of the concept of ecojustice.

43. Sallie McFague, *Super, Natural Christians: How We Should Love Nature* (Minneapolis: Fortress Press, 1997), 13, provides an illustrative argument that links the health of the environment with the needs of the world's poor.

44. Derr, *Ecology and Human Liberation,* 65–67.

45. McFague, *Super, Natural Christians,* 6 and 12.

46. Also paradigmatic is the relation of the New Testament to the Old. Although the New is genuinely new, it does not replace or negate the Old. Instead, it hermeneutically transforms the Old Testament by interpreting it christologically.

47. Kathryn Tanner has suggested that, as we have distinguished the doctrine of creation from notions of a temporal beginning of the universe (see chapter five), perhaps we might also distinguish the doctrine of eschatology from notions of a temporal end. The novelty of this suggestion makes it seem counter-intuitive; the logic, however, is compelling. Kathryn Tanner, "Eschatology without a Future?" in *The End of the World and the Ends of God: Science and Theology on Eschatology,* ed. John Polkinghorne and Michael Welker (Harrisburg, Penn.: Trinity Press International, 2000), 224.

48. Stephen Cook has argued that certain apocalyptic groups of the biblical period were not disaffected at all. At least some were part of the dominant culture of their

times. Stephen L. Cook, *Prophecy and Apocalypticism: The Postexilic Social Setting* (Minneapolis: Fortress Press, 1995), 47–50. Cook's conclusions about Jewish apocalypticism are based on a study of the social setting of apocalyptic movements throughout history. John J. Collins, *The Apocalyptic Imagination: An Introduction to the Jewish Matrix of Christianity* (New York: Crossroad, 1984), makes the point that in many cases we do not know the social settings of Jewish apocalyptic writings (18 and 29) and that the thesis that such literature arose out of crisis is too broad, holding true of many but not of all apocalyptic works (31). Carolyn Osiek, "The Genre and Function of the Shepherd of Hermas," in *Early Christian Apocalypticism: Genre and Social Setting*, ed. Adela Yarbro Collins (Decatur, Ga.: Scholars Press, 1986), further undercuts the deprivation theory by arguing on the basis of historical records that there was no political persecution taking place when the book of Revelation was written, so that the occasion of the book was not a political crisis with an entity outside the church but instead a disagreement within the church (116).

49. Stephen D. O'Leary, *Arguing the Apocalypse: A Theory of Millennial Rhetoric* (New York: Oxford Univ. Press, 1994), 62–76.

50. Leonard Thompson, "A Sociological Analysis of Tribulation in the Apocalypse of John," in *Early Christian Apocalypticism*, 166.

51. Elisabeth Schüssler Fiorenza, "The Followers of the Lamb: Visionary Rhetoric and Social-Political Situation," in *Early Christian Apocalypticism*, 130 and 134.

52. John T. Carroll, "Creation and Apocalypse," in *God Who Creates: Essays in Honor of W. Sibley Towner*, ed. William P. Brown and S. Dean McBride Jr. (Grand Rapids: Eerdmans, 2000), 260.

53. Ibid.

54. Gene M. Tucker, "The Peaceable Kingdom and a Covenant with the Wild Animals," in *God Who Creates*, 215–25, has sounded a cautionary note by arguing that two of the Old Testament passages (Isa 11:6-9 and Hos 2:18) that are commonly regarded as proclaiming an eschatological return to paradise probably do not make such extensive claims.

Bibliography

Anderson, Bernhard W. *Creation versus Chaos: The Reinterpretation of Mythical Symbolism in the Bible*. Philadelphia: Fortress Press, 1987.

―――. *From Creation to New Creation: Old Testament Perspectives*. Overtures to Biblical Theology. Minneapolis: Fortress Press, 1994.

Aristotle. *The Ethics of Aristotle: The Nicomachean Ethics*. Revised edition. Translated by J. A. K. Thomson. London: Penguin, 1976.

Athanasius. "Against the Arians, Discourse I." Translated by John Henry Cardinal Newman, revised by Archibald Robertson. In *St. Athanasius: Select Works and Letters*. A Select Library of Nicene and Post-Nicene Fathers of the Christian Church. Vol. 4. New York: Christian Literature Co., 1892.

―――. "Against the Heathen." Translated by Archibald Robertson. In *St. Athanasius: Select Works and Letters*. A Select Library of Nicene and Post-Nicene Fathers of the Christian Church. Vol. 4. New York: Christian Literature Co., 1892.

―――. "Defence of the Nicene Definition." Translated by John Henry Cardinal Newman. In *St. Athanasius: Select Works and Letters*. A Select Library of Nicene and Post-Nicene Fathers of the Christian Church. Vol. 4. New York: Christian Literature Co., 1892.

―――. "On the Incarnation." Translated by Archibald Robertson. In *St. Athanasius: Select Works and Letters*. A Select Library of Nicene and Post-Nicene Fathers of the Christian Church. Vol. 4. New York: Christian Literature Co., 1892.

Augustine. *Confessions*. Translated by R. S. Pine-Coffin. Baltimore: Penguin, 1976.

―――. "Of Holy Virginity." Translated by C. I. Cornish. In *St. Augustin: On the Holy Trinity, Doctrinal Treatises, Moral Treatises*. A Select Library of Nicene and Post-Nicene Fathers of the Christian Church. Vol. 3. Grand Rapids: Eerdmans, 1978.

Barr, James. "Man and Nature: The Ecological Controversy and the Old Testament." In *Ecology and Religion in History* Edited by David Spring and Eileen Spring, 48–75. New York: Harper & Row, 1974.

Basil. "The Hexaemeron." Translated by Blomfield Jackson. In *St. Basil: Letters and Select Works*. A Select Library of Nicene and Post-Nicene Fathers of the Christian Church. Vol. 8. New York: Christian Literature Co., 1895.

Bauckham, Richard J. *Jude, 2 Peter*. Word Biblical Commentary. Waco, Tex.: Word, 1983.

―――. "Stewardship and Relationship." In *The Care of Creation: Focusing Concern and Action*. Edited by R. J. Berry. Leicester, England: InterVarsity, 2000.

Baumgärtel, Friedrich, et al. "Pneuma, ktl." In *Theological Dictionary of the New Testament.* Vol. 6: 359–68. Grand Rapids: Eerdmans.

Berry, R. J., editor. *The Care of Creation: Focusing Concern and Action.* Leicester, England: InterVarsity, 2000.

Blenkinsopp, Joseph. *Wisdom and Law in the Old Testament: The Ordering of Life in Israel and Early Judaism.* Oxford Bible Series. Oxford: Oxford Univ. Press, 1995.

Bonaventure. *Saint Bonaventure's Itinerarium Mentis in Deum.* Translated by Philotheus Boehner. Works. Vol. 2. St. Bonaventure, N.Y.: Franciscan Institute, Saint Bonaventure Univ., 1956.

Brooke, John Hedley. *Science and Religion: Some Historical Perspectives.* Cambridge: Cambridge Univ. Press, 1991.

Brown, Peter. *The Body and Society: Men, Women, and Sexual Renunciation in Early Christianity.* Lectures on the History of Religions. New York: Columbia Univ. Press, 1988.

Calvin, John. *Commentary on the Epistles of Paul the Apostle to the Corinthians.* Translated by John Pringle. 2 vols. Grand Rapids: Eerdmans, 1948.

———. *Institutes of the Christian Religion.* Edited by John T. McNeill. Translated by Ford Lewis Battles. Library of Christian Classics. Vol. 20. Philadelphia: Westminster, 1960.

Carroll, John T. "Creation and Apocalypse." In *God Who Creates: Essays in Honor of W. Sibley Towner.* Edited by William P. Brown and S. Dean McBride, Jr., 251–60. Grand Rapids: Eerdmans, 2000.

Christian Scholar's Review 28, no. 2 (1998).

Clapp, Rodney. "The Theology of Consumption and the Consumption of Theology: Toward a Christian Response to Consumerism." In *The Consuming Passion: Christianity and the Consumer Culture.* Edited by Rodney Clapp, 169–204. Downers Grove, Ill.: InterVarsity, 1998.

Clements, Ronald E. *Wisdom in Theology.* Carlisle: Paternoster Press; Grand Rapids: Eerdmans, 1992.

Collins, John J. *The Apocalyptic Imagination: An Introduction to the Jewish Matrix of Christianity.* New York: Crossroad, 1984.

———. *Jewish Wisdom in the Hellenistic Age.* The Old Testament Library. Louisville: Westminster John Knox, 1997.

Columbia River Pastoral Letter Project. "The Columbia River Watershed: Caring for Creation and the Common Good. An International Pastoral Letter by the Catholic Bishops of the Region." 2001. See http://www.columbiariver.org/main_pages/Watershed/watershed.html

Cook, Stephen L. *Prophecy and Apocalypticism: The Postexilic Social Setting.* Minneapolis: Fortress Press, 1995.

Creeds of the Churches: A Reader in Christian Doctrine from the Bible to the Present. Edited by John H. Leith. 3d ed. Atlanta: John Knox, 1982.

Derr, Thomas Sieger. *Ecology and Human Liberation: A Theological Critique of the Use and Abuse of Our Birthright.* Geneva: World Council of Churches, 1973.

Douglas, Susan J. *Where the Girls Are: Growing Up Female with the Mass Media.* New York: Random House, 1994.

Dupree, A. Hunter. "Christianity and the Scientific Community in the Age of Darwin." In *God and Nature: Historical Essays on the Encounter between Christianity and Sci-*

ence. Edited by David C. Lindberg and Ronald L. Numbers, 351–68. Berkeley: Univ. of California Press, 1986.

Ewen, Stuart, and Elizabeth Ewen. *Channels of Desire: Mass Images and the Shaping of American Consciousness*. New York: McGraw-Hill, 1982.

Fowler, Robert Booth. *The Greening of Protestant Thought*. Chapel Hill, N.C.: Univ. of North Carolina Press, 1995.

Fretheim, Terence E. "Nature's Praise of God in the Psalms." *Creation* 3 (1987): 16–30.

Gay, Craig M. "Sensualists without Heart: Contemporary Consumerism in Light of the Modern Project." In *The Consuming Passion: Christianity and the Consumer Culture*. Edited by Rodney Clapp, 19–39. Downers Grove, Ill.: InterVarsity, 1998.

Gregory, Frederick. "The Impact of Darwinian Evolution on Protestant Theology in the Nineteenth Century." In *God and Nature: Historical Essays on the Encounter between Christianity and Science*. Edited by David C. Lindberg and Ronald L. Numbers, 369–90. Berkeley: Univ. of California Press, 1986.

Harrison, Peter. "Subduing the Earth: Genesis 1, Early Modern Science, and the Exploitation of Nature." *Journal of Religion* 79/1 (1999): 86–109.

Hasel, Gerhard F. "The Polemical Nature of the Genesis Cosmology." *Evangelical Quarterly* 46 (1974): 81–102.

Heidegger, Martin. "The Way Back into the Ground of Metaphysics." In *Existentialism from Dostoevsky to Sartre*. Edited and translated by Walter Kaufmann, 206–21. New York: Meridian, 1956.

Hengel, Martin. *Poverty and Riches in the Early Church: Aspects of a Social History of Early Christianity*. Translated by John Bowden. Philadelphia: Fortress Press, 1974.

Hessel, Dieter T. "Introduction: Eco-Justice Theology after Nature's Revolt." In *After Nature's Revolt: Eco-Justice and Theology*. Edited by Dieter T. Hessel, 1–18. Minneapolis: Fortress Press, 1992.

Irenaeus. "Against Heresies." In *The Writings of Irenaeus*. Translated by Alexander Roberts and W. H. Rambaut. Ante-Nicene Christian Library. Vol. 1. New York: Christian Literature Co., 1885.

Isaacs, Marie E. *The Concept of Spirit: A Study of Pneuma in Hellenistic Judaism and Its Bearing on the New Testament*. Heythrop Monographs. London: Heythrop College, 1976.

John Paul II. *Centesimus Annus*, 1991. http://www.vatican.va/holy_father/john_paul_ii/encyclicals/documents/hf_jp-ii_enc_01051991_centesimus-annus_en.html.

Kaiser, Christopher B. *Creation and the History of Science*. Grand Rapids: Eerdmans, 1991.

Lindberg, David C. *The Beginnings of Western Science: The European Scientific Tradition in Philosophical, Religious, and Institutional Context, 600 B.C. to A.D. 1450*. Chicago: Univ. of Chicago Press, 1992.

Luther, Martin. "Psalm 111." In *Luther's Works*. Vol. 13. *Selected Psalms II*. Edited by Jaroslav Pelikan. Translated by Daniel E. Poellot. St. Louis: Concordia, 1956.

———. "Confession concerning Christ's Supper (1528)." In *Luther's Works*. Vol. 37. *Word and Sacrament III*. Translated and edited by Robert H. Fischer. Philadelphia: Fortress Press, 1961.

McFague, Sallie. *Super, Natural Christians: How We Should Love Nature*. Minneapolis: Fortress Press, 1997.

O'Leary, Stephen D. *Arguing the Apocalypse: A Theory of Millennial Rhetoric.* New York: Oxford Univ. Press, 1994.

Origen. *On First Principles.* Translated by G. W. Butterworth. New York: Harper and Row, 1966.

Osiek, Carolyn. "The Genre and Function of the Shepherd of Hermas." In *Early Christian Apocalypticism: Genre and Social Setting.* Edited by Adela Yarbro Collins, 113–21. Decatur, Ga.: Scholars, 1986.

Perdue, Leo G. *Wisdom and Creation: The Theology of Wisdom Literature.* Nashville: Abingdon, 1994.

Postman, Neil. *Amusing Ourselves to Death: Public Discourse in the Age of Show Business.* New York: Penguin, 1986.

Ritschl, Albrecht. *The Christian Doctrine of Justification and Reconciliation: The Positive Development of the Doctrine.* Translated by H. R. Mackintosh and A. B. Macaulay. New York: Scribner's, 1900.

Roberts, Jon H. *Darwinism and the Divine in America: Protestant Intellectuals and Organic Development 1859–1900.* Madison: Univ. of Wisconsin Press, 1988.

Robinson, James M. "Jesus as Sophos and Sophia: Wisdom Tradition and the Gospels." In *Aspects of Wisdom in Judaism and Early Christianity.* Edited by Robert L. Wilken, 1–16. Notre Dame: Univ. of Notre Dame Press, 1975.

Santmire, H. Paul. "Healing the Protestant Mind: Beyond the Theology of Human Dominion." In *After Nature's Revolt: Eco-Justice and Theology.* Edited by Dieter T. Hessel, 57–78. Minneapolis: Fortress Press, 1992.

Schroer, Silvia. *Wisdom Has Built Her House: Studies on the Figure of Sophia in the Bible.* Translated by Linda M. Maloney and William McDonough. Collegeville, Minn.: Liturgical, 2000.

Schüssler Fiorenza, Elisabeth. "Wisdom Mythology and the Christological Hymns of the New Testament." In *Aspects of Wisdom in Judaism and Early Christianity.* Edited by Robert L. Wilken, 17–41. Notre Dame: Univ. of Notre Dame Press, 1975.

———. "The Followers of the Lamb: Visionary Rhetoric and Social-Political Situation." In *Early Christian Apocalypticism: Genre and Social Setting.* Edited by Adela Yarbro Collins, 123–46. Decatur, Ga.: Scholars, 1986.

Simkins, Ronald A. *Creator and Creation: Nature in the Worldview of Ancient Israel.* Peabody, Mass.: Hendrickson, 1994.

Suggs, M. Jack. *Wisdom, Christology and Law in Matthew's Gospel.* Cambridge: Harvard Univ. Press, 1970.

Tanner, Kathryn. "Eschatology without a Future?" In *The End of the World and the Ends of God: Science and Theology on Eschatology.* Edited by John Polkinghorne and Michael Welker, 222–37. Harrisburg, Penn.: Trinity Press International, 2000.

Thomas Aquinas. *Summa Theologiae.* Blackfriars English translation. Edited by Thomas Gilby. Garden City, N.Y.: Image, 1969.

Thompson, Leonard. "A Sociological Analysis of Tribulation in the Apocalypse of John." In *Early Christian Apocalypticism: Genre and Social Setting.* Edited by Adela Yarbro Collins, 147–74. Decatur, Ga.: Scholars, 1986.

Tillich, Paul. *Systematic Theology: Three Volumes in One.* Chicago: Univ. of Chicago Press, 1951–63.

Trevett, Christine. *Montanism: Gender, Authority, and the New Prophecy.* Cambridge: Cambridge Univ. Press, 1996.

Tucker, Gene M. "The Peaceable Kingdom and a Covenant with the Wild Animals." In *God Who Creates: Essays in Honor of W. Sibley Towner*. Edited by William P. Brown and S. Dean McBride, Jr., 215–25. Grand Rapids: Eerdmans, 2000.

Vincent of Lerins. *A Commonitory*. In A Select Library of Nicene and Post-Nicene Fathers of the Christian Church, series 2, vol. 11. Grand Rapids: Eerdmans, 1955.

Wenham, Gordon J. *Genesis 1–15*. Word Biblical Commentary. Waco, Tex.: Word, 1987.

Westermann, Claus. *Genesis 1–11: A Commentary*. Translated by John J. Scullion, S.J. Minneapolis: Augsburg, 1984.

Whitehead, Alfred North. *Process and Reality: An Essay in Cosmology*. Corrected edition by David Ray Griffin and Donald W. Sherburne. New York: Free Press, 1978.

Williams, Michael Allen. *Rethinking "Gnosticism": An Argument for Dismantling a Dubious Category*. Princeton: Princeton Univ. Press, 1996.

Index

ethical relation to the environment,
xiv, 81, 150, 156–58,
180, 194, 197–217, 229nn. 35, 42
evil, 18–19, 23, 79–80, 92, 93, 94, 95,
114, 115, 118, 154, 164, 166, 177,
196,
evolution, theory of, 33, 37–40,
221n. 16

finitude, xiii–xiv, 52, 56–57, 73–82,
93–96, 100, 113–21, 145–46,
150–58, 174, 199,
210
Fretheim, Terence, 202
Freud, Sigmund, 110
fundamentalism, 41

gnosticism, 14–17
Gravesande, Willem Jacob 's, 36
Gray, Asa, 39

Hellenistic philosophy, 14–19,
21–22, 29–33
history, 68–73, 80–82, 95, 110, 114,
117, 119, 120, 145, 153–54,
156–57, 165, 172, 184, 199, 211,
224n. 6
Hodge, Charles, 38
humility, 145, 173–74, 199, 201, 202,
206

identity and difference, xiii
image of God, 2, 12, 47, 49, 98, 122,
140–41, 176, 195, 203–5, 215
images in contemporary culture, 91,
185, 187, 189, 191, 192–94, 195
Irenaeus, 14–17

Jesus Christ, 1, 2, 14–17, 23, 45, 53,
98, 120, 122, 164, 165, 168,
171–72, 175–76, 184, 195, 205,
209, 213, 223nn. 40, 45
justice, 71, 175–76, 206, 208, 221n. 2

language, 91–92, 138, 141, 144, 146,
154
Leibniz, Gottfried, Wilhelm von, 34

love, 79, 83, 98, 139, 153, 158, 163,
186, 195, 205–6, 215–16
Luther, Martin, 178–79, 227n. 43

Maclaurin, Colin, 35
Marxism, 112, 119, 188
material substance, 16, 18, 113,
125–30, 196, 225n. 3
materialism and materialistic
philosophy, 18, 170–71, 187–88
McCosh, James, 40
Mersenne, Marin, 36
molecules, 62–63, 65, 67, 75, 87–88,
89, 102–3, 106, 111, 113, 224n. 2
Moltmann, Jürgen, xii
mysticism, 168–70, 172, 196
mythology, 10–12, 14, 27–28, 112,
147

narrative, 1, 2, 13, 71–73, 79, 84, 115,
218nn. 1, 2
natural law, 34–37, 39, 50, 55, 63, 65,
69, 75, 101, 103–6, 108–9, 115,
130, 177–78, 221n. 2
new creation, xii–xiii, xiv, 2, 46, 47,
83, 85, 164, 173, 184, 194, 195,
197, 209, 210–11, 212–13
Newton, Isaac, 33–37, 39, 65, 104,
130

O'Leary, Stephen D., 211
Origen, 6
Orwell, George, 97, 154

Pannenberg, Wolfhart, xii
particles, 61–65, 67, 74–75, 77–78,
87–89, 93–94, 100–101, 104, 106,
126–30, 132, 134–36, 225n. 3
personality, 110, 116
Plato, 29, 123
praise, 145, 173, 174–75, 179, 199,
201–2, 206, 217
process theism, xii
Protestants, xi, 25, 33, 37, 168,
178–80, 204, 224n. 3, 228n. 22
providence, 25, 32–33, 39
prudence, 138, 175, 197, 206–7

Printed in the United States
119917LV00001B/118/P